MONEY AND MAN

Money and Man

A Survey of Monetary Experience

By Elgin Groseclose

Fourth Edition, revised and enlarged by the Author

UNIVERSITY OF OKLAHOMA PRESS : Norman

By Elgin Groseclose

THE PERSIAN JOURNEY OF THE REVEREND ASHLEY WISHARD
AND HIS SERVANT FATHI (1937)
ARARAT (1939, 1974)
THE FIREDRAKE (1942)
INTRODUCTION TO IRAN (1947)
THE CARMELITE (1955)
THE SCIMITAR OF SALADIN (1956)
THE DECAY OF MONEY (monograph) (1962)
SILVER AS MONEY (monograph) (1965)
FIFTY YEARS OF MANAGED MONEY:
THE STORY OF THE FEDERAL RESERVE (1966)
THE SILKEN METAL—SILVER:
PAST, PRESENT, PROSPECTIVE (monograph) (1975)

Fourth edition of a book originally
published in 1934 under the title
MONEY: *The Human Conflict*

Library of Congress Cataloging in Publication Data

Groseclose, Elgin Earl, 1899–
    Money and man.

    First ed. published in 1934 under title: Money, the human conflict.
    Bibliography: p.
    Includes index.
    1. Money—History. 2. Currency question.
I. Title.
HG231.G7 1976   332.4'9   75–40960
ISBN 0–8061–1338–3
ISBN 0–8061–1339–1 pbk.

To
E. Ellice McDonald, Jr.
and
Charles A. Mason
who understand the moral dimension of
the money problem

FOREWORD TO THE FOURTH EDITION

In 1934, Joseph A. Brandt, then editor of the University of Oklahoma Press, asked me to write a work that would explain in simple terms the devaluation of the dollar that had just occurred and the events that made this devaluation necessary.

It was evident that an explanation of these happenings could not be reached through any of the monetary theories then current, all of them in eclipse with the collapse of the economic structure following the Great Crash of the stock market in 1929. A deeper examination was necessary, one that went to the nature of man's experience with money. A survey of this experience was indicated. What wisdom did the records offer?

The library shelves held an endless array of works devoted to the theories of money; only an insignificant number treated its history. Few went back beyond the times of Adam Smith for either theory or experience. Most textbooks, even today, treat the development of monetary experience as proceeding from barter to money to the institutions of credit. Yet, as the archeological evidence from Mesopotamia makes clear, institutions of credit were fully developed before those of money.

The work was published in 1935 as *Money: The Human Conflict*. In the interval the vast currents set in motion by the fiscal policies of the New Deal and the torrents raised by World War II created a new monetary landscape requiring its own geography.

These developments led to the republication of the work in 1961 and again, in a revised edition, in 1967, under the present title. This present edition incorporates further revisions by the author in order to take account of more recent happenings.

ELGIN GROSECLOSE

Washington, D.C.
January, 1976

INTRODUCTION: The Meaning of Money*

ANY discussion, to be fruitful, should proceed from an agreement upon the meaning of words and concepts. No greater confusion prevails than that surrounding the meaning of money—even among persons who are well qualified to examine the question. If this statement is doubted I would refer you to an article by that distinguished member of the *New York Times* economic staff, Mr. Edwin L. Dale, in the July 20, 1975, issue entitled, "Money Supply: A Growing Muddle," in which he states the question, "What is money nowadays?" Or one in the *Wall Street Journal* of August 29, 1975, which comments "The men and women involved in this arcane exercise [of watching the money supply]—brokers, investors, businessmen, economists and Federal Reserve officials —aren't exactly sure what money supply consists of." I would submit that if these experts do not know what money is, no one knows.

◆◈◆

This is understandable. About a decade ago certain economists, not content with leaving the matter complex, set about to simplify our understanding of money by the process of fragmenting the word—and thereby made the subject more complex.

The error into which they fell, and into which in falling they have carried the economy down into its present morass of confusion, is that of dealing with qualities and attributes rather than substance.

It is a common error of philosophers. To illustrate in the-

---

* Based on an address by the author to the Conference on "The Role of Money in Prosperity and Depression," arranged by the Committee for Monetary Research and Education, Inc., in cooperation with Clemson and Furman Universities, Atlanta, Georgia, October 2, 1975.

ology, God in the Old Testament revealed himself to Moses as Being—"I am that I am"—Being of infinite attributes, of power and compassion and justice and wisdom.[1] An ancient school of Hebrew theologians, however, impressed with God's wisdom began to apotheosize one quality as Divinity—that of Wisdom—until God ceased to be regarded as ultimate Being, and instead as ultimate abstraction. Eventually the philosophers so atomized the concept of Divine Wisdom that it became no longer understandable except by the very learned, and a vast cabalistic literature arose that for a time threatened to suffocate the Jewish faith in a fog of occult theosophy.

◄§ §►

Fortunately a later and more inspired generation threw out of the Old Testament canon the Wisdom literature, but the heresy continued to plague early Christendom under the theology of Gnosticism and its variants.

Present-day Christianity is under the influence of its own heresy—that of deifying the attribute of love to the neglect of God's justice, and half the federal government's revenues are given over to misguided subsidies generated by a so-called compassionate concern for the welfare of humanity, including the whole world—with over 150 billion dollars spent in the past quarter century in misused foreign aid benevolence.

To turn from theology and metaphysics to more tangible aspects of the subject before us, let us note that our treatment of money today is the same as that of offering a hungry man a whiff of hamburger and suggesting that he has been fed. The fragrance is not the substance.

The heresy of money, the misunderstanding of its true meaning, is that of dealing with one of its attributes rather than with its substance. I refer to purchasing power. With money you can buy things—almost anywhere—almost any time. Not everywhere, of course. It may not get you a drink of water in the Sahara; heaven cannot be bought; and there are times when one would give his fortune for another day of life. But in a stable, civilized environment the purchasing power of money is the common denominator of trade and the measure of its appeal.

But other things have purchasing power. A song, a woman's smile, the promises of kings, all have purchasing power of a sort; even the absence of substance, like the absence of two feet of stature that made Tom Thumb rich, has purchasing power. More to our proper subject, in the nineteenth century the growing use of checking accounts led to the realization that these were a form of purchasing power that was not money, but so close to it that except in times of financial panic—as in 1933—a check was as useful as money as purchasing power and usually more convenient.

The notion that checking accounts were the same as money was particularly congenial to a school of economists concerned with social control. It was also an attractive idea to politicians who look to government as the Ephesians looked to Artemis—the great, fructifying Earth Mother, cradler of mankind and dispenser of all earthly benefits.

The Constitution, it was recalled, gave Congress the power to coin money and regulate the value thereof. It was an easy step to forget the limitation of the words "to coin" and to expand on the words "to regulate." The government, it was advocated, had the responsibility to regulate the purchasing power found in bank deposits. In 1913 Congress passed the Federal Reserve Act. This gave to an independent corporation authority over the deposit accounts of member banks. It was an authority of immense latent potential. Gradually its exercise grew wider and wider and with it, its control over the economy, that is to say, the livelihood activities of society.

In the early 1960's the kind of purchasing power of which we are speaking became generally known in the trade as M_1, that is, government-issued purchasing power—note that I do not use the term "money"—plus commercial bank demand deposits, that is, deposits subject to checking or instant withdrawal.

Along with this extension of governmental authority over the economy through regulation of purchasing power represented by bank deposits went a changing attitude on the part of managers of the Federal Reserve System as to its functions. No longer was the Federal Reserve the agency of Congress whereby to regulate the value of the coinage—or even the official purchasing power—but it now undertook direct regulation of the economy.

The first major use of its leverage came in 1923, when the Federal Reserve began to exercise an authority upon prices— a function that had long been considered that of the free market place. In 1923 the Board adopted the policy of using its powers in the interest of a stable price level. This, it was argued, was a worthy and necessary undertaking and well within the responsibilities of the Federal Reserve System. This power was exercised through manipulation of the volume of bank credit. From the regulation of bank credit was only a step to the regulation of prices, including the price of money, that is, interest rates.

✥

In 1946 Congress enacted the Full Employment Act. This served to modify the Constitution by subordinating the historical federal responsibility for the common defense and the establishment of justice to that of providing a job for everyone. The Federal Reserve became a chief agency of this policy through regulating the country's purchasing power in the form of bank deposits.

Unfortunately for the regulators—and for the country—the economists discovered that there were still other forms of purchasing power that eluded regulation. There was for instance M_2, that is, M_1 plus time deposits, and there was M_3, and M-ad infinitum, because the range of items physical and intangible that have potential purchasing power is almost limitless. Thus, the current problem facing the regulators is that of how to deal with credit card money, of which there are an estimated 75 million potential purchasing power issuers. Another problem is that of *Eurodollars*, that hobgoblin of the money managers which no one has yet discovered how to manage.

In short, by dealing with this single attribute of money, that of purchasing power, economists have provided the advocates of socialistic and totalitarian government with an instrument for coercing society that is far more effective and embracing than police and secret prisons.

⋘ ⋙

To measure the distance by which the Federal Reserve has departed from its original charter I quote from the Federal Reserve Bulletin of February, 1971, discussing the policy of the Federal Open Market Committee—the instrument by which the System exercises its influence on the economy.

"The FOMC's basic concern," the Bulletin reads, "is with the real economy—production, employment, prices, and the balance of payments."

"But the Committee," the Bulletin continues, "must translate its broader economic goals into monetary and credit variables over which the Federal Reserve has direct influence. Thus, whatever emphasis is given to the financial variables that influence day-to-day open market operations, it is recognized that the immediate targets of day-to-day operations are not the goals of monetary policy but rather that those targets are set with a view to facilitating the achievement of the broader financial and economic objectives of the FOMC."

John Wesley, founder of Methodism, declared that he took the world for his parish. Here one observes how the Federal Reserve, created as a form of safety valve on mercantile credit, has taken the entire economy as its province. Under the watchful eye of this all-embracing bureaucracy the free market functions at its peril. Individual choice disappears. Perhaps one may still choose between fried and scrambled eggs for breakfast, but hardly between a two-button and a three-button jacket, since the clothing manufacturer, in producing the latter, may find his bank credit curtailed.

⋘ ⋙

The extension of political power afforded by treating purchasing power as money has led to a further grave departure from sound doctrine and practice. Since purchasing power is generally regarded as a material good, an increase in the total was regarded as wholesome and as a proper function of government. As De Lawd in the play, "The Green Pastures," said at the heavenly picnic, "Let us have some more of dat firmament."

De Lawd may provide by a wave of the hand more "firmament" for the heavenly picnickers, but it is a delusion that government, however potent, can do the same for purchasing power. Perfume is an attribute of the rose, and the only way more rose fragrance can be produced is by producing more roses. You cannot increase purchasing power by printing more pieces of paper, legended as so many dollars, or by increase of bank deposits by federal fiat. Behind each of these units of purchasing power must be a substance—and it is to the nature of that substance to which politicians and economists should address themselves.

⋞ §⋟

For many years a popular belief which has served to promote the multiplication of fiat purchasing power is that the increasing production of the economy requires a corresponding increase in the so-called money supply. For many years the computations of Carl Snyder indicating that United States industrial production rose secularly at the rate of about 3 per cent per annum was taken as a norm at which the money supply should increase. I believe that the so-called Chicago school of economists holds that money supply should increase at some fixed per centage yearly.

As one student of the subject states the proposition: "As human productivity is increased the amount of money needed to measure the exchange of human services has to be increased in just proportion to the services individuals render to one another."

But when the Federal Reserve provides the banking system with reserves by purchasing United States debt instruments with its deposit credits, it is putting fiat purchasing power into competition with the purchasing power created by the actual production of goods and services. The multiplication of such fiat or counterfeit purchasing power is the principal cause of the inflation of prices, despite depressed demand and production and high unemployment—the phenomenon of the 1974–75 recession that has so perplexed economists.

❧ ❧

Many economists delude themselves in treating purchasing power as money by calling it a function of money. This is error. A peach has the attributes of form, color, fragrance, and taste, but none of these is its function—which elementally and metaphysically is that of a carrier of seed. Likewise, the attributes of money are several, but the essential function of money is that of a carrier of value.

Other economists regard money simply as abstraction, like a statistical mean which they would relate to a commodity price index, or to a more fragile abstraction like the Special Drawing Rights of the International Monetary Fund which can best be described as an index of indexes.

The Federal Reserve note, which passes almost everywhere as United States money, is not money but equally an abstraction. This fact is evidenced by the law creating it which, however it is evaded, still declares that the Federal Reserve note is "redeemable on demand in lawful money."

The error of these concepts is that they ignore other attributes of money, notably universality. A song may have a monetary quality, particularly if sung by a famous singer, but it is evanescent and depends upon its audibility. A king's promise may buy an army, but only where the king's writ runs. Even the United States dollar, which has long been considered a universal currency, is no longer accepted everywhere, subordinate in certain areas to those more elusive abstractions known as Special Drawing Rights. Money, to be genuine, must possess more than purchasing power, it must have universality of acceptance.

Historically, only those things having the attribute of materiality have enjoyed acceptability as money. The materials may range from tobacco and wampum and cigarettes to the great stones of Yap—but only gold, silver and copper have enjoyed universality of acceptability.

ᘓᢟ ᢞᕲ

But beyond substance, or materiality, and beyond purchasing power and universality, money must have another attribute, the fundamental attribute that converts a metal into money. Like the atom, which may be substance, but substance that exists only because of a mysterious force that holds its several elements together, substance becomes money by the endowment of an attribute which, for want of a better name, we may call integrity, that is, a moral force, that of consistency which is the essence of character.

The first true moneys of Europe were pieces of metal—gold, silver, electrum—struck in pieces of uniform weight and purity. This striking or coinage first occurred in or on behalf of the temples. In the case of the Greeks it was that of the Temple of Athena, whose sacred owl is found in the early drachmas, and in Rome, that of the Temple of Juno on the Capitoline Hill. It was this temple whose sacred geese warned the garrison of the approaching Gauls, whence it was known as the Temple of Juno *Moneta* or Juno the *Warner*, and the word *moneta* attached to the coinage, from which we derive the word "money."

Early rulers, particularly the Roman, discovered that by reducing the size or quality of the coinage by insensible degrees they could increase the quantity and thereby the apparent purchasing power of their emissions. Thus began the curse of inflation which inflicts us today. When paper money was introduced into Europe from China in the thirteenth century, a new and readier means of increasing the apparent purchasing power of money became available, and with paper money emissions began the modern decline in the quality and integrity of the money that carried with it a decline in its purchasing power together with the credit convulsions, panics and depressions which periodically have afflicted the Western World.

ᘓᢟ ᢞᕲ

Today we see all about us—throughout the world, as a result of Western cultural influence—the capitulation of the money managers to the cry noted by Adam Smith, that of more money, more purchasing power—a cry which they seek to satisfy by printing more paper, progressively destroying the integrity of the money. This has gone on to such an extent that as the distinguished journals have noted, no one knows what money is. No one can say what money will buy today or tomorrow, and persons who have saved of it in hopes that it would give them a certain security of purchasing power in their old age now gaze amazed, frustrated, incredulous, distrusting not only in money, but in their distrust sweeping in all the institutions of civilization, of government, law, education and even church.

We need to return to a new valuation and appreciation of the importance of integrity, of character, in the management of money, as indeed, we need to relearn its importance in the entire economic realm of production and distribution. The understanding must spread that quantity without quality is nothing, that factory output without integrity, that is without character and consistency in the product, is worthless in the market, and without purchasing power. Similarly, money without consistency and character loses its marketability, that is, its purchasing power, just as a factory turning out quantity of product but without consistency and quality of product loses its market and purchasing power of the product.

I would propose no greater service to the profession and to the country than that monetary economists begin a revision of their concepts of money, to draw a distinction between the attributes of money and its substance and to give recognition to the mysterious and awesome force of moral integrity in its management.

◅§ §▻

Now, since a preachment without a practical application is apt to be borne on the wind, one suggestion may be offered, of an administrative nature, that a people aroused to the need for integrity in the money can adopt. It is that the Federal Reserve System be re-directed to its original function of a weathervane and safety valve on the commercial credit flow, by forbidding the Reserve banks to acquire any government obligations or to make loans on any collateral other than that arising from transactions in the production and distribution of goods.

CONTENTS

MONEY AND MAN

Book One. THE MONEY MECHANISM

W HEN our Lord was questioned on the payment of tribute, He is recorded in St. Matthew's Gospel as having asked to see the tribute money. On being shown the coin, with the image and superscription of Caesar, He said, "Render unto Caesar the things that are Caesar's."[1]

The incident is significant in monetary history for it illuminates the moral cleavage that has persisted in man's experience with money through the ages and continues to challenge all monetary doctrine and policy.

The Roman coin in the account was a *denarius*, at the time a piece of relatively pure silver and the Imperial standard of account. Before the close of the epoch, however, it had been debased to a piece of copper and the lowest status in the monetary scale. Its cultural descendant is the English *penny*, by which the name was translated in the King James Version, still signified by the letter *d* in the symbols for *pounds*, *shillings*, and *pence*.

I. Render Unto Caesar

The pages that follow are, in a sense, an account of the history of money in the hands of Caesar, that is to say, the sovereignties of history, and their capacity or incapacity for moral restraint in handling that which has been entrusted to them.

To understand the nature of the moral question raised by the incident, as distinct from the legal or economic aspects of money, we must recall the imperatives of the Jewish faith, and their influence in the continuing Judaic-Christian tradition. These imperatives had both moral and cultural content.

First, let us note the Mosaic prohibition against the mingling of diverse kinds. Thus, the devout Jew was forbidden to wear garments of mingled linen and woolen, to sow a field with

3

mingled seed, to mate cattle of diverse kinds, or plough with an ox and an ass together.[2] The economic values of these rules have often been questioned—just as monetary economists today question the value of reserve requirements for paper money emissions—but the moral value may perhaps be seen in the restraint they imposed upon the impulse to exploit to the limit the natural resources available to man.

The moral element is clearer to us in the Mosaic law against tampering with the weights and measures: "Just balances, just weights, a just ephah, and a just hin, shall ye have: I am the Lord your God."[3]

Whether the prohibitions against mingling diverse kinds applied to the metals, as to prevent alloying, is not clear. There are references in the Old Testament to brass, but generally the word refers to a simple metal and means copper.[4]

The Jews were under obligation to pay to the Temple yearly, as atonement offering, a half shekel of silver.[5] So far as is known, no coin or piece of shekel or half-shekel weight was ever struck by the Jews before the very close of Jewish national history, that is, during the Jewish War of 66–73 A.D. that ended with the destruction of the Temple. That shekel was a piece of alloyed silver weighing approximately 14.3 grams and containing 16.6 per cent copper.[6]

The extant coins were all struck within a period of five years and consequently the opportunities for depreciation or debasement were limited. We have no way of measuring the influence upon these times of the Prophet Amos' invective of nine centuries earlier against those who "make the ephah small and the shekel great, and falsifying the balances by deceit."[7]

Thus, the Jewish tradition only stated the moral question; we must look elsewhere for its practical resolution in the conditions of monetary management. Nevertheless, the statement is important for the historian of money, and clews our instant task, which we see as one of examining the phenomena of money in the light of a moral imperative, in tracing the destiny of money under one or the other influence.

II. The Economy of Money

THE difficulty in discussing the phenomena of money is the inherent one of separating the concept of money from the concept of wealth. Wealth has seemed good to mankind; a rising standard of living and a growth of material comfort have been accepted, despite the warnings of prophets and the renunciations of garret poets, as wholesome and valuable things. Indeed, poets could not exist unless someone toiled to feed them. Art requires a patron; and the creation of music, science, literature, architecture, flower gardens, and all that tends to increase the spiritual and esthetic values of life, could hardly be possible without the accumulation of a store of wealth to support this endeavor.

It is not into a consideration of the influence of wealth that we are entering, which is, indeed, a field of its own, but into its more limited expression and vehicle—money and the money mechanism. By wealth we mean the sum total of those physical goods which contribute to the welfare and happiness of mankind. By money we mean those particular items of actual or nominal wealth by which the market value of all other wealth is measured, and in terms of which, is stated. By the money mechanism we mean the functioning of money in the market place, the instruments by which its functioning is effected, and the institutions by which, in turn, the functioning of money and the instruments of money are controlled.

Money, we may freely recognize, has a useful and essential service to perform in the economic life of mankind. It has made possible the division of labor by which the man who is especially skilful in making shoes may buy with money the other articles necessary for a well-rounded life. By providing a store of value, it has made possible leisure, the saving up of wealth for a comfortable old age, or for travel or artistic endeavor. By putting contributions to the state on a money basis, rather than on the basis of service or commodities, as was common in feudal times, money has made possible strong, well-ordered governments. Money has made possible international trade, and the intercourse of nations. The economic system by which a handful of cassiterite won by a Chinese miner from the alluvial deposits of Malaya is smelted into tin in Singapore or Liverpool, which in turn is coated over a sheet of steel in Maryland, transported to Alaska, there, as a can, to enclose a morsel of salmon, then is shipped to a nitrate worker in Chile, is supported and made possible by a complex of monetary and banking transactions involving dealings in piasters, pounds, dollars and pesos, and by the media of drafts, deposits, bills of exchange, and metallic coin. Money has, in short, created the vast and complicated structure of modern economic society. And we may add—ominously—that money may destroy it.

৩৳ ৳৶

If a money economy makes possible the integration of industry, the security and leisure of old age, the establishments of government, the intercourse of nations, the focusing upon a common objective of activity in diverse parts of the world, then these things rest upon and are supported by money.

If at any point the chain is broken, if anywhere the money mechanism fails to function, the whole vast system breaks down and men in four continents may be thrown into hunger.

The removal of a bar of gold from the vaults of the Bank of England to a waiting steamship may have more influence upon the output of an assembly line in a Detroit automobile plant than the functioning of a crane which sets a motor upon that line for the waiting workmen. More men may go hungry from a rise in the interest rate than a rise in the price of bread. A bank failure may produce more misery than a plague. A change in the money standard may provoke a revolution. "It may well be doubted," said Macaulay, "whether all the misery which had been inflicted on the English nation in a quarter century by bad kings, bad ministers, bad Parliaments, and bad judges was equal to the misery caused by bad crowns and bad shillings."[1]

The stability of the modern world rests upon the stability of its money. Yet nothing is more obvious than the fact that money is not stable, that nowhere is money under control. Biologists may control the growth of microscopic bacteria in a culture; engineers, the power of exploding dynamite; electricians, the radiations in the ether, but no one has succeeded in controlling money. Yet money is, more than anything else, the creation of man, a device of his own making.

The history of civilization, said Alexander Del Mar, is the history of money. We may add that the history of money is the story of man's struggle to control it, to live with it, to bring it to do his tasks. Man lives with money, but so far it has not been a successful union.

III. The Perspective

SUCH is the complexity of the money problem that any attempt to plunge into the current conflict and to unravel the tangled threads of theory and practice is apt to result only in more confusion for the general reader primarily interested in a solution of its immediate and personal implications. We must retire to a distance for perspective. Reserve ratios, bimetallism, the gold standard, the gold exchange standard and the gold bullion standard, gold and silver purchases, price levels, inflation and deflation—these can have meaning only when examined in their historical background.

This determines our approach. Keeping an eye fixed upon the immediate struggle we shall, in the pages that follow, trace the conflict of man with money from the time that money first appeared as a formal institution of society with the purpose of obtaining what light we can upon the modern problem.

An all-embracing account of money from the earliest times to the present is, however, beyond the scope of this volume, and much that may be of interest to the strictly monetary historian or economist must of necessity be omitted.

We are interested primarily in the human experience, and the human conflict will be the thread upon which our story is strung. We shall seek, in particular, to examine the manner in which the money mechanism has subdued mankind with its fascination, to trace the phenomena of money as they have affected the social and economic life of the time, but most im-

portantly, to unravel the threads which bind the problems of
the present with the experience of the past, to match the pattern
of our present distress with that of our forebears.

&3 ૠ

When prospectors make borings at intervals and bring up a
common ore they know they have struck a vein, and by this
process they chart the underlying strata, and predict when it
will emerge. This method is implicit in our approach. We shall
make borings into the silt of history in an effort to reach the
bedrock upon which a sounder monetary philosophy of the
future may be built. We shall, where we find rich ore, cross
section and undermine with leisure until we have exhausted the
veined wealth of history. We shall seek to find in the comments
and conclusions of the leading thinkers and scholars in the field
of money a common train of thought, a vein of philosophy,
sometimes deeply submerged, but yet which may be traced in all
their commentary made in diverse ages and in diverse environ-
ments, which shall guide us in charting the drift of modern
monetary practice, and perhaps predict for us whether it is to
emerge on the hillsides of certainty or in the morass of despair
and confusion.

Book Two. THE AGE OF GREECE

THERE was a time in the Western world when money as we know it was a new thing, and its appearance was like a strange ware which men gathered in the market place to gaze upon in wonder.

It was in particular, the age of Greece—an age which in many respects resembles our own, a time when the world was young, when men were fresh with energy and enthusiasm, when there were frontiers to pass and new lands to open up to civilization, and an age when men were enterprising and self-reliant, individualistic, democratic, athletic, and full of the gusto of life.

I. Homeric Society

IN that day the Greek race was still pastoral and nomadic in fundamental attitude, but the wheeled cart had been abandoned for the fleet running, oar-driven galley, which was carrying the young men to distant and wonderful shores, while at home the shepherd was beginning to till the soil, and plant the olive and the vine.

Life was simple in this early Greek period, but it was not primitive. The civilization which was later to blossom into the Parthenon and the Erechtheum, and the sculpture of Phidias and Praxiteles, in the science of Pythagoras, the ethics of Socrates, the philosophy of Plato, and the scholasticism of Aristotle, was being firmly founded in an environment that was unclouded by a surfeit of material objects, and in experience with nature rather than artifice. Economy was direct, and devoted to serving the needs of the household. Wealth, not absent, was measured by sacks bulging with flour, jars full of wine, and heads of cattle.

Such trade as existed was very little developed. A few exchanges took place between district and district, between city and city, within Greece itself. The Phoenicians, the peddlers of

9

the sea, landed in harbors and on the beaches, and there sold the products of their own industries, or foodstuffs, raw materials, and manufactured goods which they had fetched from all the shores of the Mediterranean and the distant lands of the East. All this trade was done entirely by barter. Money was unknown. Tripods or slave girls were given in exchange for cattle, iron or bronze.

Yet it was among these peoples of the Aegean that the device of coined money first appeared in the world. Although stamped metal seems to have been used from the earliest times in China, and primitive forms of money were in use among the rudest tribes of antiquity, and although the more settled civilizations of the Euphrates and the Tigris were acquainted with the banker and debt and financial instruments, it is to the Greeks that must be attributed the inception of that imponderable thing we may call the money mechanism. With their ready adaptability, and the inventiveness for which the race was noted, they began to improve upon the complex system of barter in use in the Mediterranean, in which ingots of copper and silver were used as media of exchange, and soon were using, for their growing trade, the thing we now know as coin.

It is fortunate, in a sense, that coined money was an innovation of the Greeks, for we can trace in the history of this young race the influence of this new device upon the economy of the day, undisturbed by the complicating factors which rob its study in modern times of much of its validity. Fortunately, also, the money mechanism appeared at an age and among a people in which the intellectual capacities of man were highly developed, if their economic organization was not. Upon the phenomenon of money the Greeks focused the light of a philosophy that has never been equalled for its brilliance or lucidity. Life was new and fresh with them, and they looked upon money with an objective detachment which has never been possible for any people since. For this reason, the experience of the Greeks with money is fecund with precept and omen and lesson for a modern world that has become enmeshed in its toils. In the protean conflict that was here waged between man and money for the mastery of human destiny, we observe the pattern of all subsequent economic history, an adumbration of the recurrent defeats of the human race in its struggle against the creature of its own devising.

II. The Invention of Coinage

THE introduction of coined money in Europe appears to have occurred toward the end of the eighth century B.C.[1] The evidence leads us to believe that it did not spring full blown from the inventive genius of the Greeks, but rather that it was the adoption by the ruling powers of a desirable and somewhat obvious step in the simplification of commercial dealings.[2] Before the development of coinage the Mediterranean world had been slowly groping toward a more convenient device and measure of exchange with which to facilitate the increasing trade of the day. Oxen and sheep had apparently been used as a standard of value among the nomadic Aryans on the northern coasts of Europe, and in the towns hides, and iron and brass, and even slaves were sometimes used as media of exchange.[3] In the older communities of Babylon and Phoenicia, metal ingots bearing the stamp of the merchant who cast them passed by weight and became the basis of a highly developed banking and credit system.

By the eighth century, it seems, the more primitive forms of barter had begun to give way to one or more of the four metals —gold, silver, bronze and iron—that were beginning to appear in sufficient quantity to serve as media of exchange. Made up sometimes into useful forms, and sometimes into pieces of standard weight, they passed by weight, and rendered it possible for commerce to expand throughout the Mediterranean.

The particular contribution of the Greeks to the development of money lay in their taking these pieces of metal and casting or striking them into units of uniform weight and imprinted with the sign of state authority. The idea of stamping ingots of copper

or silver with a mark of their weight and fineness had been practiced in Babylon, but the marks were merely the certification of
the metal dealer or trader. It was when the state stepped in—in
the person of the city or the temple—and gave its seal and
certification of the weight of these pieces of metal that true
money, as distinct from barter, began, and it is to the Greeks
that we owe this development.

It is at this point, also, that the controversy begins which
persists to this day as to the source of the value of money, i.e.,
whether the value of money derives from the metal that has been
stamped, or from the seal upon the substance which is used as
money.

◆§ ৪◆

The earliest of the coinages were rude indeed. In some cases
they were crude bean-shaped ingots about the breadth of a
finger nail, bearing a punch mark, and made of a natural mixture of gold and silver, called by the Greeks "electrum" or white
gold. With the artistic instincts for which the race is noted, it
was not long before the mints of the Greek cities were turning
out coins of a beauty and character that have never since been
approached. In the fourth or third century B.C. there was struck
at Syracuse what is perhaps the most beautiful coin the world
has ever seen. The obverse is a head of Persephone, decked with
corn leaves, and surrounded by dolphins; the reverse is a
quadriga, with Victory flying above it to crown the charioteer.

◆§ ৪◆

The age which saw the development and spread of coinage
constitutes one of the most remarkable periods in the whole of
the world's history. The invention of coinage was but one aspect
of an intellectual development that embraced philosophy, art
and commerce. The full flowering of Greek genius belongs, no
doubt, to an era two centuries later, but it was in this epoch that
all that is meant by the Greek spirit and Greek genius had its
birth. Literature and art, philosophy and science, are still following the course laid out for them in these early centuries, and
commerce may also trace its modern manifestations to the
practices and precepts developed in these beginnings.

III. The First Money Crisis

WE are not so much concerned here with the character of the money that was introduced, or the standards of coinage, as with the economic effects and social consequences that followed.

We know that serious consequences did develop. The transition of Greek society from the pastoral and household economy of Homer to the money economy that followed upon the development of coinage was accompanied by an unsettlement of the habits of men, a reorientation of their ideas, and a transformation in the structure of society. It became necessary to reconstruct entirely the foundations of Greek civilization. We know that at Athens this was accomplished only at the expense of a great political revolution—peaceful, fortunately—in the sixth century B.C. and the constitution of that great body of reform with which the name of Solon is connected.

Money had, in a word, begun to exercise its fascination over the minds of men. These light, shining discs, adorned with curious new emblems and a variety of vigorous, striking images, made a deep impression upon both Greek and barbarian. And to the more practical minded, the abundance of uniform pieces of metal, each of a standard weight, certified by the authority of the state, meant a release from the cumbersomeness of barter and new and dazzling opportunities in every direction.

Not only did merchants and artisans and shepherds and farmers take readily to this new medium of exchange, with its greater convenience, and more certain value, but the growing abundance of coins gave a tremendous impetus to trade. All classes of men succumbed to money, and those who had formerly been content to produce only for their needs and the necessities of the household, found themselves going to the market place with their handicraft, or the fruits of their soil, to exchange them for the coins they might obtain.

And with this succumbing to the fascination of money, and the pursuit of profit, we find the beginnings of that enthralment of the race, the disappearance behind the horizon of history of that golden age to which Herodotus longingly referred, "when all the Greeks were still free."

＊§ §＊

The introduction of coined money produced what might be called in today's parlance "boom times" in the Mediterranean. It was an era of expansion, of the development of frontiers, of the exploitation of natural resources. While the physical results, due to the absence of the machinery and power which have characterized the expansion of European and American civilization in the past hundred years, were small in comparison to the present, and while the beneficial and deleterious results were slower, in point of time, in accumulating, the psychologic, economic and spiritual effects were the same. Cities flourished, trade was active, debtors and creditors appeared, banks were organized, and in the end there grew up a host of attendant evils resulting from an unbalanced economy based too largely on money.

The difficulties that arose in the Greek experience with money did not follow so much from an inherent defect in this new instrumentality of exchange as from the fact that, like the over-rapid and overextended development of credit in modern times, it forced a premature flowering of the commercial life of the age, and compelled the natural growth of economy to proceed at a pace faster than its results could be assimilated. The intellect and spirit of man could not mature sufficiently in the short period between the blossoming and the fruition of this device to cope with the problems it created.

The commercialization of Greece, the revolution that was carrying the race headlong from a natural or household economy into a complex world of "money economy" was not a steady process, or one which, in terms of today's tempo, would be regarded as rapid. There were, no doubt, pauses in the onward march, lulls in which men had time to contemplate the meaning of it all. Some no doubt looked back with regret upon the placid and secure times that were passing, while others regarded with repugnance those days of hard labor and tilling of the soil, and looked forward to a renewal of the onward trend, to the day when wealth would be universal and poverty annihilated. The urge could not be stayed, and the tide moved irresistibly on, carrying with it the hopes and dreams of a new era for men.

And toward the end of the seventh century B.C., the bark of Greek civilization, which had been riding the crest of a sudden prosperity, was being carried, irretrievably, it seemed, toward the dark headlands of disaster. . . .

꿔 ꏞ

We do not, of course, have commercial records of the day to permit us to chart the fluctuations in the business cycle—statistics, which, as Sir Arnold Wilson tartly remarks, the Americans collect like antiques, were unfamiliar to the Greeks—and the influences we have described were perhaps a hundred years in accumulating. We may gather that there were a number of minor depressions before the major crisis occurred which produced the final collapse of the boom and ushered in a social, political and economic revolution under Solon.

The inexorable culmination to the era grew out of the growth of debt, and sprang directly from the agricultural depression. In Attica, as in modern America, the incubus of debt had thrust its tentacles into the very vitals of society. The greater part of the peasants' holdings had come under mortgage, the evidences of which were stone pillars erected on the land, inscribed, we may understand, with the name of the lender, the amount, the rate, and the maturity of the loan. A still more insidious form of debt was the chattel mortgage—the personal loans known today under soft sounding phrases like "industrial banking" or "household finance"—by which the farmer could pledge his own person or that of his wife or his children, for the repayment of a loan. These chattels, under Athenian law, could be sold off into slavery, and such was the extent of the existing credit structure that the greater part of the agricultural population was in danger of being converted into bondage.

And while the use of money had encouraged a rapidly growing body of debt, the charges of which were an onerous burden on society, the same money economy was rendering it more and more difficult to discharge the debt. The opening of the Italian and Euxine grain trade by the Greek merchantmen was producing a market situation in which the rocky farm land of Attica had become "submarginal," and the Athenian peasants with their olive and orchard crops could not compete with the cheaper food stores from abroad.

While we do not hear them called "farm holidays" or "milk strikes," a state of affairs developed in Greece toward the end of the seventh century B.C. similar, we may believe, to that in the Middle West in the nineteen twenties. Revolution was being talked, with mutterings about "redistribution of the land," and armed insurrection was imminent.

IV. The Solonian Reform

As Greek intellect had evolved the institution of coined money, so Greek intellect was called upon to devise means of controlling it. The challenge was met with an audacity and intelligence that may even now command the admiration of the world. Solon, whose name is still a synonym for lawgiver, was the man in whose hands was placed the problem of solving the crisis that arose in Athens at the end of the seventh century.

Solon was a member of the upper classes. He had engaged in commerce and had traveled widely. His name was connected in the public mind with the recent victory at Salamis, which had been achieved either through the craft of Solon or his ability to rouse the fighting spirit of the army, and he was a popular figure who was detached from politics. More important for history, he was a dreamy-eyed poet, and it is through fragments of his poems that have come down to us that we learn a great deal of the events of the day.

The moneyed classes, the aristocracy, and the merchants, sensed the growing dissatisfaction among the masses, and in the hope of staving off rebellion, put up Solon for the archonship in 594 B.C. Probably they expected only a mild liberalism on his part; at any rate they were glad to support his candidacy, which was at the same time a popular one among the great body of voters. All parties united on Solon, each party no doubt anticipating that its particular vested interests would be his chief regard. Solon was perhaps vague in his campaign promises, for

Plutarch speaks of the "softness and profuseness, the popular rather than philosophical tone" of his poems.

՞ᢌ ᢎᢧ

Inaugurated as archon, Solon moved with amazing speed, and before the country knew what was happening, it was going through a social, economic and political revolution that completely revamped the character of the Athenian state and still amazes historians. Solon assumed extra-legal powers, and with a facility for "catch" expressions that took hold of popular fancy, issued immediately a revolutionary decree under the appealing name "Shaking Off of Burdens" (*Seisachtheia*). This decree, going at once to the heart of the money problem, tore down all the mortgage pillars of Athens and abrogated at once all agricultural and personal loans. It liberated all those debtors who were actually in slavery under previous legal adjudication, and it forbade any Athenian to pledge his own person or that of any member of his family as security for a loan.

The constitutionality of the *Seisachtheia* was widely questioned, but it was not challenged, and it solved overnight the problem of the poor debtors, the *thêtes*, tenants, and small proprietors. But of course it shattered the credit structure of Athenian economy. Deprived of the security behind their assets, and with obligations of their own to meet, the landlords and the money lenders were thrown into practical bankruptcy.

In solution of this problem, the crumbling financial edifice, Solon provided a partial moratorium by means of a debasement of the currency to the extent of 27 per cent. The *mina*, which had formerly consisted of 73 *drachma*, Solon made legal tender to the value of 100 *drachma*.*

* Some doubt exists among scholars as to whether Solon actually debased the coinage, on the ground that no evidence exists that a strictly Athenian coinage was yet in use. The common media of exchange were apparently the *drachmas* of the neighboring states of Aegina and Argus. Whether actual debasement occurred matters little, however, since it is well settled that Solon did alter the standard of payments from a *drachma*, possibly that of Aegina, which was widely circulated, to an Athenian *drachma* of lower content, and authorized the discharge of debts in the lower medium. For a discussion of this question, see Kathleen Freeman, *Work and Life of Solon* (London, 1926).

ও৯ ৪৯

The money question solved temporarily—it was to come up again and again in Greek history—Solon was now able to lay the foundation for the enduring structure of reform which brought into being that cynosure of history—the Athenian democracy. The remainder of Solon's program, his *Eunomia*, or Reign of Law, as he called it, consisting of a reclassification of the citizenship, the dissolution of the oligarchy, the codification of the laws, the negotiation of commercial treaties, we may pass over in order to examine the effects of his financial legislation.

The immediate popular reaction to the money measures of Solon is somewhat in doubt. Our principal records are the poems of Solon and the report of Androtion, whose account is borrowed by Plutarch and Aristotle. Solon's poems give of course a flattering picture of the effect of the reforms. Plutarch relates, however, that they left the people only more dissatisfied, because the emancipated debtors expected not only remission of debts but also a redivision of the land, along the lines of communistic Sparta. Charges flew about that Solon had allowed "insiders," friends of his, to learn in advance of his plans and to profit by buying up mortgaged land. The permanence of the reforms, and the reviving prosperity of Athens, are evidence, however, substantiating Solon's report, and testify to the general soundness of his program.

ও৯ ৪৯

But it is the longer range aspects of the Solonian reform that are of concern to us. George Grote, the classic historian of Greece, is of the view that:

"The *Seisachtheia* of Solon, unjust so far as it rescinded previous agreements, but highly salutary in its consequences, is to be vindicated by showing that in no other way could the bonds of government have been held together, or the misery of the multitude be alleviated. . . . . The foundation on which the respect for contracts rests is. . . . the firm conviction that such contracts are advantageous to both parties as a class, and that to break up the confidence essential to their existence would produce extensive mischief throughout all society. The man whose reverence for the obligation of a contract is now the most profound would have entertained a very different sentiment if he had witnessed the dealings of lender and borrower at Athens, under the old ante-Solonian law. The oligarchy had tried their best to enforce this law of debtor and creditor, with its disastrous series of contracts, and the only reason why they consented to invoke the aid of Solon was because they had lost the power of enforcing it any longer, in consequence of the newly awakened courage and combination of the people."[1]

The money problem was to creep up again and again in Greece. In the time of Pericles, a bulging treasury led to a vast and uneconomic expenditure on public works which perpetuated the glories of Greek civilization but did not mitigate the hardships and inequalities of the day. Hesiod complained, at a later day, of financial corruption and bribe-taking judges. Diogenes searched the streets of Athens for an honest man, and Demosthenes inveighed against the mercenary spirit of the Athenian naval commanders. Nevertheless, the general effect of Solon's money measures was to purge Greek mentality of its absorption in pecuniary values and to purify the whole spirit of Greek commerce. They created among the Greeks a saner philosophy of values and founded Greek commercial principles on a sounder basis than existed elsewhere in the ancient world. Speculative enthusiasm was apparently cured in Athens. Grote adds that though there grew up at Athens, following the Solonian reform, a high respect for the sanctity of contracts, never again do we hear of the law of debtor and creditor disturbing Athenian tranquillity. The banking system, he says, assumed a more beneficial character. The old noxious contracts, "mere snares for the liberty of a poor freeman and his children," disappeared and loans of money "took their place, founded on the property and prospective earnings of the debtor, which were in the main useful to both parties, and therefore maintained their place in the moral sentiment of the people."

Another thing stands out clearly in Greek history as the result of the Solonian currency experiment. It was never tried again.

Though here and there we find instances of currency debasement by various Greek cities, a general tradition grew up in Greek commercial policy of the sanctity of the coinage. Throughout the period of Athenian history, this one instance of formal and deliberate currency depreciation stands alone. Not only was there never any demand in Athenian democracy for new tables or a depreciation of the money standard, but a formal abnegation of any such projects was inserted in the solemn oath taken annually by the numerous *diakasts*, who formed the popular judicial body.

Upon the soundness of her money Athens built a commercial system that dominated the Mediterranean, and of the character of that commerce Augustus Boeckh says:

"The purity of the coinage promoted traffic: the merchant was not compelled to take back freight on his return voyage, although there was no lack of articles for that purpose, but he could receive and export the value of his cargo in ready money. . . . . Those articles which in other lands could scarcely be obtained singly, were in the Piraeus found together. Besides grain, choice wines, iron, brass, and other staple commodities from all the countries on the Mediterranean Sea, there were imported from the coasts of the Black Sea slaves, ship timber, salted fish, honey, wax, pitch, wool, tackling and cordage for vessels, leather, and goatskins; from Byzantium, Thrace and Macedonia, also timber, slaves, and salted fish; slaves moreover from Thessaly, to which country they came from the interior; and fine wool and carpets from Phrygia and Miletus. All the sweet productions of Sicily, Italy, Cyprus, Lydia, Pontus, Peloponnesus, were collected by Athens through her maritime supremacy."[2]

અક્ ક્ષ

The Athenian *drachma*, consisting, from the time of Solon to that of Alexander, of 67 grains (English) of fine silver, and from that of Alexander to the Roman conquest of Greece, of 65 grains, became the standard coin of Greek trade, and through the Alexandrine conquests the standard for Asia. Athenian *drachmas* moreover found their way into such distant parts of the world as India and northern Europe. Following the absorption of Greece into the Roman Empire, it became the model for the Roman *denarius*, which was originally minted at an equivalent weight and fineness. In various parts of Asia, however, the Greek *drachma* was preferred to the fluctuating Roman coinage, particularly for the Indian trade, and consequently we find it minted, under imperial auspices, far into the period of Roman imperialism. While the Roman *denarius* was constantly being depreciated, until trade in the western parts of the Empire had been reduced almost to a barter basis, the *drachma*, by the purity of its standard, kept alive the institutions of commerce in the East.

The total value to the world of the Greek commercial tradition is inestimable. Greek money and Greek commercial practices became the standard for the Levantine world. They persisted in the East throughout the period of the Roman Empire and formed a solid rock of principle in the chaotic world of Roman commercialism. And later, as we shall have occasion to discuss, when the Empire had been dissolved into its Western and Eastern halves, the Eastern half was to be resuscitated by the strength it drew from this tradition. In the long history of Byzantium we find Greek monetary policy again dominant, and to it must be attributed, as much as to anything, the vigor of this thousand-year-old empire which remained a center of civilization while Europe was sunk in medieval darkness. And finally, in the renascence of Europe, beginning in the thirteenth century, we may still trace the influence of Greek tradition in the reviving commercialism of Italy.

The Greeks, perhaps the clearest thinking of all peoples of history, met the money question and solved it, as satisfactorily as any people, by an exhibition of intellectual restraint. With one exception, they resisted the cry so common to mankind, as Adam Smith observed, to cheapen the standard of value, and thus they solved the most insidious of its evil influences.

V. A Note on Monetary Theory

WE have had occasion, in the foregoing discussion, to refer to the controversy in monetary theory as to the source of the value of money. As we go along we shall necessarily touch upon other questions of economic theory, for it is the history of the race that ideas have made events as often as events have made ideas. It seems wise, therefore, to break in upon our story this early with a discussion of abstract theory, in order that we may keep clear our concepts and terminology as we proceed.

One of the most perplexing problems in the realm both of economic theory and of practical statecraft is the nature of money. Generally speaking, the word "money" presents a very clear concept to individuals, but when we analyze that concept we find money taking such a variety of forms, and fulfilling functions so manifold, that the further we advance in our analysis the more we lose sight of what is common and what is essential.

So difficult indeed is the definition of money, and so much confusion has resulted from the attempts to define it, that economists have often abandoned the task, and limited themselves to describing money in terms of what it does, i.e., its functions. Money, therefore, is sometimes defined as anything which is generally acceptable in a community for all other goods and services, leaving to the imagination of the reader the formulation of concrete concepts of "anything." Or, in more precise terms, "the complex of those objects which in a given economic area and in a given economic system have as their normal purpose the facilitation of economic intercourse (or the transfer of values) between economic individuals."[1]

Money, in this view, is not defined as a series of objects, but a series of functions which have as the ultimate object the "facilitation of economic intercourse."

The particular functions of money are generally listed as follows:

(a) A medium of exchange, that is, a highly developed form of barter, in which money comes between the exchange of two commodities to facilitate the process. With the use of money the farmer in need of shoes does not take his bag of corn to the shoemaker, but takes it rather to the miller and from him obtains a sum of money therefor, which he gives in turn to the shoemaker. Strictly speaking, money in such a case need have no value beyond the momentary and fleeting one of a medium. Where payment for the bag of corn is made by a due bill issued by the miller, who agrees to honor it for so many pounds of flour, if this due bill is accepted by the shoemaker either because he may be in need of flour and may present it for redemption, or may in turn exchange it for leather with the tanner, the due bill has performed the function of money, and is, to that extent, money. Cases of "formal" or fiat money, with no other value than that derived from its service as a medium of exchange, are presented in the case of the paper money inflation in post-war Germany. With the German currency depreciating in the 1920's from day to day, even from hour to hour, the only value it possessed was gained by one's hurrying it to the market and spending it, and if not immediately made use of, that value was lost.

(*b*) A measure of value, i.e., a function of price, in which all other commodities and services, or objects of economic intercourse, may be embraced by a common denominator. The due bill of the miller, used above as an illustration, performs a money function in a limited sphere, but it is not a measure of value unless it is accepted generally in the community as a standard for receipts and payments of all sorts.

(*c*) A standard of deferred payments and a store of value (a carrier of value through time and space), in which present transfers of goods and services may be given a future significance, as in contracts of debt, and the fruits of present labor may be given a future value, as savings laid by for old age or emergency. No money so far devised, it may be noted, has ever succeeded in performing this function perfectly, but it may be doubted whether the failure arises from inherent defects of the thing used as money, so much as from tampering with the money in order to destroy or enhance its value—the interposition of the state or of individuals working for antisocial ends.

◦§ ◦▹

A description of the functions of money, however, is not a definition of money itself, or its own essential characteristics. Into the ramifications of this question it would be tedious to enter, and perhaps profitless for our present object, which is an objective examination of the working of the money system in the economic life of society with particular reference to the modern aspects of the money problem. The main divisions of the controversy may, however, be briefly outlined.

(a) The view that money is intrinsic, that money has a value in its very nature, and is itself an economic good, a commodity. This is the view of those who support the metallic standard, or standards of credit money (state note issues and bank credit) based upon metal and convertible freely into metal. The view is expressed in its most abstract form by Knies as follows:

"The laws of nature necessitate that for measuring, i.e., for determining the quantitative relation in terms of some quantitatively determinable object, we can employ only such an object as a measuring instrument or standard of measure as itself possesses to a special degree the quality which is to be measured. The unknown quantity in the object to be measured is then determined by the application to it of the known quantity of the same kind in the instrument of measurement."[2]

Thus, a distance of length can be determined only by a medium which in itself has length, and an expanse of surface only by an area. Such instances of measuring distance in terms of time as "an hour's journey" fall within this definition on the ground that they are but an extension of the idea, in which an "hour" becomes the length traversed in that period. Applied to money, Knies continues, "it has therefore been absolutely established that if and so far as this special quantity of *economic value* which concrete goods contain can be and is to be estimated and measured, that is possible only by means of an object which itself has economic value—that is, which is itself an economic commodity."

(b) The view that money is purely conventional, that is, without value as property, as compared with economic goods, merely a "token," and a "symbol." Among those who hold to this view are the "quantitative" theorists (the numerary theorists of former times, such as Alexander Del Mar), who believe that the value of money derives solely from the quantity in circulation in relation to the quantity of transactions to be effected. Involved in the quantity theory, and explicitly stated by many writers, is the doctrine that the substance of which money is made is irrelevant, that it is the number, and not the quality or size of the money units that counts. The idea has been expressed by Irving Fisher, a latter-day exponent, as follows:

"In short, the quantity theory asserts that (provided velocity of circulation and volume of trade are unchanged) if we increase the *number* of dollars, whether by renaming coins, or by debasing coins, or by increasing coinage, or by any other means, prices will be increased in the same proportion. It is the number, and not the weight, that is essential. This fact needs great emphasis. It is a fact which differentiates money from all other goods and explains the peculiar manner in which its purchasing power is related to other goods. Sugar, for instance, has a specific desirability dependent on its quantity in pounds. Money has no such quality. The value of sugar depends on its *actual quantity*. If the quantity of sugar is changed from 1,000,000 pounds to 1,000,000 hundredweight, it does not follow that a hundredweight will have the value previously possessed by a pound. But if money in circulation is changed from 1,000,000 units of one weight to 1,000,000 units of another weight, the value of each unit will remain unchanged."[3]

⋖§ §⋗

From this clash of opinions over the nature of money, of which the views expressed above represent the two extremes of monetary philosophy, has arisen recurrent political controversy over the "standard," and legislative halls and the council chambers of state have trembled at the thunder of dissentient argument. The view that money has no value of its own, and need have no such value, was very strongly held, especially at the time of the reaction against the Mercantilists, who held emphatically that money represented the embodiment, in quite an especial degree, of value and wealth. Locke expressed the view that humanity agreed upon giving gold and silver "an imaginary value," and Hume described money as a mere "representation of labor and commodities," as a token which serves only for the purpose of measuring and estimating the value of labor and commodities. The opposite view was held mainly by the Physio-

crats (Turgot and others), the classical school of English economists, and by their followers in France, as also by Karl Marx in
his *Das Kapital*. Roscher made the following pointed and fre-
quently-quoted remark in regard to the contrast of these two
views: "The false definitions of money are divisible into two
groups: those who regard it as something more, and those who
regard it as something less, than an economic commodity."[4]

(c) A third view synthesizes these two extremes and holds
that money must possess intrinsic value, but that it derives an
additional value from its use. An exponent of this view was Benjamin M. Anderson, Jr., who wrote:

"We conclude, then, that money must have value to start
with, from some source other than the money function, and that
there must always be some source of value apart from the money
function, if money is to circulate, or to serve as money in other
ways. But this is not to assert the doctrine of the commodity
school, that its value must arise from the metal of which it is
made, or in which it is expected to be redeemed. Nor is it to deny
that the money function may add to the original value. On the
contrary, the services which money performs are valuable
services, and add directly to the value derived from non-
pecuniary sources. Value is not physical, but psychical. And
value is not bound up inseparably with labor-pain or marginal
utility."[5]

For our immediate interest, it is to be noted that the philosophical problems of the money mechanism were not overlooked by the clear-thinking Greeks. Aristophanes remarked
the phenomenon which is now described as Gresham's Law,*
and Aristotle states the gist of the value problem in his *Politics*.[6]
Money, as it arose in history, was originally natural, deriving its
validity from the fact that the objects used as money possessed
intrinsic worth, either for use or ornament, or from its connection with religious and customary observances. Such was the
case with gold and silver, with cowry shells and wampum, with

* "In our Republic bad citizens are preferred to good, just as bad
money circulates while good money disappears."—*Frogs.* p. 717.

even the *fei*, or great stones the size of a mill wheel, used by the natives in the island of Uap. But what made these substances money, in the sense of performing all the monetary functions, was the sanction of society, either by custom or by fiat of the state. When the Greek city placed its emblem upon an ingot of metal and thereby certified to its weight and fineness, the ingot became money in an enlarged sense and capable of functioning on an extended scale. That certificate of the state is a definite and important addition to its value, and as society grows in complexity, and the money function increases, the contribution of the state rises geometrically in importance. In an ideal state of society, perhaps, the intrinsic quality of money might entirely disappear, and be replaced by the value derived from the control of the state. But for that to occur, the control of the state would need be perfect in authority and god-like in intelligence.

What is of immediate importance in the study of money is not a resolution of these diverse theories, or a determination of the relative contribution of social sanction and intrinsic value in the money mechanism, but an appreciation of the means by which the control of money by society may be perfected. Money is a human institution, and as humanity does not live by logic, neither does the money mechanism subject itself to logical analysis and dissection, much as the economist might desire it to. The proper study of money, and its control, must be by the historical approach, by patient study of the manner in which man has lived with money in the past. In this study lies more fruit for hope than all the charts of prices and trends and ratios of statistical and theoretical economics.

Book Three. THE ROMAN EXPERIENCE

Fᴿᴼᴹ the monetary experience of the Greeks, it is natural for us to pass westward to Rome, the mistress of the ancient world. The Roman experience with money is of importance to us for we are, in a sense, the residuary legatee of Roman civilization, of Roman concepts in law, politics and administration, and particularly of Roman concepts of money. And in passing to Rome our attention inevitably focuses upon the great monetary crisis of the third century A.D., escaping, for the moment, the historical events that led to that debacle.

I. Crisis In the Empire

Tʜᴇ situation of the Roman Empire in the latter half of the third century was a condition of depression and despair to which the modern world, with its dips in the business curve, its paroxysms of commercial expansion and contraction, can present no parallel. Trade was stagnant, the imperial treasuries were empty, money was depreciating, and trade, such as existed, had almost reverted to a barter basis. Everywhere land was falling to waste, untilled, empty, gaunt, the water courses dried and the poplars sere and yellow, the walls crumbling under the elements, the huts and cottages deserted and succumbing to ruin. Peasants had forsaken the soil, seeking the greater safety of the town or city, where, if employment was not to be had, there was free corn and amusement. The vast estates, which had been built up under the influence of slave labor, the imperial system, and commercial economy, were untended and falling into desuetude, the slaves running away and revolting, the hired managers, sensing the "end of things" and the futility of effort, hastening to line their pockets with such profits as could still be eked out, and the patrician owners, fearful of the stability of the régime, taking their liquid capital, their gold and silver and jewelry and hiding it against the day of inevitable collapse.

In the cities and towns, misery was assuaged by the circus, while disease spread and hunger and rioting waxed. The craftsman could no longer ply his trade, for the iron, the leather, and the wood could not be obtained. Sea trade was at the mercy of roving pirates and had practically ceased to exist. Public wealth and private wealth, both struck at their sources, were vanishing. The authority of the government had disappeared, the country was in chaos and anarchy, the army had lost its discipline, and on the frontiers the barbarians were unhindered in their depredations of the Roman provinces.

"The accumulation of miseries," writes Léon Homo, "which was reinforced by terrible natural catastrophes, plagues and earthquakes, spared none of the regions of the Empire, and, as was to be expected, produced the most disastrous effects in the economic domain. Shortage of production and impossibility of movement . . . . money shortage and high cost of living . . . . depopulation and general ruin—the whole economic fabric of the state was cracking and seemed likely to break up at any moment."[1]

And in the words of Ferdinand Lot, "The Empire from the third century onward is a preparation for the Middle Ages."[2]

II. The Money Problem Appears

To understand the causes of the commercial collapse of the Empire, it is necessary that we trace briefly the appearance and early manifestations of the money problem in the Roman Republic.

The Romans were a military people, and had been slow to adopt the use of the new device of coinage, which the Greek traders, with their shiny, silver *drachmas*, had been slowly popularizing in Italy. Not for two hundred years after its first introduction, or well into the fifth century B.C., do we find coinage supplanting, in the domestic transactions of the Latins, the use of bronze or copper by weight. Even then, the implications of coinage were not assimilated, its proper use and functions were not grasped, and, almost immediately, we begin to note the effects of its more pernicious influences.

It is during this same century that marked the introduction of copper coinage that the money question protruded itself into Italy. From the first, the problem of debt was an aggravating cause of the Social wars and the early struggles between the plebians and the patricians. And while the institution of debt is more ancient than the institution of coinage, or even money, the consequences of debt were sharpened and embittered by the ease of going into debt which circulating capital, like coin, provided.

The early debt problems grew out of the military organization of Rome. The Roman army was originally a militia, whose service was temporary. The citizens were called up at the beginning of each campaign, and at the end they returned to their homes, without receiving any pay. Every man had to provide his own equipment. The citizens recruited had to leave their fields and their beasts. Since they got no pay, the cost of the campaign fell on every man. If they returned safe and victorious, they often found their farms neglected, their fields ravaged and their cattle driven off by the enemy.

This calamity prevented them from sharing in the profits of victory when the war ended favorably at Rome. As they were without resources they borrowed, and fell into debt. In Rome the laws on debt were very hard. This was, without any doubt, one of the causes which contributed to ruining the middle class and swelling the mass of the poor, the landless, the proletariat.

In 375 B.C. we hear of the first debt cancellation—a practice which later became frequent as one crisis followed another in the growing commercialism of the Republic and the Empire. This was one of the famous Licinian Rogations, a program of reform advanced by Licinius, one of the people's tribunes. In 342 B.C. as a measure to cope with the growing money problem, Roman citizens were forbidden to accept interest at all, but they managed their usurious practices by arranging loans through the Latins and dummies of other Italian states.

⇜§ ९⇝

Meantime, the growth of money and liquid capital, as a result of the military successes of the legions, combined with a fiscal system which was never equipped to cope with the problems of money economy, was creating new difficulties. With the final defeat of Carthage by the series of exhausting Punic wars, and the transfer to Rome of the commercial and financial hegemony of the Western Mediterranean, money began to take on new importance.

Rome, as a result of its military power, was in today's language, a creditor on international account, with a heavy balance of payments in its favor. Tribute payments and proconsular revenues, and such less legitimate gains as the booty of victorious generals and the profits of provincial tax farming found their way to Italy both in the form of money and in the form of a flood of imports with which domestic industry could not compete. The result was stagnation in agriculture and domestic manufacture. Thus, as money poured in from abroad, poverty and debt increased—a paradox that has not been limited to Rome.

To solve these problems, the Licinian laws were repeatedly revived, particularly during the period of the Gracchi—Tiberius and Caius (133–121 B.C.)—and Caius tried to introduce a complex program including increased taxation of the provinces (with the idea, it is supposed, of setting the financiers against the landowners), the starting of enormous public works to give employment, and increased distribution of subsidized cheap corn. Still another recourse which was attempted—as it has been attempted since in history—was that of price fixing.

The aediles had, and frequently exercised, the authority to fix prices within the city. To the political logic of the Romans it was easier to solve the demands of the depressed classes by arbitrary measures against speculators and honest traders than by attacking the fundamental question of a sound fiscal and economic system.

⇜§ ९⇝

Meantime, the inequalities of classes and the social strife and unrest were fostered by the growth of speculation, the indulgence in non-productive commercialism and the mad scramble for money. Roman political policy gravitated around the quest for treasure. In the maneuvers of Caesar with Pompey and the Senate, for instance, may be traced an astute play to get hold of the gold mining regions.

Banking and speculation appeared on the scene. The sale, purchase and exchange of money were growing important since Rome had become a center for a swarm of foreigners from every city and country. The Roman monetary system was gradually being extended, and Greeks and Orientals who came to Rome with gold or silver money struck in their own countries had first of all to exchange it for Roman *denarii*. This was a source of great profit to the bankers, or *argentarii*, because of the great varieties of coinage brought to them.

Another activity of the bankers was the organization of companies to bid for state monopolies. As public expenditure increased, the tax farm, or revenue collecting agencies, became a lucrative privilege. The shares of these companies were widely held—by senators, smaller nobles and commoners—and trading in the shares became even more profitable than money changing. Some companies, like those which had the tax farm of Sicily, and which had such influence at Rome that it was impossible for the provincials to obtain justice against the organized, methodical spoliation which was practiced, were immense earners. But the fortunes of war, the invasion of a province, like that of Asia by Mithridates, rendered the shares highly risky; and the vicissitudes of foreign affairs were immediately translated into the commercial crises of Rome. There were cases of absolute financial panic.

III. King of Shreds and Patches

ROMAN administration, despite its achievements in the fields of politics and law, never succeeded in erecting a monetary system. It is quite likely that imperial policy never took cognizance of money, except to use it for its own ends, and never appreciated its importance in civilized economy. At no time, in the long period that Rome was the center of the Mediterranean *imperium*, was there any defined monetary policy, or was there exercised over the money mechanism any authority except of the most capricious character. It is doubtful, in fact, whether the Romans had any conception of money, or its functions. Certainly their understanding of it was most superficial in comparison with the well defined philosophy of the Greeks.

ᴥ§ §ᴥ

In reviewing the monetary system of the Romans during the imperial period we note at the outset the absence of uniformity in the coinage. Only toward the very end of the Empire, in the time of Diocletian, do we find the sovereign prerogative of the state asserting itself over the coinage. Among the reforms which that monarch introduced, in a vain effort to stem the tide of disintegration, was the absorption of the currency system into the imperial administration.

ᴥ§ §ᴥ

When the curtain of history opened upon the imperial scene, in the age of Augustus Caesar, the money of the Empire consisted of three metals—gold, silver, and copper. At the top of the scale was the imperial *aureus*, a gold coin which Julius Caesar had originated, weighing at the start one-fortieth of a *libra* (say 126 English grains) or of a size approximating the old five dollar gold piece or the present English sovereign. Below the *aureus* was the *denarius*, a silver coin which had been introduced in 277 B.C. in imitation of the Athenian *drachma*, but which was now somewhat lighter (approximately 60 grains as compared with the 66 of the *drachma*), and which may have had an official ratio of 25 to the *aureus*. Below the *denarius* was the *sestertius* or *sesterce*, theoretically one-fourth of the *denarius*, struck both in silver and in bronze; and finally the *as*, a copper piece equivalent to one-fourth of a *sesterce*.

The Empire was nominally—though never very effectively —on a gold standard. Actually, it was on a bimetallic, or tri-

metallic, standard, with three metals—gold, silver and copper—
all in use and with no effective ratios maintained among them.

Gold was the standard for imperial payments and taxes were
exacted in gold, or in silver and copper, at a constantly increasing rate for gold (set by official money changers connected with
the imperial office), and gold was used for donations to the
army. For empire trade, and particularly for the foreign trade—
with India, Persia and China—which was becoming important,
silver was the accepted medium, while for the ordinary transactions of the city and among the poor, copper was the common
denominator of value.

We may understand the absence of system in the coinage by
reference to the various authorities exercising jurisdiction over
the mints. The emperors jealously maintained the prerogative
of gold coinage, and all the *aurei* struck bore their effigy, but
from want either of foresight or of will, the coinage of silver and
copper remained at the mercy of a host of diverse authorities.
Augustus had made some half-hearted attempts to unify the
coinage, but the Senate, chief antagonist of imperial power,
shrewdly asserted its ancient prerogatives, and Nero, around
A.D. 54, returned to it the authority of which it had been deprived by Augustus. During the reign of Nero, the mark of the
Senate (S. C.) again appeared on all gold and silver, and down
to the time of Diocletian all bronze minted under the imperial
authority was "with the consent of the Senate."

❧ ❧

In the East, Roman monetary ideas never took hold, and the
peoples in that part of the Empire insisted with considerable
pertinacity on the retention of their own mints. In this they were
aided by the demands of foreign trade, in which Roman coins,
because of their inferiority, their adulteration with base metal,
and their irregularity in weight, were everywhere suspect; and
for the Eastern Mediterranean, and the trade with India, Greek
drachmas continued to be minted—at Caesaria in Cappadocia,
Antioch in Syria, Tyre in Phoenicia, and occasionally in a few
other towns, until well toward the time of Diocletian.

For the great mass of local transactions copper continued to be the chief medium of exchange, and either as the result of a positive policy of cultivating local favor or out of ignorance of its consequences, the emperors allowed to numerous provincial cities the right of striking copper and bronze coins. Some of these were in the nature of commemorative medals, and none of them was legal tender beyond a limited area. Later, however, these bronze coins of Eastern cities became the only trusted coins in the Empire, and were circulated widely, even in the northern parts of Europe.

◄§ §►

In addition to the gold coinages of the Emperor, the silver of the Senate and the important trading cities of the East, and the bronze and copper of a long list of lesser cities, we find that generals in command on the frontiers were frequently permitted to strike money. During the Republic, in the year 91 B.C., the generals had been authorized to coin moneys in their own name, and from the time of Sulla they occasionally issued gold coins in the provinces.

◄§ §►

Finally, among those who exercised power over the money system, must be mentioned the mint masters and money changers. Early in the Republic the mint masters had come to exercise considerable authority over coinage. At the time of the introduction of silver coinage, in the third century B.C., the Senate had set up a body of Mint Commissioners to regulate the coinage. The Mint Commissioners quickly assumed autocratic powers and after the last Punic War they began to stamp on the coins their own monograms rather than the insignia of the Republic. The authority they exercised was not easily to be surrendered, and because of their organization into a powerful guild, they were able to defy the emperors. When, for instance, Aurelian attempted to reform the coinage in A.D. 274 they resisted his efforts, revolted, fortified the Caelian hill in Rome, and the Emperor wrote that he lost the lives of 7,000 soldiers in their subjugation.

◄§ §►

Such was the failure of the Romans, in dealing with the money mechanism, that its simplest problem—a uniformity of the standard—they never succeeded in solving. Money, which rules the destinies of men more than any Caesar or *basileus*, remained in Rome a "king of shreds and patches." It is now necessary to examine the failure of the emperors, despite the autocratic power at their command, the wealth of philosophy and administrative ability at their beck, to meet and treat with the money mechanism in another of its insidious manifestations.

IV. Imperial Impotence

To the fond admirer of Roman civilization, schooled in a reverence for Roman probity and justice, it will come as a shock to find how impotent the government was to resist the temptation to profit by the nefarious practice of currency debasement. The administration which could fling a highway from the Pillars of Hercules to the Bosporus, and erect the Colosseum and the temple of the Sun at Baalbek, and formulate the principles of law assembled in the Corpus Juris and the Pandects, could nevertheless stoop to plugging silver *denarii* with iron, and washing copper with gilt, and palming off on its citizens the most thinly disguised counterfeits of honest coin. The practice of currency debasement pervades the history of Roman administration. Hardly had money appeared in the Street of Janus, than began the vicious practice that was to work such havoc in the Empire, and by the tradition it gave to Europe, to multiply the misery, the confusion and the blight of medievalism.

The earliest Roman money was the *as*, theoretically a *libra*, or a pound of copper. Originally, *aes* were rude lumps of copper unadorned with any effigy or stamp, and passed by weight. When the practice of stamping ingots of copper or bronze was introduced into Umbria and Italy, in the middle of the fifth century B.C., the metals were made up into pieces of defined weight, known as *as signatum* (stamped copper), and passed by tale. During the succeeding century the bulky *as signatum* was supplanted by a heavy round coin—the *as grave*—and coinage as an institution was fairly started.

With coinage and metal pieces passing by tale rather than by weight, appeared the surreptitious debasement which has so long been the curse and temptation of those in charge of money. By the middle of the third century, the *as* weighed no more than four ounces, and at the time of the first Punic War, after the year 241 B.C., it weighed but two ounces. Sometime later, at an uncertain date, but possibly 89 B.C., it was reduced by 75 per cent, or to half an ounce, and at the beginning of the Empire, it had been generally supplanted by the new *sesterce*, equivalent to four *aes*.

The Roman *denarius* had, under the Republic, enjoyed a somewhat better fate. It had been introduced in 277 B.C., after the defeat of Pyrrhus had made Rome undisputed master of Italy, and tribute was beginning to flow in quantity toward the Seven Hills. The adoption of silver coinage may have been the result of these more abundant supplies of the metal, and if so, it would give the lie to the excuses of money scarcity offered for the recurrent debasement of the *as*. Possibly it arose from the necessities of an expanding trade, and a distrust abroad of the fluctuating Roman coinage. It was in silver *drachma*, or its equivalents, that what we should now call the international exchanges were settled. The great unit of account in the Hellenic world was the Attic *drachma*, issued by Athens, the purity of which was unquestioned, and it was an unconscious tribute to the superiority of Greek commercial policy, and acknowledgment of the necessity of conforming the Roman coinage to a world standard, that the silver *denarius* of Rome was modelled, as to weight and fineness, after the Athenian *drachma*.* This meant a weight of about 66 grains. By the beginning of the Empire period, however, the *denarius* had been reduced to 60 grains in weight.

"In reviewing the causes which contributed to the decline of

---

* Compare the present-day practice of "backward" countries in tying their currency systems either to the dollar or to sterling. The name *denarius* derives from the fact that it was originally issued as equivalent to 10 of the copper *aes*.

the wealth and the diminution of the population of the Roman Empire," says George Finlay, "it is necessary to take into account the depreciation of the coinage, which frequently robbed large classes of the industrious citizens of a great part of their wealth, reduced the value of property, produced confusion in legal contracts, and anarchy in prices in the public markets. The evils which must have resulted from the enormous depreciation of the Roman coinage at several periods can only be understood by a chronological record of the principal changes, and by remembering that each issue of a depreciated coinage was an act of bankruptcy on the part of a reigning emperor."[1]

The imperial coinage, instituted by Augustus upon the foundations laid by Julius Caesar, was undisturbed for seventy-five or eighty years; but with the accession of Nero (A.D. 54) we note the first official step in its deterioration. Nero reduced the size of the gold *aureus* from 40 to the *libra* to 45, and reduced the *denarius* from 84 to the *libra* to 96 to the *libra*.

Succeeding emperors increased the quantity of alloy in the *denarius*, and it is under the Antonines—the so-called golden age of Rome—that the deterioration became marked. Under Trajan and his successors the *denarius*, which up to the time of Nero was 99 per cent pure silver, dropped to 75–80 per cent. Under Septimus Severus (proclaimed Emperor A.D. 193) the depreciation became worse. In the silver coins the base metal rose to the proportion of 50 to 60 per cent, the fine silver content of the *denarius* dropping to around 26 to 32 grains (against an original fine weight of 66).

By this time the fluctuations in the value of money were seriously affecting foreign commerce, especially with India, where by now, of Roman money only the gold seems to have been acceptable. Although in domestic transactions the legal tender value of the coinage was supported by the imperial authority, and the coins were given a forced circulation within the Empire, after the time of Septimus Severus the *denarius* ceased to pass the frontiers. In the North good silver was demanded, and the coins of purer silver disappeared over the border.

◅§ ৡ►

As the third century advanced, the depreciation became so rapid that it is characterized by Mommsen as a *chute*. The gold piece, which had apparently retained something of its original weight, was being surreptitiously, if not officially, adulterated. Probably the standard was kept by minting coins at full weight for the army, but it appears that other gold coins issued for treasury payments contained up to 50 per cent base metal. Caracalla (A.D. 215) officially reduced the value of the *aureus* from 45 to 50 to the *libra*.

From Caracalla to Gallienus (A.D. 215–268) the monetary system was in a state of the utmost confusion. The *denarius* had gradually been so reduced in size and in silver content that even the imperial authority could not give it validity. Caracalla therefore introduced a new silver coin, the *argentus antoninianus*, weighing 60 to the *libra*, or about 84 grains, and as the *denarius* gradually sank in value and became eventually a copper coin, the *antoninianus* became the principal silver coin of the Empire. The *antoninianus*, however, soon began the same dizzy downward course as the *denarius*, the base metal content increasing, until by the end of the reign of Gallienus, it too was no more than base metal washed over with silver. A large number of these coins went into hoarding.

"Little by little the other moneys, at first those having an actual value, then those without value, were drawn down by this whirlpool and disappeared into the gulf," says Mommsen. "It is not an exaggeration to say that in the last half of the third century there existed no longer in the Roman Empire any money having an intrinsic value corresponding to its nominal value, not even a piece of brass or billon."[2]

◅§ ৡ►

With such a chaos of coinage—depreciated gold, debased silver, copper masquerading as silver by a thin wash of tin, coins of less than their stamped weight, coins plugged with iron, silver coins so alloyed with copper that they passed for copper —one wonders how trade was carried on, what was the standard of value, in what medium money accounts were kept.

Due to the variations in the ratios between copper, silver and gold, arising from varying supplies of the metals and the estimate placed upon them, as well as the varieties of coins in use as the depreciation continued, a third measure of value had been introduced, the money of account. This was the *sestertius* or *sesterce*, which was nominally one-fourth the *denarius*, but actually was an imponderable—since the actual coined *sesterce* was constantly fluctuating—derived from the bullion or intrinsic value of a *sesterce* that once, but no longer, existed, and the current rate of exchange of depreciated coins. It was a system somewhat like that found in China where accounts might be kept in *taels,* a unit of weight varying from province to province, but discharged in depreciated dollars, copper and brass *cash,* or in *sycee* (silver bars).

The *denarius* at its original rate of one twenty-fifth of an *aureus* was also used as money of account, but as the coined *denarius* continued to depreciate until it was nothing more than a piece of copper circulating at 500 to 525 to the *aureus*, and as the *aureus* was likewise debased, the money of account became merely a symbol, a twenty-fifth of an *aureus*, which in turn did not exist except as a division of the *libra.*

⊷§ §⊶

Money had also different values according to its purpose. *Denarii* could legally be tendered at a certain rate in discharge of commercial debt, but at another rate—a lower one, of course —for taxes; while for foreign trade it had a third rate, its bullion value. In imperial payments the same accounting prevailed in reverse order. The silver *denarius,* for instance, during the days when it was still silver and in good repute, was current for 16 of the copper *aes,* but was paid to the legion at the rate of 10 *aes*— the rate of exchange constituting in effect a bonus to the military. Later, when they were no more than pieces of tin-washed copper, they were paid out by the imperial treasury in discharge of debts at the rate of 25 to the *aureus*; but in the payment of taxes they were received at 500 to 525 to the *aureus.* Pure metal coins were struck for army pay and debased coins for other purposes. The imperial mints deliberately mixed a certain proportion of plated coins (base metal washed with silver) among the more honest, and all had to be accepted at the official rate.

◅§ §▻

Greek *drachmas* had continued to be coined, at Caesarea in Cappadocia, Antioch in Syria, Tyre in Phoenicia, and occasionally in a few other towns, but this relatively pure money was itself drawn into the general crisis. The admission of the *tetradrachmas* of Antioch into the money of the Empire, under the reign of Gordian III, the same favor accorded by Philippus to a portion of bronze struck in Syria, finally the cessation of these diverse coinages toward the epoch of Gallienus; all this is perfectly explained, says Mommsen, by the efforts of the government to raise the value of the imperial money. "To accomplish this," he says, "it assimilated new moneys which still retained an appearance of real value; it should necessarily result that soon these moneys would likewise disappear, as had the Roman *denarii* of silver and billon, as had the *sesterces*. It is what took place. In this terrible period, one sees disappearing at the same time the last vestiges of political institutions which had up to now survived in the Empire; even ancient civilization had already begun to disappear."[3]

◅§ §▻

A pathetic commentary on the times is the large quantity of Roman money that went into hoarding, the finding of which has enriched the cabinets of collectors. The hoards secreted toward the end of the third century consist almost solely of copper. In these patina encrusted pieces one reads the frantic uncertainty of the age—the emperor an embezzler, the government a liar, and frightened men clutching at bits of copper as the sole reality in a crumbling world.

◅§ §▻

It is difficult to say what was legal tender money during the decline of the Roman Empire. What had been intended to be purely local issues circulated widely throughout the Empire as full value coins preferred to imperial money. The bronze of the

East, which was of considerable weight and excellent material, drifted westward, and large numbers of bronze coins of Syria and Egypt have been found on the banks of the Rhine where the legions were encamped. Bronze also found its way into the melting pot, with the result that bronze money, rare in the time of Commodus (A.D. 180–193) largely disappeared towards the last quarter of the third century. The old copper *as* had ceased to be minted in A.D. 217 and the most abundant medium of exchange was the *antoninianus*, now (A.D. 270) a copper coin with about 2 per cent silver.

Generally speaking, copper coins only were legal tender, and these were nearly always issued at an overvaluation. Some of the emperors, while they paid out overvalued copper coins for government disbursements, required the revenues to be collected in silver, while others demanded payments into the treasury to be made in gold; but these measures were soon abandoned as impractical. So long as they could, the silver producing provinces were compelled to pay in silver, and the gold producing ones, in gold. But, after that, neither legal tender laws nor robbery could bring forth gold or silver. The aborigines had been stripped, the mines were worked down to the last phase of Roman mechanical and metallurgical resource, the depositories at Rome had been plundered, the bulk of the precious metals had gone to Asia. There was nothing left to make money of but copper, and towards the fourth or fifth centuries even this metal became scarce.

V. Struggle Against Chaos

AGAINST this creeping paralysis that was benumbing not only trade and industry but the government and the army, a number of the later emperors frantically struggled. Aurelian had attempted in A.D. 274 what seems to have been an experiment in "managed currency," was bitterly opposed by the speculators and money changers, and lost 7,000 troops in quelling the revolt. Diocletian, the most absolute of all the emperors, was born and bred a soldier, but he recognized the importance of the money question and attempted a general recoinage. Despite his autocratic exercise of power, however, he was unable to achieve any uniformity in the weights of his coins, either of gold or silver; the money mechanism had so far disintegrated that the best he could do was to reëstablish, not a coinage, but uniform standards of weights and measures. Mommsen blames "audacious frauds, half measures of reform, simultaneous issues of gold by colleagues, and often by rival rulers on different bases, or the infidelity of officers charged with the control of money."

᪥

The disintegration continued, and there seemed no power great enough to stop it. The treasury was empty, agriculture prostrate, industry demoralized, trade stagnant, and the only commercial activity was a maddened, consuming, parasitic speculation. In A.D. 301 Diocletian issued his famous price fixing decree as the last measure of a desperate sovereign.

Only portions of this decree have come down to us—fragments here and there turned up by archaeologists—but enough to reveal it as one of the most unusual documents in history. The discovery of portions in the farthest corners of the Empire confirms its widespread application, and the language of the preamble reveals, in words most explicit, both the terrible degree of economic collapse and the vagueness and superficiality of Roman economic philosophy:

For, if the raging avarice . . . . which, without regard for mankind, increases and develops by leaps and bounds, we will not say from year to year, month to month, or day to day, but almost from hour to hour, and even from minute to minute, could be held in check by some regard for moderation, or if the welfare of the people could calmly tolerate this mad license from which, in a situation like this, it suffers in the worst possible fashion from day to day, some ground would appear, perhaps, for concealing the truth and saying nothing; . . . . but inasmuch as there is seen only a mad desire without control, to pay no heed to the needs of the many, ... it seems good to us, as we look into the future, to us who are the fathers of the people, that justice inter-

*vene to settle matters impartially, in order that that which, long
hoped for, humanity itself could not bring about may be secured
for the common government of all by the remedies which our
care affords. . . . . Who is of so hardened a heart and so untouched by a feeling of humanity that he can be unaware, nay
that he has not noticed, that in the sale of wares which are exchanged in the market, or dealt with in the daily business of the
cities, an exorbitant tendency in prices has spread to such an
extent that the unbridled desire of plundering is held in check
neither by abundance nor by seasons of plenty. . . . .*

⊸§ §⊶

As more and more fragments of the decree have come to
light, and scholars have been able to reconstruct the document,
we are able to realize its importance to the historian as indicating, more surely than the bellicose narratives of ancient historians, the true state of Rome at this period. The decree, by the
very completeness of the list of articles whose prices it regulated,
must have been felt in every village and countryside in the imperial domain. The prices of all articles of trade, from a measure
of beer and a bunch of watercress to a piece of genuine purple
silk and pure gold in bars, and of services from the shaving of a
man or the shearing of a sheep to the fees of a lawyer for presenting a case, were set out in detail.

⊸§ §⊶

The price fixing decree of Diocletian was a failure, and was
abandoned within five years. It cast economy into too rigid a
mold, with the result, in the West at least, of further disintegration. From the crisis of the third century, the Western Roman
Empire never recovered. By the fourth century money had
fallen to the degraded position of *ponderata*, when it was customary to assay and weigh each piece. And by the seventh
century, the weights themselves had been so frequently degraded that it was no longer possible to make a specific bargain
for money. There was no law to define the weight of a pound
or an ounce, and no power to enforce the law if one existed.
Under these circumstances money became extinct. Nor, as Del

Mar recounts, was it the only institution to perish; all institutions had perished. There was no government except the sword, there was no law; there were no certain weights and measures. Exchanges were made in kind, or for slaves, or bags of corn, or lumps of metal, which men weighed or counted to one another, holding the thing to be sold in one hand, the thing bought in the other.

No more fittingly can we close this chapter on the failure of the Romans to cope with money than by quoting the words of Antoninus Augustus, cited by Del Mar, "Money had more to do with the distemper of the Roman Empire than the Huns or the Vandals."

Book Four. THE BYZANTINE ACHIEVEMENT

AN empire that existed as a political entity for more than
eleven hundred years, whose capital was not threatened
by an invader for a period of nine hundred years, whose rulers
were regarded with awe from the tips of Brittany to the Punjab,
whose commerce extended from the China Sea to the Atlantic,
and whose money was the unquestioned standard in the camps
of the Huns on the Danube and in the ports of the Arabian Sea,
cannot be regarded but with wonder and admiration.

I. The Fabric of Empire

SUCH was the empire of Byzantium, which rose like a phoenix
from the ashes of Roman civilization. During the long era of
medievalism, when Europe was the camp ground of the barbarian, when it seemed that the lamp of civilization might at any
moment be extinguished, it hurled back assault after assault
upon its frontiers and maintained itself as the repository of
ancient culture and the traditions of Greek and Roman
civilization.

Such an empire must have sucked its strength from deep and
spreading roots. Armies do not breed of themselves, and courts
and emperors and robed ecclesiastics and stately churches and
magnificent palaces and baths and far flung embassies are not
supported without industry and commerce, and industry and
commerce depend upon a sound and well-managed money.
Among the contributory factors to the Byzantine achievement
certainly the character of the money and, more particularly, the
character of the monetary administration, must be given a
large place.

It was in the year A.D. 325 that Constantine laid the foundations of his new capital on the banks of the Bosporus—the New

Rome, the imperial city of Constantinople. With spear in hand he marked out the boundaries, and on such scale that his courtiers exclaimed in astonishment, "How long, our Lord, will you keep going?"

"I shall keep on until He who walks ahead of me will stop," replied Constantine.

It was also in that year that the Emperor, with the same prescience of the future grandeur of the empire he was creating, enacted his great reform in the currency system, and thereby laid the commercial foundations upon which the political strength of the empire rested. Constantine had, indeed, recognized, long before, the importance of stable money as the basis of stable empire. Twelve years earlier, when he was but a local satrap, he had reformed the coinage in the provinces over which he exercised authority.

But to examine the reconstruction of money in Byzantium requires us to refer, for a moment, to the Emperor Diocletian.

৺৾ ৡ৵

Among the reforms introduced by Diocletian was his great scheme for the reorganization of the imperial administration. Two *imperators*, or *augusti*, were established, one to rule over the Asiatic portions of the Empire, the other to guard the European dominions; and the entire machinery of government was placed under imperial authority. Among the various functions absorbed under the imperial establishment was that of coining money, previously exercised, as we have seen, by a host of conflicting authorities. Henceforth, the familiar letters S. C. are no longer seen on the copper coins, and everywhere was the diademed effigy of the ruling emperor. For the first time in Roman history a universal and uniform coinage became possible.

The division of authority between two imperial households soon extended itself into a geographical and political severance of the realm. Under Constantine, the ruler of the Eastern Empire took up his permanent residence at Byzantium, which thereafter remained the capital of an empire which preserved the name and tradition of Roman civilization.

II. Splendor of the East

THE significant thing about the division of the Empire by Diocletian—from the standpoint of monetary economics—is that
it permitted the revival of a tradition which had long been submerged. The eastern half of the Empire, embracing the Asiatic
provinces, had from the time of Alexander been Greek in character, culture, and to a large degree, language. After the split of
the imperial administration, Greek influence again became
paramount in the East. Greek became the language of the court
—the *imperator* or *divus* becomes *basileus*—and Greek became
the renascent culture.

With the dominance of Greek influence in the imperial administration, we find returning to authority, after a submergence of 500 years under Roman domination, the sound philosophy of commerce and money, which we have traced in a preceding chapter. This Greek tradition of sound money, while it
had been submerged, had not been extinguished.

ఆర్ ইశ

We have already noted how, during the era of Gallienus, the
bronze coins of the East were so superior to anything of Roman
production that, though they were coined only for local use,
they were circulated as far as the Rhine and the Danube, where,
apparently in lieu of a better coin, they were utilized for troop
payments. Greek mints had still been operating within the preceding fifty years, and the last, the Alexandrian mint, had only
been closed by Diocletian.

As Greek commercial tradition revived we find a cessation
of the continual debasement of the coinage that had marked
the history of Rome. Constantine had reformed the coinage by
the establishment of a new gold piece called the *solidus*, or
nomisma, and a new silver piece called the *miliarense*, and by
continuing the coinage of the copper *follis* originated by Diocletian. This system, in its general outlines, was not tampered
with by succeeding emperors. Gradually it became fixed upon
the gold *solidus*, weighing approximately 65 grains,* which was

* It is significant of the Greek tradition that the weight of the new

minted at this standard for eight hundred years; and under the name *bezant*, it circulated from Ceylon to the Baltic.

It was a more honest coin, and a more honest commercial ethic than the world had witnessed for a long time, that we find in Byzantium.

∾ঔ ৡ∾

One important influence of the return to honest coinage was the reappearance of the precious metals in circulation. In the latter years of the Roman Empire, gold and silver had, as we have noted, so far disappeared from circulation that practically all payments were made in copper. Gold and silver now came out of hoarding and returned to the channels of trade.

Certain it is that gold was never scarce in Constantinople, despite the fact that large amounts of *bezants* were shipped abroad and used as media of payment throughout Europe. The amount of specie in existence during the ascendancy of the Empire (A.D. 716–817) was tremendous—so great indeed that no degree of extortion could have collected these sums unless the people had been wealthy and great commercial activity existed. We have some figures on the treasury assets. They amounted, during the regency of Theodora, to 1,099 centenaries of gold (a centenary was one hundred *libra* weight of bullion), 3,000 centenaries of silver, and in addition plate and gold embroidery containing 200 centenaries of gold.[1] If the Roman *libra* may be taken as 5,040 grains, and the silver valued at a ratio of 14 to 1, the whole was equivalent to nearly 1,589,000 troy ounces.

Some light on the actual size of this hoard is afforded by comparison with other famous treasures of history. The famous ransom—the roomful of gold—paid to Pizarro by Atahualpa, the last of the Incas, is estimated to have been no more than 185,000 ounces of gold, and the total gold extracted by the Spaniards from Peru, not more than 231,000 ounces. Lexis estimates, basing himself in the main on Soetbeer, that between

gold *bezant* corresponded very closely with that of the Attic silver *drachma*, the great unit of account in the Hellenic world.

1522 and 1547 the gold produced and plundered in Mexico amounted at the most to 922,000 ounces.[2]

The total amount of gold collected and delivered by France to Germany in payment of the five-billion-franc war indemnity exacted by the Treaty of Frankfort of 1871 did not exceed 2,600,000 ounces.[3] The famous German War Chest, established in the Harz mountains, contained only 1,383,000 ounces of gold at the outbreak of World War I,[4] and the gold reserves of the Bank of England in August, 1914, amounted to less than 10,000,000.

◈ ◈

Not only was money in abundance at Constantinople, center of a far flung political and commercial hegemony, but the *bezants* struck with the imperial seal became the accepted medium of exchange throughout the civilized world. Indubitable evidence of the regard for Byzantine coinage are the *nomisma* with names of the Byzantine emperors of the fourth, fifth, and sixth centuries which have been found in southern and western India, and in the Mongol hoards which were uncovered during the Indian Mutiny of 1856.[5] The bulk of these coins, incidentally, were not carried to India by Byzantine merchants, but by Persians and Abyssinians, who evidently regarded them as more generally acceptable than the productions of their own mints.

And in Europe the *bezants* served in all important payments where gold passed hands. Either because of respect for the authority of the Eastern Empire, as Del Mar believes, or because of the prestige of the Byzantine gold and the profusion with which it was minted, the European princes and feudal lords never minted gold on their own account. In England, for instance, we learn from the exchequer rolls of the Middle Ages, payments in *bezants* were the ordinary thing where gold was used.[6]

◈ ◈

Of the prestige of the Byzantine coinage, we have the testimony of Cosmas Indicopleustes, an Egyptian merchant of the sixth century, who traveled widely, perhaps as far as Ceylon, and whose work *Christian Topography*, is a leading source material for historians. He writes:

"The Roman Empire hath many privileges in that it is the first of empires, and that it first believed in Christ, and that it doth service to every branch of the Christian economy; and there is yet another sign of the power which God hath accorded to the Romans, to wit, that it is with their gold piece that all nations do their trade; it is received everywhere from one end of the earth to the other; it is admired by all men and every kingdom, for no other kingdom hath its like."[7]

And Cosmas tells an interesting story in illustration of the profound respect commanded in India by Byzantine money:

"The King of Ceylon, having admitted a Byzantine merchant, Sopatrus, and some Persians to an audience and having received their salutations, requested them to be seated. He then asked them: 'In what state are your countries, and how go things with them?' To this they replied, 'They go well.' Afterward, as the conversation proceeded, the King enquired: 'Which of your kings is the greater and the more powerful?' The elderly Persian, snatching the word, answered, 'Our king is both more powerful and the greater and the richer, and indeed is King of Kings, and whatsoever he desires, that he is able to do.' Sopatrus, on the other hand, sat mute. So the King asked, 'Have you, Roman, nothing to say?' 'What have I to say,' he rejoined, 'when he there has said such things? But if you wish to learn the truth you have the two kings here present. Examine each and you will see which of them is the grander and the more powerful.' The King, upon hearing this, was amazed at his words and asked, 'How say you that I have both kings here?' 'You have,' replied Sopatrus, 'the money of both—the *nomisma* of one, and the *drachma*, that is, the *miliarense* of the other. Examine the image of each and you will see the truth. . . . .' After having examined them, the King said that the Romans were certainly a splendid, powerful, and sagacious people. So he ordered great honor to be paid to Sopatrus, causing him to be mounted on an elephant and conducted around the city with drums beating and high state."[8]

ക§ ई∾

A sound coinage was of course but one aspect of a commercial policy devoted to the encouragement of industry, the investment of capital, and the organization of enterprise. Banking was
brought under a more wholesome ethic. No longer do we read of
unregulated banking and the frauds of the money interest. Exchange was brought under imperial monopoly, and the money
changers, like many of the commercial fraternity of the Empire,
were organized strictly into guilds under imperial auspices, with
fees limited and the exchange rates fixed by law.

The *Book of the Prefect* contains a series of provisions concerning bankers and money changers in the capital of the
Byzantine Empire. In order to be admitted into the society of
bankers, the testimony of honorable men had to be forthcoming
to answer for the candidate that he would do nothing contrary
to the rules—that is, that he would not file or clip either the
solidi or the *miliarensia,* that he would not issue false coin, and
that if any public service prevented him from carrying on his
business he should not install any of his slaves in his place as
director of the bank. Infringement of these rules was severely
punished: the delinquent's hand was cut off. The money
changers were bound to denounce to the prefect the unlicensed
changers, *saccularii,* who prowled about the highways with their
money bags; they might not discount anything on the gold if it
was of good alloy and stamped with the authentic imperial effigy;
they should take it for what it was worth if it was not good metal;
the penalty was chastisement with the whip, cropping off the
hair and beard, and confiscation. They were compelled to denounce false money and the receivers of it.[9]

Debt apparently had no large place in Byzantine economy.
Under the influence of Aristotelian concepts of money, as
handed down in Greek philosophy and passed on in the structure of Christian economic teaching, it is likely that interest was
regarded with repugnance, and that debt, although it existed,
was an inconsequential factor in commercial transactions.

Among other important contributions of Byzantine administrative policy to the commercial weal of the Empire was the
guild system, in which production, prices, and methods of work
were meticulously regulated and which provided a pattern for

the later guilds of Europe. The Rural Code, which broke entirely with Roman law tradition, accorded the peasant and small landowner privileges which this class of society had never before enjoyed.* Likewise, the Nautical Code, or Rhodian Sea-Law, attributed to the time of Leo III (A.D. 717–741), but developed sometime between A.D. 600 and A.D. 800, was of great benefit to navigation and became the model for the navigation codes of Europe.

❧ ❧

The dominance of Constantinople lasted for the better part of 800 years—a period longer than the historical era of Rome. Toward the end, however, evidences of decay became manifest. And we need not look into the chronicles of military campaigns for the evidence. The coins that have been handed down tell the story. The first signs appear in the reign of Alexius Comnenus (A.D. 1081–1118). Alexius was unpopular, and his unpopularity is attributed to the frauds he committed in adulterating the coinage. Alexius paid the public debts in his own debased coinage, but he enforced the payment of taxes, so long as it was possible, in the pure coinage of the earlier emperors. The ruin produced by these measures at last compelled him to adopt new regulations for collecting the land tax; and the credit of his coinage became so bad throughout all the countries in Europe in which Byzantine gold had previously circulated that the Emperor was compelled, in all public acts with foreigners, to stipulate that he would make all his payments in the gold coin of his predecessors.

The decline of Byzantine commerce in the Mediterranean is attributed by George Finlay to these measures of Alexius, which ruined the credit of the Greek merchants and transferred a large

* The Rural Code has received its greatest attention from Russian scholars (much of whose work has not been translated into English), partly because of the mooted question of Slavonic influence in Byzantine institutions, partly because of the influence of Byzantine communal land theories in later Russian rural economy and political policy. See A. A. Vasilev, *History of the Byzantine Empire* (University of Wisconsin Studies, Madison, 1928).

quantity of capital from the cities of the Empire to the republics of Italy.*

In A.D. 1204 the Venetians, who had been growing in importance and who had a grudge to even with the Emperor, succeeded in diverting the Fourth Crusade into an attack upon Constantinople. The City and the Empire fell; and though it was later reconstituted and continued to exist as an independent power for another 250 years (until the final sack by the Turks in 1453), it never recovered its commercial importance. Byzantium ceased, from 1204, to be a world center of civilization.

ৰ্গ ২৯

Such was the strength of Byzantine finance that in a period of eight hundred years, from Diocletian to Alexius Comnenus, the government never found itself compelled to declare bankruptcy or to stop payments. "Neither the ancient nor the modern world," says Heinrich Gelzer, "can offer a complete parallel to this phenomenon. This prodigious stability of the Roman financial policy secured the *bezant* its universal currency. On account of its full weight it passed with all the neighboring nations as a valid medium of exchange. By her money Byzantium controlled both the civilized and the barbarian worlds."[10]

ৰ্গ ২৯

The Byzantine Empire is an example of sound commercialism and testimony that money, if handled properly and with due restraint, can be made to serve the highest purposes of man. In its commercial institutions and commercial philosophy lay a great part of the secret of its long continued vitality. And a principal feature of that commercial philosophy was the tradition of sanctity of the coinage—the idea that it is the duty of the state to avoid tampering with the money mechanism for personal or political objects, and that the duty of commercialists is to use money with restraint, as a means and not as an end.

* George Finlay, *op. cit.*, III, 63. In the treaty with Bohemund for the evacuation of Byzantine territory, signed at Deavolis in 1108, Alexius was obliged to stipulate that his payments should be made in *bezants* of the coinage of Michael (Anna Comnenus 328).

Book Five. THE MIDDLE AGES

IN the dark and seemingly bottomless quagmire of the Middle Ages, through which Western civilization had to pass before reaching the firmer ground of a new day, most of the institutions of antiquity perished, and among them money. Money, indeed, was perhaps the first to disappear in the tremulant depths, although, as we shall see, the monetary tradition of Rome was to remain, like a floating scum, to poison the economy of modern Europe in the freshness and vigor of its rebirth.

I. Passage of Avernus

WE have already traced the gradual disintegration of money in Rome. By the end of the fourth century it had practically disappeared in Europe, and with it went all the fabric of organized commerce and industry. Law courts and libraries, schools and posts and inns, even the organization of armies, all disintegrated in the miasmic atmosphere or were sucked down into the paludal mire. The Roman Empire had been split in twain, and then into many fragments, each of which became a separate kingdom; the kingdoms in turn became divided into numerous counties and duchies, and the latter into still more numerous realms. The world dwindled and the commonwealth "became the duke's courtyard." Over the Europe that had basked in the deceptive effulgence of the *Pax Romana* swept wave after wave of barbarism, producing convulsions in society like the social revolutions of the modern age, engulfing everything not of the most solid substance, leaving in their wake, as they receded, the detritus of a destroyed civilization.

This long period of decay and convulsion and racial migration lasted in Europe for some seven or eight hundred years. While its boundaries cannot be precisely defined, roughly they

may be marked by the fall of Rome in 476—although the northern provinces of the Empire had long earlier passed into other
hands—to the fall of Constantinople in 1204, which signalized
the removal of the commercial center of the Mediterranean
from the Bosporus to the city states of Italy, the recommence-
ment of gold coinage in Europe, and the revival of money
economy.

◦§ §◦

When European civilization began finally to emerge from its
intellectual coma and economic misery, and money, among
other institutions of the past, began to evolve itself anew out of
the fading gloom of medievalism, it appears to have been rein-
stated in the same tentative manner that it fell. The order of
falling was from money to bullion, and from bullion to barter.
The order of revival was much the same. It began with the
fixation of weights, and money was weighed in the scales and
assayed or tried by combustion. Following this came pieces or
sums with the names of weights—to wit, pounds, shillings, and
pennies (dennies or *denarii*) which passed by tale, and which,
although they never contained the weights of metal indicated
by their names, afforded by means of these names a ready conception of their relative proportions of value.

Some memory of Roman institutions was carried across the
gulf of the Middle Ages in the designation of weights and the
division of money standards, as weights and money slowly revived. The Roman pound, or *libra*, survived as a conception of
weight; but its actual standard, even in Roman times, is today
a problem baffling to scholars, and when it was revived the *libra*
became different things in different localities. Each locality had
its own variation of the standard, and weights had to be qualified
by prefixing the name of the town or locality in which they were
current, as for example, the *livre* of Tours, the Cologne *mark*
and the pound sterling (*Esterling*).*

◦§ §◦

* Such a system prevails in many regions of Asia today. Despite the
spread of the metric system under the influence of authoritarian govern-

Toward the end of the Middle Ages, three standards of account, at least for weighing the precious metals, had risen to enough prominence to become the basis for currency in the chief countries of Europe.

In France, two standards of weight for money had come into prominence, the *livre* or *poid de marc* of Paris, which was the capital of the Frankish kings, and the *livre* of Tours, the principal trading city toward the Arabian border at the west. The *livre tournois* was about a fourth lighter; and either because of the profits to be derived from coining money according to the lighter standard or, as some scholars assert, to take advantage of the higher relative value of silver to gold in the nearby Moslem dominions, the feudal barons enjoying the mint franchise preferred to do their minting at Tours according to the Tours standard, while at Paris the French kings attempted to keep up a tradition of the better weight standard. By the time of St. Louis (d. 1270) the *sol* of Tours had become generally known as the *gros deniers d'argent* or the *gros tournois*, and in Germany, as the *groschen*, and it became for a while a standard of coinage which was widely imitated. The distinction between the *livres tournois* and the *livres parisis* was maintained until the days of Louis XIV, when (1667) it was abolished and reckoning by a single *livre, sol* and *denier* was established.

Due to the fluctuations in weights and coinages, and especially the practice of lowering the standard of weight for money to bring it in correspondence with a debased coinage, it is almost impossible to assign modern equivalents to the various *livres* in use. The Paris *livre* or *poid de marc* was equivalent originally to 7,555 English grains,[1] but the *livre* as a weight soon parted company from the *livre* as a unit of money. D'Avenel states that in 1200 the *livre tournois* designated 98 grams (1,512.336 grains)

ments and their Five Year Plans, local measures persist. Thus, in villages in Iran, work may be measured by one *batman*, grain by another, and vegetables by a third, while the standard may take its name from the city of its principal usage. In China, as late as World War I, merchants had to be familiar with the weight of a variety of *taels* and the commodities to which they applied. Vestiges of these differences remain in the English system of weights and measures, as in the ounce *troy* and the ounce *avoirdupois*, and the long ton and the short ton.

of fine silver, but that by 1600 it had fallen to 11 grams.[2] The unit of weight (for metals) eventually became fixed upon the *mark* of 4,608 French grains (3,777.5 English grains) divided into 8 ounces. It is upon this *mark* that most of the tables of French coinage down to the Revolution were based.

In Germany, the standard of most common acceptance, which subsequently became the standard for weighing metals, was the Cologne *mark*, which at the beginning of the nineteenth century was equivalent to 3,608 English grains. The origin of the *mark* is unknown but it is conjectured to have been a degenerate descendant of the Roman *libra* in Venice, and to have weighed originally around 4,000 English grains. As the medieval period wore on, it partook of the general degradation of weights, falling in Venice to 3,681.5 grains, and in Germany generally from 3,681.5 to 3,608 grains, at which latter weight it made its way into Denmark and England in the ninth century. Its weight was fixed in Cologne at 3,608 grains by edict of Charles V in 1524, who declared it the standard of weight for the precious metals throughout his German empire. Charles was at the same time King of Spain, and the *mark*, after some further degradation (falling to 3,557.5 grains in Valencia and 3,550.5 grains in Castile), was fixed in that country generally at 3,550.5 grains, and at this weight found its way to America where it was used to measure and coin the vast metallic productions of the newly-found continent.[3]

The pound avoirdupois of 7,000 grains in use in the English-speaking countries is apparently derived from the "old commercial" pound of 7,600 grains formerly used in Amsterdam, Hamburg, and Paris, and used in England for the assize of bread until 1815, and in Scotland for general purposes until late in the nineteenth century. The Anglo-Saxon pound, sometimes called the "moneyers' pound," sometimes the "pound tower," contained 5,400 grains and was used in the English mints previous to 1527. In that year Henry VIII issued his second coinage (Act of 18th Henry VIII), and the pieces were weighed by the *troy* or *troyes* pound of 5,760 grains, and this has continued to be used for weighing the precious metals in England ever since.[4]

⋘ ⋙

In addition to a vague conception of a *libra*, which survived in Europe, some memory was also retained of the Roman division of the coinage. In Byzantium, where civilization was still flourishing, and whose contacts with Europe were numerous if not vital, the *libra* was coined into 72 *solidi*. When Charlemagne attempted, in imitation of Roman imperialism, to reestablish his own coinage throughout his dominions, he instituted a system based upon a *libra*, divided into 20 *solidi*, each consisting of 12 *denarii*. A gold *solidus* seems to have been provided for, but he never got beyond the coinage of a silver *denarius*, and with the growth of feudalism, the break-up of his empire, the multiplicity of coinages by local princes and feudal lords, all that remains of his system is the traditional division of the unit. This survives in the English system of pounds (£), shillings and pence (originally dennies, and still abbreviated as *d.*) and in the *livre*, *sou* (or *sol*), and *denier* which were the reckoning in France until superseded by the metric system at the time of the French Revolution.

⋘ ⋙

As money slowly reestablished itself in Europe, we find a multitude of provincial and feudal mints springing up. Every petty baron or princeling decided to perpetuate his name or rule upon a piece of metal. The right of issuing money is a special prerogative of the sovereign power. It is enough to say that as this power gradually collected itself in petty feudalities on the map of Europe, like drops congealing on a window pane, the first emblem of its new-found majesty was a mint and a coin. As sovereign authority gradually coalesced and extended its sway over larger and larger territory, its first task was to recover the exclusive right of coinage. But it was a long and difficult task. In France, the Merovingians had been compelled to delegate the right of coinage to counts, bishops, and cities. One writer declares that members of the ancient corporation of moneyers of Rome (the Mint Commissioners), whose signature was the official guarantee of coinage, continued to coin in their own name and to their own profit from a great variety of types.[5]

In the seventh century there might be reckoned in France hundreds or perhaps thousands of mints uncontrolled and offering no guarantee. Throughout western Europe the position was analogous; lords, prelates, and municipalities claimed to be absolutely independent in coinage matters.

Charlemagne, in his capitulary of 805, had prohibited every mint except the royal one, but his successors had not been able to maintain the sovereign authority, and according to letters patent in 1315, twenty-nine lords of France appear to have retained the right of coining money and determining the law, weight, stamp and value of the different specie.[6]

And toward the end of the Middle Ages there were in Germany, according to Karl Helfferich, 600 mints working.[7] Most of these mints struck small silver or copper, and their diversity of sizes and shapes and fineness renders them almost impossible of cataloguing or defining. It is, in fact, not until the thirteenth century that it is possible to construct any intelligible story of money in Europe. That century was marked by the sack of Constantinople by the Crusaders in 1204, the end of the Eastern Empire, as such, and the transfer of the commercial hegemony of the Mediterranean to Italy. The capture of Constantinople and the establishment of the abortive Latin Empire on the Bosporus marked the end of the *solidus*, or *bezant*, as the universal standard of international trade, and prepared the way for the introduction of gold coinage into Europe.

❧

The attendant circumstances of this transfer and their influence upon the monetary history of Europe are to be found in the history of the Crusades and of the commercial growth of the petty independent states which sprang up from the political confusion of Italy. The German invaders of the Peninsula had not swept away city life, as did their cousins in the provinces of northwestern Europe, and several of the older cities, such as Milan and Genoa, important in Roman times, continued to exist. Venice, founded during the disorders of the fifth century, began to attract settlers because of its comparative impregnability. The survival of these cities and the founding or revival of others was possible because of continued contact by sea with the civilized East, and toward the eleventh century they were sufficiently strong to throw off feudal and church authority and to organize local city states upon the basis of a commercial aristocracy. No sooner did they achieve each their little autonomy than they threw themselves with redoubled energy into the development of the trade with the East. Florence and Venice, Pisa and Genoa, led the way and reaped the fruits; and it was in her most flourishing time, when she had conquered her rivals and was enjoying a prosperous and active trade, that Florence resolved upon the coining of gold.

The influences which collected in the Italian city states, arising from their contacts with the East, molded and transformed under the peculiar forces of their own development, and finally emanating throughout Europe, were to affect profoundly the course of European civilization—in art, in commerce, in politics, in money—so profoundly in fact that the economic revolutions of today are but the distant convulsions produced by the subterranean conflict of the fire of Italy and the water of Europe.

⊷❧ ⧉⊷

The concatenation of events that produced throughout Europe the almost simultaneous revival of gold coinage in the thirteenth century is attributed to various causes. According to some, the foreign trade of the Italian republics must have become so extensive as to demand a currency medium of higher denomination than silver; or that trade must have developed in such directions as to tap gold-using or gold-bearing regions that could supply the Italian mints.[8]

Alexander Del Mar, however, offers another theory of the correlation of the two events. According to his view, the coinage of gold has, since it first appeared in the monetary systems of the world, been the incontestable prerogative of sovereignty, and during the long period of the Middle Ages such was the majesty of the Eastern Empire, so powerful the tradition of Roman grandeur, so impuissant the multitude of feudal authorities, that no prince had the presumption to place his own seal and signature upon a piece of gold money. Even in those isolated cases where gold was coined by other princes, such as the coinage of Clovis, that of the kings of the Cimmerian Bosporus, or the coinages of the Roman generals, Roman suzerainty and majesty were acknowledged by placing upon the coins the imperial insignia.[9]

•§ §•

The reintroduction of gold into the coinages of Western nations is marked by the minting of the gold *florin* of Florence in 1252. Clovis had struck some gold coins of excellent quality, and Charlemagne may have issued a few, but Florence was the first state of modern Europe to establish a continuity of gold coinage. Genoa followed closely upon Florence in issuing gold, probably the same year, and in 1254, or possibly earlier, Louis IX of France (St. Louis) commenced the coinage of *louis d'or*. Five years later (1257) Henry III of England imitated the *florin* in his gold pennies, while more than thirty years later Venice instituted the coinage of gold *zecchinos* (corrupted later into *sequins*). It was not until some seventy-five years later, in 1328, that gold coinage appeared in Germany, signalized by the issues of the Emperor Louis IV, surnamed "Bavarian," closely imitating the *florin* of Florence. In Moslem Spain gold coinage had prevailed since the Moorish invasion in the eighth century, but the first gold coined by Christian powers was the *oro gran modulo* (*doblas de oro*) of Alfonso XI of Castile (1312–1350).

By the middle of the fourteenth century, therefore, we find the institution of money fully reestablished in Europe, with gold, silver and copper coins in circulation.

•§ §•

Hardly, however, had money as an institution of organized economy, as a social mechanism, been reestablished, than it began to disintegrate under the destructive influences handed down from Rome, the sciolism of the age, and the moral infirmities of rulers.

II. The Color of Gold

THE reappearance of money in Europe and the transition of society to a money economy was accompanied by the same phenomena that we have observed in early Greece and in the Roman commonwealth. Everywhere men were dazzled by its form, by the opportunities it offered for the accumulation of wealth, for the ease of movement, for the loosening of old ties and habits. Europe became money-mad; for the pursuit of spiritual peace was substituted that of the pursuit of the precious metals; the authority of the old morals and ethics were sensibly weakened, and life took on an unrestrained search for the pleasure, the ostentation, the movement, and the power that money offered. More than armies, or capable government, or sound administration, or a contented citizenry, as the bases of a prosperous and ordered society, was the presence and authority of money.

With seeming suddenness one principle became the dominant chord and theme of contemporary thought and practice, and this principle was incorporated, like a heraldic device, in the attitudes of the day, by the phrase *pecunia nervus belli* (money is the sinews of war). It became the dogma of philosophy, the motto of princes, the adjuration of ministers. Gold, as the most precious of the metals, was elevated into the pantheon; the quest for the yellow metal became the occupation of alchemy, of statecraft, of war, of exploration. Letters-patent were freely issued by the kings to alchemists, permitting them to employ the means which they discovered "by philosophic art" to change impure metals into gold and silver, or to make gold and silver with mercury. It was so with Edward III, Henry VI, and Edward IV of England, and with the kings of France, and the German and Italian princes. The libraries of the day were filled with volumes treating of the transmutation of the metals, crowding out the earlier works on the destiny of the soul, the nature of divinity, and the duties of the Christian life. Money became the basis of political philosophy, and Botero, Bodinus Besold, Ammirato, and other publicists of the epoch argued the need for money—even above man-power—for the successful prosecution of war or state administration. The search for treasure, in the earth, in the crucible, in the Indies, and on the high seas, became the universal mania; and the voyages of the early explorers were not so much to discover spices as precious metals, or lands where the precious metals were abundant.

⋞§ §⋟

No sooner had Columbus taken formal possession of the island of Hispaniola than he asked the wondering natives for gold. "This fatal word," says Del Mar, "so fraught with misfortune to the aborigines that it might fittingly furnish an epitaph for the race, and so tainted with dishonor to their conquerors that four centuries of time have not sufficed to remove its stigma, seems literally the first verbal communication from the Old World to the New."

Gold, indeed, became a fetish. "We allow the color of gold to be the noblest in the world," wrote Honoré Bonet, in his *Arbre des batailles*, speaking of the colors of armorial bearings. "Now, this is the reason: gold of its own nature is bright and shining, and it is so strengthening and full of virtues that the doctors give it as a sovereign remedy to those who are weak even unto death. And so it represents the sun, the which is a very noble body if we consider it in regard to light, for the law says there is nothing more noble than brightness. . . . . And the ancient laws formerly ordained that no man in the world should wear gold except princes."

⋞§ §⋟

Perhaps nothing better illustrates the power of money in the Middle Ages and the mercenary quality of that period than the growth of the *condottieri*, or professional undertakers of war, and the general dependence of medieval princes upon the use of mercenary troops. For a long period wars were waged and states maintained by the use of bodies of professional soldiers, largely Germans, Swiss, and Spaniards, raised and equipped chiefly by Italians, and serving in any land or under any banner which could assure them of pay, and devoting their lives as a sacrifice to any prince whose only claim upon their loyalty was a full purse.

By the use of such mercenaries the French kings and German emperors expanded their authority, and the Thirty Years War was largely conducted. They remained an integral part of the French military system until the final downfall of the monarchy and were employed by the English government during the War of the American Revolution. The characteristic of the system is preserved in such terms as the *Ribauds* of the thirteenth century, or the *Routiers*, the *Écorcheurs*, and *Retondeurs* of the fifteenth, and is nowhere better summed up than in the famous phrase, "blood for money; no money, no Swiss!"

❧ ❦

It is natural, under the influences and circumstances of this "raging avarice," that the mechanism of money should be utterly uncontrolled: there was no authority strong enough to assert itself over a territory of any consequence, and such authority as existed was without the courage, or the wisdom, or the morality, to undertake the control of money. It was an era of the most flagrant debasement, of money tampering and manipulation. No one seemed to recognize the evils that were being piled up for subsequent generations by this practice, and if they were recognized no one seemed to care. "Many princes, both in the Middle Ages and later in the sixteenth and seventeenth centuries," says Richard Ehrenberg, "did a roaring business in currency depreciation."

❧ ❦

The right to clip, degrade, or debase the coinages, or to change the standard, was looked upon complacently as the prerogative of sovereignty. To debase the currency became, as it were, a crown right, and the process was given a sonorous Latin name, *morbus numericus*, as though it were a phrase of canon or civil law, an ancient and hallowed practice. Up to the reign of Charles VII, the "seignorage," i.e., the profits realized from the coining of money, was one of the chief revenues of the French crown. The idea was generally accepted that when the necessity of the state so required, the king could not only increase the seignorage, and raise still greater sums in the manufacture of money, but might also impair the coins by diminishing their worth. By some this process was considered a source of revenue that was prompter, easier and less burdensome than any other. At the end of the thirteenth century the situation was so harassing that the towns pledged themselves to pay heavy taxes in order to obtain from their overlords the assurance of sound currency. This was the *moneyage*—a tax levied triennially as a recompense for the king "not to alter or debase the coin, which he was entitled to do by his prerogative."

ﻋﺞ ﻓﻌ

The difficulty in tracing the actual course of the depreciation is complicated not only by the lack of historical records and the confusion in those that exist, but by the variety of forms employed to achieve the ends.

Three general methods were employed for the debasement of money. The most common, during the earlier period, were *la mutacion du poids*, which was a reduction of the weight or standard of the specie without diminishing proportionally its current value—the surreptitious debasement so common in Roman history—and *la mutacion de la matière*, which was a change in the standard.

A more subtle method, involving no actual tampering with the coin, was *la mutacion de l'appellation*—a change in the legal denomination or standard of value, a practice also hoary in antiquity—the method no doubt used by Solon, and used even in modern times, as in the devaluations of the United States dollar in 1934 and subsequently.

The gold *florin*, for instance, was originally struck at 53 grains, and it was of absolute fineness. As the process of wear and tear and abrasion went on, and the coins in circulation became less than the nominal standard, it became customary to buy and sell and enter into contracts on the basis of the standard or perfect *florin*, and its subdivisions, and accepting or tendering at a discount the actual coins in circulation, depending upon their degree of abrasion. The ideal or standard *florin* became the "money of account" in which books were kept and transactions predicated. This "money of account" received official sanction

in 1321 when the ideal or standard *florin* was officially designated as the "*florin* of the public seal" (*fiorino di sigillo*).
Florins were tested and counted into small leather bags, which
were fastened up and sealed with the seal of the city. These were
known as *fiorini di sigillo* and were used in the payment of large
sums. Current *florins* were then given an official rate of discount
to these sealed *florins* at which they should circulate. Gradually,
of course, since the bulk of the circulation consisted of the worn
coins—the greater value of the sealed bags rendering them useful only in large transactions—the *fiorini di sigillo* came to be
more a concept than an actual measure. This method of officially valuing the current coinage in reference to the theoretical,
founded upon sound principle, thus came to be used as a device
for readjusting the ratio between gold and silver, which was
beginning to be a problem; and then, as the money of account
drifted further and further away from an actual coin, and its
concept as a physical unit was gradually lost, it became the
vehicle for currency depreciation. On the pretext of adjusting
the ratio between gold and silver, or to take official cognizance
of a deteriorated state of the outstanding circulation, or as an
accompaniment of a "recoinage," the value of the money of
account was gradually lowered. By this process the gold *florin*
was gradually raised, between 1252 and 1534, from 20 *soldi* to
150 *soldi* of account.

In the sixteenth century, so far had the Italian states fallen
away from the former probity of their currency policy and practice that Bernardo Davanzati declared in his *Lezione delle
monete*, which appeared in 1588, that the disorder of the monetary system had within a period of sixty years made away with
a third of the public wealth.

❦

In France, the price of a *mark* weight of gold was gradually
raised from 44 *livres de compte* in 1309 to 171 *livres de compte*
in 1342. At this point of depreciation a new *livre de compte*,
equivalent to four of the old, was instituted to an accompaniment of a solemn declaration on the part of the government "to
adhere to good money, as in the halcyon days of St. Louis, etc.,

etc." In the terms of this new *livre* the price of the *mark* of gold was again brought to 44 *livres*. By 1419 the price of gold in terms of the money of account had again risen to 144 *livres*, when it was again reduced by one-half or to 72 *livres* by the introduction of a new *livre de compte*. Again the *livre de compte* continued to decline, and in 1709, just before the French currency came into control of John Law, it took 576 *livres* to buy a *mark* of gold. Between 768 and 1764 the *livre* of Charlemagne had declined to one sixty-sixth of its original value, according to the tables prepared by the Abbot of Bazinham,[1] in which some forty different and distinct debasements are presented, or one on the average of every twenty-five years, while omitting many surreptitious and gradual debasements occurring between the major depreciations.

The course of depreciation in Germany was as definite as in France. To draw one instance out of an uncharted mass: the standard of Hamburg and Lübeck, the principal trading towns, was a *schilling*, originally coined as one-sixteenth of the Cologne *mark*, each *schilling* consisting of 12 *pfennige*. The coin and the standard soon parted company, the *mark* being retained as a unit of account, the *schilling* both as the name of a coin, and as a subdivision of the *mark*. In 1255 the two cities, recognizing the state of depreciation, agreed, as a sort of monetary union, to coin the *mark* of fine silver into 38 *schillingen* 10 *pfennige*: in other words, the *mark* of metal became equivalent to 2 *mark* 6 *schillingen* 10 *pfennige* of account. The course of depreciation of the *mark* of account may be indicated by the following table showing the number of *mark* of account commanded by a *mark* weight of fine silver:[2]

Date	Mark	Schillingen	Pfennige
1226	2	2	0
1255	2	9	5
1293	2	9	8
1305	2	15	5
1325	3	0	9
1353	3	10	11
1375	4	3	0
1398	4	15	2

Date	Mark	Schillingen	Pfennige
1403	5	1	11
1411	5	12	5
1430	8	8	0
1450	9	12	2
1461	11	8	10
1506	12	8	0

It is frequently assumed that England was comparatively free from this constant and universal practice of money alteration. The Norman kings rarely tampered with the coinage. Their coins were all of one class—silver pennies, sometimes including half-pennies, but usually pennies only. These did not constitute the only money in circulation, but the only money issued by the king. In addition to silver pennies, there were coins issued by the nobles and ecclesiastics, commonly base silver coins, of local course and circulation, and the gold coins of Byzantium.

With the reign of Henry II (Plantagenet), however, evidence of frequent debasements appears. It is worthy of remark, that this period which marked an enlargement in the authority and dominions of the English kings ushered in also an era of profligate monetary practice. The kings themselves now began the practice of coinage tampering which had heretofore been limited to the ecclesiastical and vassal mints. The process reached a culmination in the reign of the first three Edwards. In 1310 the Commons petitioned and represented to Edward II that the coins were depreciated more than one-half. Between 1300 and 1464 the weight of the silver penny dropped from 22 grains in weight to 12 grains.[3] And Del Mar observes in England an innovation in the method of debasement. This was a marked difference between the content of a coin as provided by law or mint indenture and its actual content, as found by weight or assay of perfect specimens still extant. For example, the mint indenture of 1345 provided that the Tower pound of silver, .925 fine, should be coined into 22.5 pennies. This would make the gross weight of each penny 24 grains, and the content of fine silver 22.2 grains, whereas Del Mar found by examination that the actual coins in good condition weigh but 20 grains and contain but 18.5 grains of fine silver, and that this same thing held true in the case of other coins of the period.[4]

III. Course of the Dinar

THE failure of European philosophy to understand money, or of government to control it, or of business to resist its temptations is nowhere better illustrated than in the currency history of medieval Spain. Here in the Iberian peninsula the sounder traditions of the East met and were subdued by the wayward practices of the West; here again occurred the same conflict between Hellenic philosophy and self-control and the license and mismanagement of Rome.

While Roman civilization was slowly dying in the West, a new civilization was being born in Arabia. In the Arabian peninsula, at the beginning of the seventh century, arose a religious leader—Mohammed—who, in a few short years, united the diverse and disunited peoples of Arabia and established a great religious, social, economic, and political movement that was to flame like a beacon throughout Western Asia for the next two centuries, invade Europe, and for five hundred years more to constitute the most brilliant civilization of the Mediterranean.

ঙ§ ৡ৯

The Hegira, or flight from Mecca, occurred in 622. In 633–639 the whole of Syria was subdued; in 638–639 Egypt was conquered; in 637–651 Persia was overrun; in the interval between 647 and 689 every organized state of Africa, westward to Carthage, was reduced; in 692–698 Carthage was captured; between 698 and 709 the remainder of Northern Africa, including Mauritania, to the Atlantic was subdued; and in 711 the Arabs entered Spain, so that within a century from the beginning of Mohammed's conquering career their power was firmly established over a territory which stretched uninterruptedly from India to the Western Ocean.

The wellspring from which flowed this tide of conquest is

found in the religious inspiration of Mohammed's teaching, but the sources of the remarkable civilization that was established in its wake, which we know as Saracenic, were many and diverse. The religious teachings of the Prophet were derived in part from Jewish and Christian tradition; the political administration was copied, with modifications and refinements, from Persia; science and philosophy were derived from the Greeks; mathematics perhaps from India.

❧ ☙

Among the institutions which the Arabs borrowed from the Greek civilization of the eastern Mediterranean was the highly developed commercial system with its well regulated money economy. We have already told of money in Greece, the development of Hellenic monetary philosophy, and the traditions of sound currency which were established in the Hellenized portions of the East—traditions that somehow managed to survive the centuries of Roman imperialism and that were revived and purified at Byzantium.

To support the expanding commerce of their Empire, the Arabs adopted bodily the Byzantine currency system. At the outset of their national career they employed chiefly copper coins of their own design, but founded on the Byzantine type and system. The gold coins employed were those of the Byzantine Empire, and the silver ones those of the Sassanian kings of Persia (which, in turn, were based on the Greek *drachma*), whose empire they had overthrown at the battles of Kadisin and Nehavend. In 691 or 692 the Caliph Abd-el-Malik inaugurated the regular Moslem coinage, which thereafter was issued from all the mints of the Empire. This consisted of gold *dinars* weighing 65 grains, .979 fine or approximately the size of the *bezant*, and silver *dirhems* of 43 grains, .960 to .970 fine. This currency was carried into Spain when the Arabs overran the peninsula in 711, and soon supplanted the diverse and heterogeneous Gothic moneys in use.

❧ ☙

The period of Saracenic dominion of Spain was, with the ex-

ception of the short interval in which the treasures of the New
World were flowing into Spanish coffers, perhaps the most brilliant and prosperous that land has ever experienced. The seat
of government was at Cordova, which in the course of a few
years became the richest, most learned, and most brilliant city
in the world. The lands of Spain were brought to a thorough
state of cultivation; fruits, vegetables, cereals, and commercial
plants were introduced from Asia; irrigation was extended from
the foothills to the lowlands; an infinite number of manufactures
and other industries were established; the gold, silver, copper
and lead, iron and quicksilver mines of Andalusia, Jaen, and
other districts were reopened and worked by free laborers; and
in addition, an immense trade with the Levant which employed
more than a thousand ships was maintained from Barcelona
and other ports.

وهی فهی

There were of course weaknesses in the Arab civilization: its
virtues were largely borrowed rather than native; the religious
and philosophic base of the system was a rigid dogma which did
not allow sufficient room for growth; and the fertile energies of
the movement had no doubt exhausted themselves, like the
febrile blooming of a transplanted flower, before they could be
renewed from the inner sources of the race.

Toward the end of the tenth century the Saracenic political
administration began to decline, split among numerous warring
sheiks, and with the reviving power of Europe, Spain in the next
two centuries passed over into Christian hands. As the Saracens
withdrew from the peninsula, they left behind them the culti-
vated lands, the irrigation ditches, their commercial organization, and in particular their money system.

Unfortunately, our knowledge of the monetary system in
Saracenic Spain is fragmentary and incomplete. We know practically nothing about the monetary regulations, the legal ratio
of value adopted from time to time between gold, silver, and
copper, the laws of legal tender and seignorage, or the quantity
of money in circulation. Apparently, the system consisted of
gold, silver, and copper, the integer and the tale relations of

which are undetermined. At first there were 10 of the silver *dirhems* to the gold *dinar*; but afterward the ratio is supposed to have been raised to 18 or even 20. The earliest *dinars* which were circulated in Spain had Latin inscriptions on them, possibly to familiarize the inhabitants with the new coinage.

We do know, however, that during the four centuries that the Saracenic rule continued, the gold coinage was retained very near its original weight and purity, and although this feat alone may not indicate a stability of money or the most enlightened currency practice, it does bear witness to a self-restraint in dealing with the medium of exchange and a rigorous adhesion, despite all temptation to the contrary, to the best traditions and concepts of the day. The mere maintenance of an unadulterated coinage may not be evidence of "scientific" currency practice, but it is the best testimony the age could offer of a sense of moral responsibility and an intellectual restraint in dealing with the money mechanism.

❧ ❧

The *dinar*, the coinage of which had been instituted by the Caliph Abd-el-Malik in 691–692 at a weight equivalent to 65 English grains, was still minted at 64.5 grains in Spain at the beginning of the eleventh century. Under the Moorish dynasty of the Almoravides, which lasted from 1094 to 1144, the *dinar* was struck at an equivalent of 60 to 61.75 grains. As such, but under the name of *maravedi* (derived from *almoravides*), the Arabian *dinar* was adopted by the Christian conquerors of Spain as the basis of their currency, but its weight was immediately reduced; and it was struck at an equivalence of 56 grains.

Hardly had the authority and the coinage prerogative passed from Moslem to Christian hands when the *dinar*, which had been retained at substantially its original weight for 450 years, was immediately subjected to the most profligate and unrestrained debasement. By the time of James I of Aragon (1213) the *maravedi* had sunk to 14 grains. Under Alfonso the Wise the *maravedi* was reduced to 10 grains, and at that size it had become too small for circulation and, of course, for further debasement. Accordingly it was converted into a silver coin weighing about 26 grains. The silver *maravedi* now began the same headlong course downward in size and fineness that had attended it as a gold coin. In 1368, at the accession of Enrique II, it weighed less than 17 grains; by the time of Juan I, eleven years later, less than 14 grains; by the time of Enrique III, less than 7 grains. On the accession of Juan II in 1406 the silver *maravedi* contained only 3.35 grains fine silver, and by the time of Enrique IV (1454), only 1.49 grains fine silver. The *maravedi* had of course ceased long earlier to exist as an independent coin, and was merely a unit of account in which the value of the actual coinage was measured. The process of depreciation was effected by "recoinages," in which new coins and new denominations were introduced, but the *maravedi* was retained as the common measure of value, and as such descended further and further in grade until it became no more than the most minute unit of account in the monetary system. Its value was raised slightly at the time of the great reformation of the currency instituted by Ferdinand and Isabella to represent 1.52 grains of silver, but afterward it resumed its downward course, and at the beginning of the nineteenth century represented no more than 0.62 grains of silver.

❦

In the fortunes of the *maravedi*, as a gold coin maintained at from 60 to 65 grains weight for a period of 400 years or more under Arab control, to a unit of account representing less than 1.5 grains of silver in the first four hundred years of European control, is summed up the story of money as it was handled in Europe from the time of its reappearance after the close of the medieval period down to the beginning of the modern era.

The secret of the currency disorganization of medieval times is to be found in the confusion in the eyes of nearly everyone between money as a mechanism and money as a commodity. Everywhere was an ignorant and foolish desire constantly to increase the number of units of money in one's possession, without reckoning what those units might represent—the same universal desire that led Adam Smith to comment in 1776, "no complaint is more common than that of a scarcity of money."

To the unrestrained desire to increase the quantity of money in circulation—by princes, in order to enlarge their revenues; by merchants, their profits; and by laborers, their wages—is to be attributed the inability of medieval, or modern Europe, to exercise sane and proper control over the money mechanism.

IV. False Dawn

HERE and there, amid the confusion of practice and the sophistry of thought, appeared the beginnings of a more intelligent approach to the question of money. This re-orientation of attitude among thinkers was occasioned by the misery which the currency manipulations were producing among all but a few favored classes. By the middle of the fourteenth century parts of Europe were almost in stagnation as a result of the monetary malpractices of their rulers. According to an official document of 1361, in France, the currency tampering had become so frequent and so aggravating that "it was with difficulty a man might know from day to day what coins he should disburse."[1] France was not the only sufferer: nearly every country was affected, and the extent of the evil might be measured by the complaints of the people and the protests and denunciations of the publicists.

The chief remedy lay in the limitation of the central power and in the continual vigilance of the subjects. Some countries exercised it. The Italian republics, as a result of their contacts with the East, had absorbed something of the Byzantine-Hellenic tradition, and as a rule maintained an honest currency system. The Florentine gold *florin*, for instance, was never debased, in spite of numerous adjustments in the minor coinage and changes in the rates. England did not suffer too many disastrous experiences. In Holland, at the beginning of the fifteenth century, Jacqueline of Bavaria had to promise not to make any change in the coinage without the consent of the towns of Dort, Leyden, Haarlem, and Delft.

The frequent debasements in the currency had begun to pro-

duce a series of memorials emanating either from towns or from
private persons. Pierre l'Auvergnat deplored the hardships upon
lesser folk—peasants and laborers and artisans—of receiving
bad money for their labor and products, while the towns of the
South of France went so far as to declare that it would be "the
work of the Holy Ghost" to get back to the coinage of St. Louis
and never after to depart from it."[2]

In the latter part of the fourteenth century appeared Nicole
Oresme's famous treatise, *De origine, natura, jure et mutatione
monetarum* (Treatise on the Origin, Nature, Law and Mutation
of Money). With an exactness and clearness of idea, this greatest of the scholastic economists declared that money should not
be debased without serious reasons of public utility; and he advanced proof that it does not belong to the prince but to the
community, and to the private persons into whose possession it
comes. Others—Diomede Caraffa, Andreas de Rampinis, and
Gabriel Biel—began to give their attention to questions of
monetary practice. Juan de Mariana, a German and a member
of the Jesuit order, boldly attacked the mischievous administration of Philip III of Spain, which had issued a new billon currency of much less value than the old one. Mariana, also, insisted
upon the rights of the people in the face of royal power. According to him, the coinage should be as stable as the weights and
measures, if confusion in business affairs was to be avoided.

◄§ §►

It is possible that the growth of economic philosophy and a
keener analysis of the problem of money might have followed
upon these early speculations and warnings, and money eventually brought under intellectual control, had it not been for the
discovery of America.

The discovery of America in 1492, and the enrichment of
Europe by the spoils of treasure in precious metals that found
their way throughout Europe, had a tremendous effect upon the
politics and economy and attitudes of Europe. The desire for
liquid wealth which the reviving use of money awakened, far
from being satisfied by these seemingly limitless resources, was
fanned into a consuming passion. Whatever intelligence was be-

ginning to work in the field of monetary practice was immediately lost, whatever morality was growing up was cut down; and we find at this period the introduction of new refinements of the money mechanism, new methods by which its power could be multiplied while its value was lessened. From now on we note the beginnings of those practices which Despaux calls *inflation fiduciare* and *inflation rentière*—that is, the use of paper money to expand public purchasing power and the use of commercial credit to expand private purchasing power.

Book Six. THE EMERGENCE OF CREDIT

A PECULIAR quality of our economic civilization is that it is founded upon an institution—the taking of interest—which was regarded with disapprobation and suspicion by the shrewdest thinkers of antiquity, among them Aristotle and Cicero. Its use was restricted to strangers by the Mosaic Code and was condemned outright for a thousand years by the Christian church. It was outlawed as well by civil law until the sixteenth century.

The growth of credit, under which fair name have gone the institution of interest-taking and its dark shadow, debt, and the influence it has had upon the money mechanism, will be more fully developed in succeeding chapters. Here, only its beginnings, and its first reception as an instrument of commercial and financial power, will be dealt with.

I. Death of a Philosophy

Until the reign of Henry VIII in England interest-taking had been forbidden by both the canon and the civil law. The statutes of Alfred, of William the Conqueror, of Henry II, of Henry III, of Edward I, of Edward III, and of Henry VII had prohibited the lending of money upon any interest whatsoever, as an offense punishable by penalties ranging from forfeiture of chattels, lands, and Christian burial, under Alfred, to a loss of all substance, whipping, exposure in the pillory, and perpetual banishment, under William the Conqueror.

The law of England was representative of the European attitude in general on the subject of interest. The French laws against usury, which continued in effect long after their abrogation in England, were known as the most severe in Europe. Both French and English civil law derived from canon law, in which,

78

for 1,500 years, prohibition of usury had been a central doctrine.[1]

꿋 ୫

These interdictions against the taking of interest, which it is the fashion of modern economics to regard as an especial mark of the ignorance and superstition of medievalism, were not capricious or unreasoned; rather they may be regarded as among the finest intellectual fruit of moral philosophy. Certainly it was no casual or incidental condemnation which the church visited upon the offense. Its heinousness was the subject of a vast literature, of disputations carried on ardently from generation to generation, and age to age. Aristotle, upon whose philosophy the thinking of the churchmen was largely based, was familiar with the effects of debt and interest in commercial Greece; the money economy of his day was highly developed, and the Solonian revolution was recent history. The church had risen from the ruins of a civilization that had crumbled under a mismanaged money, and the church fathers saw about them the terrible effects of commercialism gone mad. What has confused modern economic historians about the attitude of the church on money and interest is that the Schoolmen spoke in terms which are not familiar to modern economics, and this has given rise to the interpretation that they were legalists and logicians, rather than objective students. It is true that they condemned interest-taking because "it is contrary to Scripture; it is contrary to Aristotle; it is contrary to nature, for it is to live without labor; it is to sell time, which belongs to God, for the advantage of wicked men; it is to rob those who use the money lent, and to whom, since they make it profitable, the profits should belong; it is unjust in itself, for the benefit of the loan to the borrower cannot exceed the value of the principal sum lent; it is in defiance of sound juristic principles, for when a loan of money is made, the property in the thing lent passes to the borrower, and why should the creditor demand payment from a man who is merely using what is now his own?"[2]

But they also had a keen appreciation of the true nature of money economy, and the distinctions between money and wealth which confuse so many today. The distinction they grasped was expressed by Gratian: "Whosoever buys a thing, not that he may sell it whole and unchanged, but that it may be a material for fashioning something, he is no merchant (i.e., exempt from condemnation). But the man who buys it in order that he may gain by selling it again unchanged and as he bought it, that man is of the buyers and sellers who are cast forth from God's temple." By very definition a man "who buys in order that he may sell dearer," the trader is moved by an inhuman concentration on his own pecuniary interest, unsoftened by any tincture of public spirit or private charity. He turns what should be a means into an end, and his occupation "is justly condemned, since in itself, it serves the lust of gain."[3]

If the condemnations of the churchmen against interest are based upon narrow logic and legalistic concepts, the explanation is undoubtedly not that they failed to see the problem objectively, but that the rhetorical modes of the day were in a straitjacket, and they were compelled to find in legalistic concepts and express in narrow rationalizations the sanctions for the condemnation which arose out of a natural and instinctive repugnance to the evils they saw about them.

•§ §•

Gradually, beginning in the thirteenth century, after the fall of Constantinople and the rise of capitalism in Italy, a gradual relaxation began to develop in the attitude toward the subject of interest. In the literature of the time is revealed the process by which the prohibition was nibbled away. If a man might not charge money for a loan, he could, of course, take the profits of a partnership, provided the risks of the partnership were also assumed. A rent charge might be bought, for the fruits of the earth are produced by nature, not wrung from man. Compensation might be demanded if principal was not repaid at the time stipulated. Payment might be required corresponding to any loss sustained or gain foregone from being deprived of the use of the money. Annuities might be purchased, on the theory that the payment is contingent, and so speculative, not certain.

These various practices and evasions began to find their defense in the sophistry of logic. The leading church fathers, themselves by now commercialists and politicians, developed a legalistic basis for the practices. The doctrine of *damnum emergens* that arose was based on the theory that if a lender suffered loss by the failure of a borrower to return a loan at the date named, compensation might be exacted. By the doctrine of *lucrum cessans*, if a man, in order to lend money, was obliged to diminish his income from productive enterprise, it was claimed that he might receive in return, in addition to his money, an amount exactly equal to this diminution in income. These two concepts of "actual loss incurred" and "certain gain lost" were the basis of the idea of *interesse*, or interest, which originally was a penalty exacted from the borrower for neglect to pay the debt at a certain time. After a time, it came to be the practice that loans were made nominally without interest, but the lender actually received, under the name *interesse*, a regular percentage for the whole period of the loan, the borrower by a fiction being assumed to be guilty of culpable neglect (*mora*) for the period. "What remained to the end unlawful," says Tawney, "was that which appears in modern economic textbooks as 'pure interest' —interest as a fixed payment stipulated in advance for a loan of money or of wares without risk to the lender."[4] The essence of usury was that it was certain, and that, whether the borrower gained or lost, the usurer took his pound of flesh.

ఆర్ ఏ

With the Reformation, the canonical doctrine came up for review. The general trend of the opinion of the reformers was that loan interest was a parasitic profit, admitting of no defense before any strict tribunal, but they consented to a practical compromise with the frailty of man, believing that interest was tolerable as a concession to his imperfection.

This change of view was crystallized in England in the reign of Henry VIII by an act (37 Henry VIII, c. 9) which legalized the taking of interest on the ground, as the act declared, "the statutes prohibiting interest altogether had so little force that

little or no punishment ensued to the offenders." A charge of
10 per cent per annum for the use of money was made legal and
anything over this amount was forbidden as usury.[5]

Although the act was subsequently repealed, some years later
in the time of Edward VI (but reenacted in 1571 by 13 Elizabeth, c. 8), and the legalization of interest did not appear in
Europe until the following century, the year of the Act of Henry
VIII, 1545, may be taken as a convenient date to mark the
beginning of modern price economy.

ᴥᔕ ᔑᴥ

Today debt is the very woof and warp of the fabric of modern
commerce, to which the gaudy pattern of material achievement
is merely tied like the strands of colored wool in an oriental
carpet. Hardly a venture is undertaken, or a transaction consummated, from the building and furnishing of a shelter to the
laying of a trans-Atlantic cable, the building of a steamship or
the erection of a factory, without the powerful stimulus of credit.
Without credit, or debt, our civilization could not be sustained—
at least in its present complexity of organization and movement
—and the mere repayment of debt, on a universal scale, is, in
the opinion of leading economists, sufficient to disrupt the
machinery of business and to produce the cataclysms and the
convulsions we term depressions.

Because our money system is today based more upon credit
than metal, upon the institution of commercial banking rather
than that of coinage, upon debt rather than wealth, it is necessary, in the pursuit of an analysis of the historical working of the
money mechanism, to turn from the consideration of coinage
and currency, which were the chief aspects of money in ancient
and medieval times, to that of debt, its growth, and its present
complexities.

II. The Perquisite of Sovereignty

THE institution of debt and interest-taking is of course very
ancient, and had become prevalent in Europe long before the

abrogation of the legal prohibitions against it. Tacitus mentions the limitation on interest in the third century B.C. In Byzantium, where the influence of the church was subordinate and subservient to the state, the ecclesiastical repugnance to interest-taking was inarticulate, but apparently the interest rates, and the terms on which debt might be contracted were closely supervised by the state authorities. The code of Justinian forbad *illustres* to ask more than 4 per cent, while traders were limited to 8 per cent, and others to 6 per cent, while bottomry ran up to 12 or 12.5 per cent.[1]

In Europe, however, due to the decay of society and the disappearance of money, together with the influence of church doctrine, money debt had been relegated to a minor rôle, and had become a nefarious practice of the Jews which honest folk regarded with horror. And when finally it did reappear as an institution of European society, the circumstances under which it was introduced were not such as to surround it with regard or veneration, or to permit its development in a restrained and orderly fashion. Debt, like money, which it serves as handmaiden, was accompanied in its growth in Europe by malpractices and mishandling to which it seems never to have been subjected in the older civilizations. Once the restraints of ecclesiastical dogma and intellectual discipline were thrown off, debt like money, became uncontrolled, unlicensed, and subject to no authority but that of the commercial passions.

A form of debt, of a salutary character, was growing in Italy, under Byzantine influence, in the form of bills of exchange and the practice of *commenda*, which involved the use of credit for short terms; but the growth of a body of permanent debt—the type that weighs like the burden of Atlas on modern society, a burden which is never extinguished, but seldom alleviated, and constitutes a cankerous drain on the social system—is to be traced to the financial practices of medieval princes and governments.

◄§ ﴾►

We have already called attention to the sudden and overpowering greed for liquid wealth which swept over Europe with the renascence of money and the instruments of money economy. This passion for money, which manifested itself in an ever-growing ostentation, a luxury in food, and other sensual gratifications, had, it must not be forgotten, other far-reaching and compelling motives. The gradual concentration of political power, and the increasing expenses of the state in administration, justice and diplomacy, were too diverse and heavy to be met by the feudal organization of economy, the system of financing the state by services and by taxes in kind. The general obligation of all citizens to bear arms, which was the basis upon which the feudal forces were built, proved incompatible with the increasing economic development, particularly the growth of city life; and for the hire of the ubiquitous mercenary troops by which the kings of Europe maintained their authority and extended their dominions, money was a prime necessity.

To the aid of statecraft and its demands for more and more money came the pseudo-philosophies of the age with their dictum, *pecunia nervus belli*—money is the sinews of war—and the exhortations to princes to lay up treasure. Diomede Caraffa, Ghillebert de Lannoy, Saba da Castiglione, Scipione Ammirato, and Lelio Zecchi all echoed the words of Giacomo Trivulzio's reply to the question of Francis I as to what was necessary for carrying on war in Italy: "Most Gracious King, three things must be ready—money, money, and once again money" (*denaro, denaro, e denaro*).

Only Machiavelli, the much maligned, stood up against this pernicious doctrine, and combatted the general opinion, declaring that good soldiers may help to find gold, but that gold does not produce good soldiers. Machiavelli urged that the strongest resource of a well ordered state was the presence of a trained militia drawn from the citizenry.

꿿 꿾

The limited money income of the princes and the inflexible character of their fiscal systems were inadequate to provide for their increasing financial needs, and numerous expedients were resorted to. We have already discussed the widespread currency debasement which was practiced. The rough and ready expedient of the sale of crown lands had even in the feudal state outrun the bounds of expediency. The practice of financing state needs by grants of land had, in addition, been a great war breeder. It forced the princes into still more extensive military expeditions for the purpose of acquiring more land for their disposal. State and administrative offices were sold as another recourse, until the administration was encumbered with a crowd of useless attachés who could not be got rid of, and the tradition it engendered—of office, once acquired, being a permanent possession of the incumbent—has remained to harass the governments of modern Europe and to nullify the most well-intentioned efforts of ministries to limit public expenditure.

Faced with the limitations of a fiscal system which no intelligence seemed capable of modifying to meet a changing age, together with a commonly held view that a prince was morally bound to supply the requirements of his administration from his own patrimony, the expedient of borrowing was adopted, and the doctrine was fostered that the prince had the right to compel his subjects to lend him money. During the latter centuries of the Middle Ages, and especially from the thirteenth on, princes more and more contracted the habit of obtaining forced loans from those among their subjects who relied on their protection or were in some other way dependent on them, and who also had liquid capital at their disposal. Forced loans were particularly in favor among princes of absolutist tendencies, such as Louis XI and his successors on the French throne, but such loans appeared in other countries of more liberal tendencies. As late as Henry VIII, Elizabeth and James I, the forced loan was common in England, and not until 1628 did Parliament compel the English Crown to abandon it as a financial expedient.

৵৽ ৾৽

The first of the forced loans of which we hear was, however, not by a prince but by the Republic of Venice, in 1171. The restrictions placed by the Byzantine emperors in Constantinople upon the Venetian merchants there—who are said to have numbered some 200,000 in all, including retainers and families—induced the republic to prepare for war. A forced loan was decreed, and inspectors were appointed to collect sums in proportion to income. The state paid interest at 4 per cent every six months. The Chamber of Loans (*camera degli imprestiti*) was instituted to bank the money and pay the interest. The scrip delivered to creditors could be negotiated, and repayment was effected by periodical redemption.

Frederick II frequently resorted to loans as an extraordinary expedient, and we know that in the short period between September, 1239, and March, 1240, he borrowed to the extent of nearly 25,000 ounces of gold. Innocent IV obtained 200,000 silver *marks* by similar methods, and St. Louis contracted various loans for his crusades against the infidels. On certain occasions he sent into some town of the East, and to Acre more particularly, an authority to borrow in his name. The Grand Masters of the military orders of the Temple and the Hospital were commissioned to find money lenders, and it was at Paris that the repayment was effected on presentation of the letters of authorization, together with the receipts delivered by the Patriarch of Jerusalem and by the Grand Masters.

This sort of financing could not be supported without the system of farming out the taxes and the pledging of individual branches of revenue. This led to a frightful degeneration of the financial system, which led in turn to the repeated heaping up of debts.

❧ ❦

But the results of these methods of covering state expenditure were more destructive and pernicious than the breakdown of the system of public finance. The system resulted, if not in a "death a-borning," at least in the anemic and feeble growth of a real concept of credit and debt and its proper place in economic society; and this stunting of intellectual growth in the realm of one of the most important departments of modern economy arose from the casual attitude of the waxing governments toward their loan obligations. Instead of being regarded as the last resource of a harassed treasury, and to be treated, when incurred, with a sanctity and regard for their terms, loans were regarded as a prerogative of sovereignty, a legitimate method of raising revenue, a form of "tax anticipations" which should be repaid if convenient but allowed to default, or be passed on to subsequent generations, if inconvenient to meet. The institution of debt, in a word, became, and still remains, in the traditions of the modern world, not a recourse of distress and extremity, but a facile means of obtaining present goods on an easy confidence in a roseate-hued future prosperity.

"The princes and their advisers seldom had sufficient economic foresight and insight to be deterred by higher considerations from the momentarily desirable state bankruptcy," says Ehrenberg. "Even in the second half of the eighteenth century the jurists were by no means agreed on this point whether a prince was bound to recognize the debts of his predecessor."[2]

ᴇᶠ ᶠᴇ

Toward the middle of the fourteenth century French subjects tried to safeguard themselves from the exactions of forced loans and the inevitable defaults, and from 1350 to 1358 the charters of some of the towns contained a clause that the king was not to compel their inhabitants to make him loans.

Edward III in 1339 defaulted on a loan of 1,355,000 gold *florins* obtained from the Italian firms of Peruzzi and Bardi, while at the same time the King of Sicily defaulted on a loan of close to 200,000 gold *florins*, and iniquitous measures had just then been taken in France against Italian bankers generally. In 1546 the Republic of Genoa reduced the rate of interest and deferred payment. The government of Philip II of Spain repudiated its debts on three occasions. On the first occasion, in 1566, the creditors of the state received only from 10 to 14 per cent of their due. The administration began by annulling every lien in respect to guarantee of loans on the revenues of the state, and offered to supply an annuity of 5 per cent per annum. Twenty years later the government again repudiated its obligations and resorted to the most arbitrary measures, even issuing an attachment on the gold and silver coming from the Indies, gold and silver on the security of which banking houses had lent. In 1595, Philip II became a bankrupt for a third time.

"It is characteristic that the funded debt of the Spanish Crown in the sixteenth and seventeenth centuries increased chiefly through the repeated state bankruptcies," comments Ehrenberg.

Portugal showed herself as little trustworthy. In 1557 the King of Portugal effected a partial repudiation, accompanying his act by a pious appeal to conscientious scruples, and by citing the dogma of the theologians that he would be guilty of usury if he paid interest higher than 5 per cent.

III. Development of Credit Instruments

A DISTINCTION is properly made by the commercial community between short term commercial debt and long term capital obligations, and between these two and public debt. While in essence they are all various forms of obligations to pay in money sums due in the future, and while they all so overlap that no definite boundaries can be drawn between them, yet each category has its own distinctive characteristics, and generally its own distinct market in the financial bourse. All three are children of money economy, and what is of more importance, they have all become vital components in the complex mass which today constitutes the money mechanism. To understand money as it functions in modern society it is necessary to go beyond gold and silver and copper, the coinage prerogative, seignorage, the gold-silver ratio, and reserve ratios—problems which have been the preoccupation of classic economists—and to examine the institution of debt in its historical setting, and its modern implications.

Commercial debt, especially short-term commercial debt, made its appearance in Europe as a product of Italian capitalism and the commercial renascence which began in that area and spread thence throughout Europe, while capital debt grew out of a combination of short-term commercial debt, and its instrumentalities, and instrumentalities which in turn were a result of the concussion of expanding Italian capitalism and medieval guild economy. Commercial debt made its appearance under more favorable auspices than public debt, which we have examined. Perhaps this is because Italian commercialism grew up under the influence of the older Byzantine and Arabic-Hellenic tradition. In its earlier stages the processes, the instruments, and the institutions of commercial debt managed to acquire, before Italian commercialism had overshot itself in an orgy of profit making, enough character and stability to survive, in some of their original purity, the mishandling which they were later to receive.

⊷ ❧

The financial system that developed was an individualistic system, in contrast to the coöperative ideals of the medieval guilds, and, in the view of some, its narrow, individualistic and antisocial practices, expanding under the influence of *laissez-faire* philosophy and the mercantilist doctrines of the early modern era, explain the twentieth-century disenchantment with capitalism, the rise of dictators, with their dogmas of fascism, socialism, communism, and their variants, and the popular acceptance of a new bondage. The commercial heritage received from Italy, says Jacob Strieder, is primarily "a frame of mind," but it implies also "the whole sum of practical models in business furnished by the Italian merchants in the fields of exchange, wholesale trade, industry, colonial administration, and high finance."[1]

⊷ ❧

For the first three and a half centuries of the commercial renascence of Europe—say from 1252, which marks the reintroduction of gold coinage, to 1596, when the Bank of St. George of Genoa collapsed—the Italians were the bankers of Europe. What brought them into prominence as bankers and financiers was the fact that, lying nearer to the Mediterranean and being in closer contact with Byzantium, they had become the principal traders of Europe, bringing down from the north amber from the Baltic, tin and wool from England and silver from Germany, and forwarding in exchange the spices, silk, soap, wax, refined sugar and glass of the East, and in addition, increasing amounts of their own manufactures.

The Crusades had brought the Italian merchants directly into the Greek-Arabian world, which they had formerly known only through the Byzantine market and the mediation of the Byzantine traders.

Merchants in oriental goods had begun to appear in Italy in increasing numbers from the eleventh century on. A revival of commerce in Flanders, Germany, France and England had widened the market, and the growing demand was naturally satisfied largely through the Italian cities. A large part of the industry of the Orient was being transplanted to Italy also.

As money grew in importance not only as a medium of exchange but as an object of barter and trade, an insensible transition occurred in the character of the operations of the Italian merchants. Confining themselves at the outset to purely commercial transactions, it was not long before they were embarked upon financial undertakings. Much of their commerce had consisted of gold, silver and precious stones from the Orient. Presently exchange was added, and above all, lending at interest. A class of professional money changers grew up, recruited from such towns as Asti and Chieri, who, under the collective name of Lombards and Cahorsines, established their 'change counters in all the European trading cities of the Middle Ages. Their transactions soon brought them into competition with the pawnbroking business of the Jews, and in these usurious practices they, like the Jews, were not always free from odium and persecution.

It was not long before, in many places, corporations of *cambisti* were formed for exchange and deposit, and the great family merchant corporations, such as the Bardi and the Peruzzi, with their extensive system of branch houses throughout Europe, began to convert their trading establishment into huge private banking institutions. In the thirteenth and fourteenth centuries the Italian banker-merchants covered the civilized world with a network of communications. They had their correspondents; they received notices of political events, of combinations, and of chances.

◈◈

An important factor, in addition to the trading activities, which contributed to the growth of Italian merchant banking, was the papal financial system. The Roman Catholic church had in the course of the Middle Ages become an international organization with a gigantic administrative system. The Roman See had, partly involuntarily or partly on its own initiative, risen to problems of important political policy, of the waging of war, and the like.

For such a development, a carefully built up system of papal taxation including all of Christendom had early become indispensable. It was founded chiefly under Innocent III, about the beginning of the thirteenth century, on the basis of tithes, Crusade contributions, taxes imposed by the papal bureaucracy, and perquisites of all kinds, levied on all Christendom, but particularly on the clergy.

"The great Italian merchants," says Strieder, "with their trading counters in all the European centers, furnished ready and satisfactory instruments for the collection and transfer of all these dues. It was inevitable that these merchants should also supply loans to the Pope in times of financial stress. Even more often, they performed this function for the upper ranks of the clergy, who were not always in a position to pay the various levies demanded by Rome except by means of advances from the bankers. On the other hand, the financiers who were connected with the papacy sometimes accepted deposits from the treasury of the Papal See, when rich yields or an economical and able administration had given rise to a surplus."[2]

◄§ §►

The commercial system of Italy reveals itself in the far-reaching, systematically thought out trading practices, in the organization of trading companies, in the introduction of double entry bookkeeping, and particularly in the credit mechanism that was developed. The model for the banking and commercial practices of Europe, until the rise of modern banks of issue, is to be found in the practices of the money changers of Italy. In addition, the Italians developed several forms of corporate bodies; multiplied maritime contracts; placed insurances on practical bases—ceasing to employ them as stipulations accessory to other contracts; developed the bill of exchange; took fresh steps and surrounded commercial transactions with guarantees and penalties, including the revival of the principle of bankruptcy.

Most of these developments were borrowings from Byzantium or the Saracenic world, but they were modified under Italian influence, adapted to the more individualistic character of the Italian system, and in some respects were broadened and rendered more supple and universal in application. It was not until later, when the merchants had become almost wholly bankers, and were competing with the Jews in pawnbroking, and financing the requirements of princes and prelates, that the excesses and abuses began to creep in which remain as a canker to modern economy.

◄§ §►

Perhaps the most important instrument of money developed by the Italians is the bill of exchange. Although forms of the bill of exchange were known to the Assyrians of the ninth to seventh centuries B.C., and the *publicani*, the bankers of the Roman world, employed certain means of effecting the payments of money abroad, it is to the Florentine merchants or, according to some authorities, the Genoese merchants, of the twelfth century that its origin as a document of modern usage is to be traced. In that century we find the appearance of the bill of exchange under its various forms—the bill payable to order, and the promissory note; the ordinary bill drawn in the money of the country where it is payable, and the bill payable in another country at the rate current when due; the bill payable in a place specified, or where cargo was discharged; the bill to mature at date fixed, or after sight.

The bill of exchange was invented by the necessities of daily affairs, and by professional experience it was developed quite apart from any intervention of public authority, and around it grew up a customary law to meet all the exigencies of its use. The influence of the jurists over its growth was lacking, although before long exchange, with its complicated operations, raised many delicate problems in which at every moment the question of usury came to the surface. It was in this connection that the jurists, and the theologians in particular, took up the subject, studied and discussed it. The legislator in turn busied himself with the bill of exchange. Nevertheless, as late as the middle of the sixteenth century the law did not concern itself with the bill of exchange other than to limit itself to approval of regulations made by the bankers themselves.

According to Nys, the effect of legal regulation, which began in the sixteenth century, impaired some of the most useful features of the bill. "Thanks to custom," he says, "the bill of exchange was assuming, toward the end of the Middle Ages, a quasi-universal character; and when, in the sixteenth century, special legislation followed closely on special legislation, the result was the disappearance of one of the prime conditions of the bill of exchange—facility of circulation. A so-called anarchy was followed by excessive regulation injurious to trade, and to repair the mischief it was necessary to wait for the impulse of the nineteenth century towards legislative uniformity."[3]

᳐ᔆ ᔆᵔ

The exchange contract in its primitive form, the *contractus permutationis* or *cambii*, was that by which a trader about to go on a journey borrowed in specie of the country he was leaving a sum repayable in the country of his destination. In the documents of oldest date the title contains an acknowledgment of the receipt of a sum, and of the obligation to restore it at an appointed term; but the characteristic nature of the transaction consisted in its extending from one place to another. In 1157 mention occurs at Genoa of a transaction resulting in a promise of payment in Tunis. We have also a bill of exchange of 1200, according to which a sum received on loan was to be repaid at Messina one month after the arrival of the borrowers' vessel in Marseilles or some other Provençal port.

The bill of exchange was in frequent use by the middle of the thirteenth century, but at this time its form was that of a document certified before a notary. At the end of the fourteenth century, however, it approached the form now in use. Bills of exchange were, however, drawn only by bankers and money changers who had branches or agents in the place stipulated for payment. The protest continued for a long while to be effected in the presence of a notary. In London the protest was often lodged after inquiry made on the doorstep of the shop of one of the many scriveners, or public clerks, a kind of solicitors, that dwelt in Lombard Street. The object of the questions put was to find out if anyone offered himself to take up the obligation and pay the bill.

The importance of the bill of exchange in the money mechanism lies in the fact that it is the one form of debt upon which, experience has demonstrated, a system of payments may be built with safety in conjunction with a metallic money. Theoretically, it provides a basis for realizing the ideal of the managed-money advocate, that is, a money related to the commercial transactions of mankind, rather than to a commodity the supply of which is stable but the demand for which is extremely fluctuating. The bill of exchange may be regarded only remotely as an instrument of debt; rather it is an instrument of exchange, and its use as an instrument of exchange is best illustrated in the modern use of the acceptance, which in commercial practice is an order drawn by a shipper of goods upon the purchaser for payment to a designated individual (or bank) of the amount of the purchase. In such a case, the only element of debt in the instrument is the fact that time elapses between the moment the instrument is drawn and the moment it is presented—no more than the interval required for the postal delivery of the bill. When it is a time acceptance, the bill may run for a limited period, thirty, sixty, ninety days, or even up to one year or eighteen months, but in sound practice only so long as the orderly marketing of the goods requires. As debt, it is an extremely short-term debt, the maturity being short enough to avoid the hazards of changes of value in the unit of money, the great danger in the body of long-term debt outstanding. Furthermore, in sound practice, its extinguishment is not based upon future productive ability, something which experience has demonstrated to be extremely hazardous under the tempo and shift of modern economic forces, but upon goods actually above ground and already in the course of marketing. There have been, of course, abuses in the use of the bill of exchange, particularly in bankers' bills, created largely to speculate in money, and in the use of bills of exchange to finance the carrying of excessive inventories, as was common during the decade 1920–1929, but these are abuses subject to intellectual control, while other forms of debt are not only subject to abuse, but also subject to economic forces which mankind has not yet learned to control.

IV. Growth and Modification of the Banking Function

CONNECTED with the development of banking instruments is the growth of banking as an independent function, rather than as an appendage of mercantile establishments.

Banks of deposit had been known in early Greece; and in Egypt, as adjuncts of the public granary system, under the Ptolemies, they had developed into a highly comprehensive system.[1] They had appeared in Damascus in 1200, and in Barcelona in 1401, but it is to Venice that we owe those traditions and sound principles of commercial banking which we find more fully developed in the Bank of Amsterdam and the Bank of Hamburg.

Venice was ultra-conservative, and the money changers and merchant bankers were subjected to much more rigid regulation than elsewhere. As early as 1361, an edict of the Venetian Senate forbad bankers to engage in mercantile pursuits, thus separating the banking business as an independent function. Thirteen years later, to prevent bankers from engaging in trade through dummies, they were forbidden to create credits against certain commodities. Later restrictions required the bankers to open their books to inspection, to keep their current funds in view and make all payments over the counter (*sopra il banco*), and to put up a security with the state as guarantee of their liabilities. The reserve against deposits was repeatedly raised, as banks continued to become involved, and, in 1523, stood at

25,000 *ducats*. In 1524, the institution of bank examiners to supervise the operations of banks was created, and two years later the use of the check, by which one banker paid off his deposits by a draft on another banker, was forbidden.[2]

The various attempts to regulate private banking were unsuccessful. The laws enacted disclose the presence, in Venetian private banking, of precisely the same evils and mistakes as those with which later centuries have had to struggle. In 1584, the failure of the house of Pisani and Tiepolo for 500,000 *ducats* brought private banking to an end. The commercial importance of Venice was too great to be left to the winds of financial malpractice, and the Venetian Senate resolved upon radical banking legislation. A state bank was established, the *Banco della Piazza del Rialto*, which assumed the deposit business of the private bankers. The act was opposed by the banking interest, was repealed, but reenacted in modified form in 1587.

The *Banco della Piazza del Rialto* was founded upon the principle of safe deposit, a principle unfortunately largely submerged in modern banking practice. Lending of deposited funds was not practiced. The bank sought to make no profit from the use of its credit, and merely undertook to keep the money of depositors in safety, and to pay it out or transfer it to others at the will of the owner.

The profits of the bank were derived from fees for effecting transactions on its books, for the negotiation and discounting of bills of exchange, for notarial services in connection with the protesting of drafts, and from the bank's services as money changer. As Venice was an important commercial entrepôt, a great variety of currencies were constantly being received by the merchants. The bank accepted these various moneys, sorted, valued and discounted them, crediting the client on its books with the proper sum in Venetian money of account, or returning to him current Venetian money. Sums standing on the books of the bank to the credit of a customer were so much more certain in character and amount than the sum of a certain number of the worn and debased coinage in circulation that deposits came to bear an *agio*, or premium, over the actual money. Payments were made *del giro*, that is, by transfer on the books of the bank from the account of one customer to the credit of another, or by actual cash paid to the depositor in settlement of the deposit liability. The more important method was of course the transfer on the bank's books.

The *Banco della Piazza del Rialto* dominated Venetian banking until 1619. In that year the Republic, pressed for funds, agreed to discharge a contract in bank credit, and for this purpose organized the *Banco del Giro*, famous in Venetian history. Though nominally based upon the same principles as the older institution, it was at the outset burdened with a deposit liability for which it held no corresponding specie. Bank credit as a monetary influence had, therefore, appeared, and when in 1637 the *Banco della Piazza del Rialto* was absorbed by the *Banco del Giro*, the concept of banking as strictly a deposit and warehouse function began to disappear.

܍ ܀

Public banks of deposit had been springing up—and falling —all over Europe in the fifteenth and sixteenth centuries, but it is not until the foundation of the Bank of Amsterdam in 1609 that we find a return to the rigorous principles of the *Banco della Piazza*—the idea that bank deposits are the property of the depositor and not to be used for the private profit of the bank, that the prime responsibility of a bank of deposit is that of safe-keeping.

The deposit principle at Amsterdam arose, as in Venice, out of the confusing variety of coins in circulation and the dissatisfaction with the operations of the exchange brokers. In 1608, the city forbad the holding of deposits by the bankers, and the following year created the Exchange Bank (*Amsterdamsche Wisselbank*), later known as the Bank of Amsterdam, with a banking monopoly in the city. The Bank of Amsterdam was simply a warehouse for coin. The bank accepted deposits only at their bullion value and granted credit for the amount in lawful money, subject to a proper charge for handling. Payments in Amsterdam came to be made universally in bank money, which commanded a premium over actual coin, and a merchant was practically obliged to have an account there.

The affairs of the bank were kept secret by the small committee of the city government which was charged with its administration; but to preserve the character of the institution the burgomasters and council of Amsterdam were required to take oath annually that the treasure was intact. It was generally supposed until the last half of the eighteenth century that the bank had sacredly fulfilled its obligations to keep in its vaults the exact amount of coin and bullion represented by the bank money outstanding. In 1672, when the French king was at Utrecht, the bank paid so readily as left no doubt of the fidelity with which it had observed its engagements, and the prestige of the institution rose enormously.

Nevertheless, the bank had begun surreptitiously to use its power in various lending operations. As early as 1657 individuals had been permitted to overdraw their accounts, and later enormous loans were made to the East India Company. The truth became public property in the winter of 1789 and 1790. The premium on bank money, which was usually kept above 4 per cent, fell to 2 per cent, and in August, 1790, disappeared altogether. In November, the bank was admitted to be insolvent and its debt was assumed by the government of the City of Amsterdam. It officially ceased to exist on December 19, 1819.

✌️ 👉

Of only one bank, of all those founded in northern Europe, can we say with certainty that the true principle of deposit banking was maintained inviolate. That was the Bank of Hamburg. It was the last survivor of the medieval banks. For two and a half centuries it succeeded in carrying on the principles of the Bank of Venice and the Bank of Amsterdam. Accounts could be opened only by a Hamburg citizen or corporation and could be transferred only upon his appearance in person or by attorney with a transfer order. The principle upon which the bank was conducted was the granting of a credit on the books for the silver or gold deposited. No loans were made and no notes or other liabilities were created beyond the amount of coin and bullion on deposit. So faithfully was the rule adhered to that when Napoleon, on November 5, 1813, took possession of the bank, he found 7,506,956 *marks* in silver held against liabilities of 7,489,343 *marks*. A large part of the treasure was removed, but when the freedom of the city was restored in 1814, the bank resumed business with unimpaired credit. The thefts of Napoleon's forces were made good in 1816 by a transfer of French securities. Thereafter, however, modern banking methods were gradually introduced and a capital of about 1,000,000 *marks* was accumulated in addition to the buildings. The bank survived the storm of the crisis of 1857, which carried down so many of the banking institutions of Europe, but finally fell when the banking and monetary system of Germany was reorganized after the establishment of the German Empire in 1871. Incidental to the creation of the empire was the establishment of the gold standard, and the bank was ordered to liquidate its accounts in fine silver by February 15, 1873. The latest reference to the existence of the Bank of Hamburg is found in the proceedings of the Hamburg Senate on October 13, 1875, declaring their purpose to sell to the Bank of Germany for 900,000 *marks* the buildings of "the venerable institution which had performed such great services to German trade."[3]

With the disappearance of these older banking institutions, founded upon the honorable concept of the inviolability of funds left on deposit, a new type of banking began to grow up, based, in England, upon the unprincipled practices of the goldsmiths, and fostered by the deceptive theories and practices of John Law in France. It is from these later developments, rather than from the Italian beginnings, that modern note issue and central banking takes its origin. Central banking, however, did not really begin its growth until the nineteenth century, and we therefore reserve for later discussion its characteristics and its influences in money economy.

V. Beginnings of the Money Market

THE transition from medieval Italian commercialism to modern

price economy would not have been possible, but for one institution contributed by the guild system of northern Europe. The
organized security exchange, upon which the liquidity of modern wealth depends, and which has become, in modern times—
and in America particularly—a critical and significant adjunct
of the money mechanism, was a development of the medieval
trade fair. It was not until the sixteenth century that the commerce in money, money instruments, and negotiable instruments
of debt and ownership, had become localized in a "stock exchange." Yet it is characteristic of the impetuosity with which
Europe took to money economy, as well as the unprincipled
character of money dealings, which we have noted in the case
of coinage and public debt, and to a lesser extent in banking
transactions, that hardly had security exchanges been organized
when they were subjected to the same uncontrolled excesses
which we have observed in other departments of the money
mechanism. We shall have occasion to observe some of them as
we trace the development of the security exchange.

⋘ ⋙

Among the institutions developed by the guild system of
medieval Europe was the fair. The fairs were periodic meetings
of merchants and traders for the purpose of exchanging their
wares, and were held wherever the roads of commerce crossed
and wherever sufficient order and authority existed to provide
security for the merchants. These periodic markets date very
far back: five great fairs were held yearly in Arabia long before
the time of Mohammed, and in Europe during medieval times
they appeared at the chief halting places on the commercial
routes from East to West, from Kiev to the British Isles. Often
the fairs coincided with pilgrimages; indeed, the pilgrimages instituted by Islam were as commercial in nature as religious, and
the pilgrimages to the shrines of the saints in Catholic Europe
early became commercial in character. The reviving institution
of law began to give special consideration to the fairs and the
necessity of protecting merchants on their way to and from these
assemblies. The "Truce of God," which was solemnly confirmed
at the Council of Clermont in 1095, frequently renewed, and

ratified for the last time by the third Lateran council in 1179 as a general law for Christendom, forbad at any time the use of violence toward merchants, who were placed upon the same footing as priests, monks, lay brothers, and pilgrims.

It was natural that these fairs should become centers of financial transactions, particularly as the principal function of banking was connected with bills of exchange, that is, remittances to and from foreign parts. In these fairs, merchants in each commodity or branch of commerce had their own meeting place, and the meeting place of the merchants in bills were called "fairs of exchange." Here the bankers bought and sold their bills and fixed the rates of exchange for the various parts of Europe. At Piacenza, for instance, a resort frequented by the Milanese, Tuscans, Venetians, and Genoese, fifty or sixty representatives of the greatest firms gathered every three months. To gain admittance a security of 2,000 *crowns* had to be deposited, while, in order to be able to take part in the fixing of rates, it was necessary to have a counting house and to lodge a further security of twice that amount. The fair lasted eight days; the bankers dealt successively with the acceptance of bills of exchange, the fixing of the rate of interest, and compensation.

Attempts of governments to fix by legislative enactment a maximum for the rates of exchange were occasionally made, but the business was too quicksilver-like and eluded their pains. It was easy for the business, like Hamlet's ghost, to shift its ground; dealing with a commodity of universal demand, and practically weightless,* the merchants could easily take up their stand in places where the regulation was laxer. As such a result, we find, by the middle of the sixteenth century, the growth of the great Antwerp bourse, where financial transactions were practically unlimited, either by government or custom, or by the objects of the transactions themselves.

* By the use of clearing-house mechanism and a form of money of account (the *scudo di marche*), it was unnecessary for the merchants to bring actual money to the fairs, and Rafaello di Turri writes that the bankers who settled accounts of hundreds of thousands of gold *florins* had scarcely enough money for a few days about them. "The creditor," he adds, "dreads nothing so much as receiving money." Nys, *op. cit.*, pp. 213–214.

୰ଽ ଽ୰

Antwerp had risen to importance as a "fair" city early in the sixteenth century. Already an important center had existed at Bruges—from whose fairs we get the name "bourse"—but the silting up of the Zwin, hindering the loading and unloading of sea-going ships in Sluis, the port of Bruges, caused a migration of the merchants to Antwerp. The first great movement of foreign merchants from Bruges to Antwerp took place in 1442, but even in 1553, Bruges had not lost entirely its international importance.

A more important factor in bringing the merchants to Antwerp was the license they enjoyed there. The trade in Bruges had been free in comparison with the restrictions prevalent in other cities of the Middle Ages, but in comparison with the absolute freedom enjoyed by the foreign merchants in Antwerp, Bruges seems medieval. For instance, in Bruges the brokers were a monopolistic corporation, but in Antwerp they were free. In Bruges, only sworn money changers could engage professionally in money changing or *giro** bank business. In Antwerp, on the other hand, the Charter of 1306 granted this right to all burghers, and in the city's prime there were practically no restrictions on the trade in money, precious metals, and bills. The city authorities gave trade all the freedom possible, and such regulations as existed originated almost entirely with the merchants themselves.

Foreigners flocked to Antwerp to trade, and though there were fewer Italians and Hanseatics than at Bruges, great numbers of Portuguese, Spanish, English, and German merchants took their places and were now the leaders in business. In the course of four decades Antwerp became a trading center such as Europe has not witnessed before or since; for at no time in

* Literally, "circular banking," the transfer of sums from one person to another upon the books of the bank. *Giro* accounts, in modern (European) banking represent non-interest bearing balances kept with the central banking institution for the settlement of indebtedness through transfer from one account to the other without the use of checks or currency, and corresponds somewhat to clearing-house transactions in American banking practice.

European history has there been concentrated in one market to such a degree the trade of all the commercial nations of the world. It is said that more than five hundred vessels sailed in or out of the port in one day, and that the English merchants employed more than 20,000 persons in the city. The poet Daniel Rogiers said of the Antwerp exchange, "One heard there a confused murmur of all languages, one saw there a motley mixture of all possible costumes; in short the Antwerp bourse seemed to be a little world in which all parts of the great were united."

❧ ❧

The absence of trade restrictions in Antwerp effected a significant change in the character of the fairs. In the fifteenth century Antwerp had two fairs—the Whitsuntide fair in the spring, and the St. Bavon's fair in the autumn—which were used chiefly by the English merchants for their cloth trade; later there were four fairs; but with the migration of the Bruges trade to Antwerp, the seasonal character of the fair broke down, and business was transacted the year around. Since trade was free the year around, there arose the "continuous fair."

Another important alteration was the growth of trade by samples, which obviated the necessity of bringing vast quantities of actual wares to the city. Gradually, with the growth of standard types, we find appearing the true bourse, where dealings are consummated without displaying the wares themselves, but by the use of securities representing the wares.

The use of the word "ware" suggests a produce exchange as the earliest and most important form of the exchange. Produce of various kinds, especially pepper, did form an object of exchange dealings in Antwerp; and there was a considerable development of the produce exchange later in Amsterdam; but the produce exchange, as a distinct type, did not reach its full development until the nineteenth century.

The "ware" which formed the main object of trade on the Antwerp exchange was lendable capital, represented by various paper instruments. Princes who desired to borrow money, and who formerly would have applied to individual financiers like the Fuggers, turned to the exchange of Antwerp or of Lyons, where lendable capital from all over Europe was collected. Through the medium of the exchange a French king could and did borrow money of a Turkish pasha; and it is said that payments amounting to a million *crowns* were made in a single morning without the use of a penny of cash.[1]

∽ই ইॐ

We see adumbrated, even eclipsed, at Antwerp, all the forms of financial manipulation with which the modern world has become so familiar that they are accepted as a matter of course. An interesting tract of the *Licentiate Christoval de Villalon*, printed in Valladolid in the year 1542, describes the speculation in exchange that had developed: "Of late in Flanders a horrible thing hath arisen, a kind of cruel tyranny which the merchants there have invented among themselves. They wager among themselves on the rate of exchange in the Spanish fairs at Antwerp. They call these wagers *parturas* according to the former manner of winning money at birth (*parto*) when a man wagers whether the child shall be a boy or a girl. In Castile this business is called *apuestas*, wagers. One wagers that the exchange rate shall be at 2 per cent premium or discount, another at 3 per cent, etc. They promise each other to pay the difference in accordance with the results. This sort of wager seems to me to be like marine insurance business. If they are loyally undertaken and discharged, there is naught to be said against them. But there are many ruinous tricks practiced therein. For dealing of this kind is only common in merchants who, holding much capital, perhaps draw a bill of 200,000 or 300,000 *ducats* in Flanders or Spain and conclude on one of those wagers, whereby one leaves the other free which of the two transactions he will carry out. By their great capital and their tricks they can arrange that in any case they have profit. This is a great sin."[2]

Arbitrage, or dealing in the differences between prices or rates of exchange in different places, was a modified form of this speculation. This had been done in the medieval Italian towns, but never on such a scale as at Antwerp. Maritime insurance had also been practiced in Italy, and later in Portugal. It grew so enormously in Antwerp that in 1564 six hundred people were making what one writer calls a "fat living" out of it. There were no companies, but a number of people often insured the same vessel. Premiums became more or less standardized, but frauds were so common that an attempt was made in 1559 to regulate the business by law. Life insurance was also in use, limited chiefly to fixed periods (called term insurance today), such as the duration of a journey by land or sea. This also led to frauds, and even to crime.

A great deal of speculation went on in pepper, which was a barometer of trade, like steel operations today. The pepper trade was a prerogative of the king of Portugal, who sold the cargoes of the East Indian fleets to large syndicates which thereby obtained a monopoly at second hand. They often bought the cargoes while still at sea, gave the king of Portugal, who always needed money, large advances, and repaid themselves by charging a high price. They were able to regulate the price in their own interest at Antwerp, where the bulk was disposed of, or at any rate until the arrival of a new fleet from the East, which then set the price. These two factors, the interest of the syndicates and the amount of the new imports, determined the price of pepper, and as both were incalculable, as were a number of other factors, such as war and peace, the price of pepper was extremely speculative. All sorts of methods were used to divine the course of the pepper market, and we find astrological prognostications flourishing, and "market forecasters" and other equivalents of today's chart readers that swarm in the brokerage establishments of Wall Street. And we find merchants of the highest sagacity and good sense, such as Lienhard Tucher, giving close heed to these absurd prophecies and systems of prophecy.

Such an atmosphere was the breath of life to promoters and adventurers, as well as to captains of industry, finance, and commerce. Lotteries flourished. People could be found to bet on anything, including such matters as the sex of children yet to be born. Some transferable "securities" appeared to represent capital, and commodities were also sold by grades, without the use of samples. Negotiable stock did not precede bourses, however—the evolution was rather the converse.

◆§ §◆

The speculative coloring which dealing in commodities assumed injured it in the eyes of many solid merchants, and the liquidity of capital and the growth of machinery of exchange, rather than stabilizing trade and strengthening the fabric of commerce, as is so lovingly claimed by the defenders of unregulated bourses, only served to destroy the substance while it exalted the illusion. We have evidence of this in an opinion rendered by fourteen Paris jurists in 1530 on the question as to whether certain forms of business then practiced at Antwerp were allowed by canon law. It is based on testimony given by Spanish merchants resident in Antwerp. The evidence adduced that many of the richest firms no longer liked to deal in commodities, unless all the merchants were unanimous in believing that there was good prospect for profit; and the reasons they gave not only are witness to the speculative character which trading had assumed, but they serve as a penetrating explanation of many of our modern commercial vicissitudes:

(1) It was very troublesome to export or import commodities, to warehouse and resell them, a process needing investigation of the buyer's credit, while the number of sound firms dealing in commodities was declining.

(2) It was too risky, for they feared to lose their capital, or get it "frozen."

(3) Finally, it did not offer so good nor so sure a profit as dealing in money and bills. Therefore they engaged increasingly in the latter.[3]

A few decades later Lodovico Guicciardini, a man of good economic sense, who in other respects was full of enthusiasm for the greatness of Antwerp's trade, confessed that the dealings in money at Antwerp were now a public danger. "Formerly the nobles, if they had ready money, were wont to invest it in real estate, which gave employment to many persons and provided the country with necessaries. The merchants employed capital of this kind in their regular trade whereby they adjusted want and superfluity between the various countries, gave employment to many and increased the revenue of princes and states. Nowadays, on the other hand, a part of the nobles and the merchants (the former, secretly through the agency of others, and the latter openly in order to avoid the trouble and risk of a regular profession) employ all their available capital in dealing in money, the large and sure profits of which are a great bait. Hence the soil remains untilled, trade in commodities is neglected, there is often increase of prices, the poor are fleeced by the rich, and finally even the rich go bankrupt."[4]

"We know in the main this picture is a true one," says Ehrenberg. "The merchant class of the medieval centers mostly turned their energies to dealing in money. The people who were their successors, the Spaniards and the Portuguese, did not know how to profit by this change. They borrowed the capital necessary for world trade from the former and had to give back to them the lion's share of the profits. The trading nations of modern times, the English and the Dutch, had not yet laid hands on the heritage of the Mediterranean cities. Guicciardini's pessimistic view of his own times is easily understood."[5]

◈

With the breakdown of the restrictions against interest-taking, which was pretty general by the middle of the sixteenth century, the loan business came prominently to the front, and at Antwerp, Lyons and to some extent in other cities, obligations of princes and cities and the great merchants became an object of trade and speculation. The great merchants, such as the Fuggers, whose credit was unquestioned, would borrow in one market and lend in another where the rate was more favorable. Most of the losses from the speculative excesses of the day were the result of these merchants' overstraining their credit to engage in risky ventures, carrying down with them the community which had advanced them money on "deposit." This was the case with Höckstetter, who tried to corner the mercury market and ruined his "depositors" as well as himself. It was the case with the Bank of St. George and the Peruzzi of Genoa whose advances to Philip II of Spain involved most of Genoa, and practically ruined the position of that city as a financial center when Philip defaulted in 1595. This process was cloaked under the name of deposit business, and although it differs consider-

ably from modern bank deposit business, it bears more re-
semblance to such business than currently prescribed banking
theory would have us believe.

VI. Appearance of the Joint-Stock Company

WHEN, toward the end of the seventeenth century, the true stock
exchange made its appearance, as distinct from the older bourses
in which commodities as well as financial instruments were dealt
in, everything was prepared for the blossoming of all the speculative machinery and practices which have become so significant
a part in the modern scheme of money economy. The restrictions
against the taking of interest had broken down, and bonds of
public and private borrowers had become a familiar object of
trade. One further thing was required to prepare Europe for the
wild speculative inflation that marked the opening of the
eighteenth century—the joint-stock company.

The joint-stock company was an outgrowth of the "regulated
company," which in turn was a development of the partnership
and limited associations of the merchant guilds. Societies had
existed in the first part of the Middle Ages with social and religious objects, and about the eleventh century, with the springing up of trade, commercial guilds arose. The Anglo-Saxon
word "guild" means a "contribution to a common fund" and
came to be applied to the society itself. The dangers and difficulties of trade led the merchants to unite in bands for a journey,
after the fashion of caravans now found in the unsettled countries of the East. Some of the early guilds subjected the members
to regulations like the following: Everyone was obliged to carry
armor, a bow, and twelve arrows, on penalty of a fine; they must
stand by and help one another when they set out for a journey;
in case one member had not sold his wares the others must wait
one day for him; if one was imprisoned or lost his wares on the
road the others must ransom him.

The organization was probably temporary at first, and the
company of merchants dissolved at the end of the trip; but as

such caravans became more regular at any place there grew the tendency to permanence of organization. These merchant guilds were at first also private associations, formed privately by the merchants to protect themselves; but they received public recognition and became part of the town government as the town saw the advantage it could get from them in pushing its trade and protecting it against the efforts of rivals. They included not only professional merchants, but all who bought and sold, including many artisans. Of the nine members who belonged to the Shrewsbury merchant guild in its earliest period two were fishermen and one was a butcher.

∽§ §∾

Along with the growth of the merchant guilds arose various forms of commercial associations, particularly the partnership. The need of association was felt because it was necessary that a merchant or his representative accompany his wares on the road. It was often difficult for a merchant to look after a commercial venture in person; he could not trust it to a hireling; and the slight development of the carrying and commission profession made it impossible for him to leave it in charge of persons who nowadays make it their business to attend to such matters. The merchant therefore would associate with him someone who could represent his interests, generally a member of his family, and family partnerships were the prevailing form of association at first.

A more developed form of the association was the *commenda* (from the Latin *commendare*, entrust). The common form of the *commenda* was an agency commission given to a commercial traveller allowing him to take abroad certain goods, at the owner's risk, and to dispose of them in his discretion. It was a sort of silent partnership in which the principal, or *commendator*, supplied capital in the form of money, wares, or a ship, while the agent, or *tractator*, contributed only his personal services to the enterprise. The profits were usually divided one-fourth to the *tractator*, three-fourths to the *commendator*.

The *commenda* was of Arabic origin. It existed in the time of Mohammed, and it became the mainspring of Moslem trade.

It was common throughout a great deal of Asia and Africa long before the Christian merchant learned to use it and to profit by the facilities it offered. In Europe, it was first adopted in the south, on the Mediterranean coast, and spread from there northward. As the circle of its operation grew wider and commerce increased, it became one of the most general forms of association. In the fifteenth century it was all but universal.

‌‌

By the sixteenth century we come to the "regulated company." Among the reasons for the rise of the great commercial companies was the exposure of distant commerce to armed attack by pirates, privateers and formal enemies of the nationals, which consequently required a greater military force for its protection than a small group could afford. Partly because of these dangers, partly because of the natural perils of the sea under the conditions of navigation at the time, partly because of the very novelty of the commerce, distant trade was very hazardous. As a result, associations of merchants were organized for carrying on trade in these parts. These associations came to be required by European governments, which assigned a certain field to each company in which it was given a monopoly, and in that field trade by individuals and by other associations was prohibited. The purpose of this was partly to give a certain character to the trade of the nationals in the foreign country, by eliminating unscrupulous traders and those who went out on single ventures and with no idea of building up a permanent trade, but also to diminish the risks of distant commerce by assuring to those who spent money in developing it the full fruits of their labor. An additional reason was the ease of taxation and regulation which the regulated companies offered.

The regulated company was merely an association of merchants who secured admission by paying the entrance fee and giving obedience to the rules. Each merchant traded on his own capital and kept his profits for himself; there was no pooling of capital and profits. It was an organization similar to a modern stock exchange.

Among the earliest of these companies was the English Muscovy Company, organized in 1556 for trade in Russia. During the course of the next several decades they began to appear in increasing numbers, among them the Company of the Levant (1581), the Company of Africa (1588), the East India Company (1599), the Virginia Company (1606), and the Company of North America (1606). French companies appeared a little later, the first, apparently, being the *Compagnie du Canada*, organized in 1599. After that they began to multiply and by 1642 twenty-two had been formed. Louis XIV created nearly forty, largely by the process of merger and reorganization. So effectively had the world been parceled out and monopolized by these regulated companies that by 1600 in England, for instance, an independent merchant had the whole world, save France, Spain and Portugal, shut against him.

⋘ ⋙

The passage from the regulated company to the joint-stock company was a slow process of transformation in the character of the regulated company arising from the demands for associations with greater permanence and stronger authority over their members. Early examples of the joint-stock company are to be found in Italy, but the company form developed north of the Alps only after the founding of the Dutch and English East India companies about 1600.

The English East India Company, organized in 1599 as a regulated company, was made over into a joint-stock company by degrees, and could not be regarded as permanently established on this basis for over fifty years.

The Dutch East India Company was the first of the true joint-stock enterprises. It began in 1602 as six semi-independent groups representing as many cities, with a loose and somewhat vague general administration to join them. Not until 1652 were its shares put on the market. They were taken up to a considerable extent by the capitalists of Antwerp who no longer had use for their money at home.

These early company enterprises were highly successful, and by 1700 England and Scotland together had 140 joint-stock companies with a total capital of £4,250,000. Most of the companies were small, of course, and three-fourths of this amount represented the capital of the Big Six—the East India, the African, Hudson's Bay and New River companies, and the Bank of England and the Million Bank. The first two voyages of the English East India Company netted 95 per cent, although it took over nine years to close the accounts.[1]

The Dutch East India Company was more consistently profitable. Its dividends were as follows: 1605, 15 per cent; 1606, 75 per cent; 1607, 40 per cent; 1608, 20 per cent; 1609, 25 per cent; 1610, 50 per cent; 1613, 37 per cent. In 1622 it paid a dividend of 22 per cent in cloves.[2]

⋖§ §⋗

With the organization of the Royal Exchange in London in 1698, the modern stock exchange makes its appearance. The Paris Bourse was organized in 1724 and by this time the bourse of Amsterdam had achieved the same general structure by evolution. These new exchanges, limited in their operations to dealings in shares and money instruments, together with the shares of the regulated and joint-stock companies which were beginning to be traded in, offered new possibilities for speculation which soon attracted, and then absorbed, public attention. The methods of manipulation which had been developed into an art on the older bourses were now adapted to these newer objects of attention, and it was quickly discovered that dealings in shares offered larger opportunities for gain, on a slenderer capital, than the older forms of arbitrage and exchange speculation. Traders speculated on a rise, or fall, or a combination of both. Systems of news gathering and forwarding by which traders could obtain advance information of important events affecting the price of securities, became highly developed. London speculators, for instance, got word through private channels of the signing of the Treaty of Ryswick in 1697 a day before the British ambassador arrived with the official announcement, and made fortunes in buying up Bank of England stock, the fate of which hung on the outcome. The sudden jump in the quotations from 84 to 97 was not explained until the following day.

Underhand methods of trade were common. Speculators

would set afloat rumors to depress the price of securities, and then buy in. One day during the reign of Anne in England a well-dressed man rode furiously through the street proclaiming the death of the Queen. The news spread and funds fell; the Jewish interest on the exchange bought eagerly, and were suspected later of having been responsible for the hoax, though it was not proved against them. The Englishman, Child, who made a fortune in speculating, and who was called in a pamphlet of 1719 "the original of stock jobbing," would have one set of brokers spread rumors of disaster, and sell a little of his stock publicly, while another set bought for him "with privacy and caution," and in a few weeks he would reverse the process and come out 10 or 20 per cent ahead.

These manipulations resulted in what were regarded at the time as enormous fluctuations in the quotations, although in comparison to modern stock market movements they would hardly be regarded as extreme. The shares of the East India Company, for instance, moved within a range of £200 to £37 in the five years 1692 to 1697, while the range of quotations on the African Company shares was from £52 to £13, and on the Hudson's Bay Company, from £260 to £80. A number of stock jobbers got prison sentences as a result of manipulations, but no visible effect was noted in the price movements that followed.

By the dawn of the eighteenth century, the materials were all prepared for the first credit inflation of the modern world. Because of the influence it had upon the use of money and the mechanism of money in modern times, it becomes necessary to examine the manifestations of this "bubble era" in some detail.

Book Seven. THE GREAT PAPER MONEY EXPERIMENT

The name of that ardent Scotsman, John Law, is short. His career was likewise short: he was Comptroller General of France for less than five months in the year 1720. The space of time during which he bestrode the financial world of Europe like a Colossus scarcely exceeded five years at the most. The financial mania that swept over the continent at his touch flamed and died in less than two years. His epoch is usually dismissed by historians with a short passage on the "bubble era"; and by economists, if discussed at all, it is treated as a freak in the hothouse growth of modern finance.

I. Basis of the Idea

But the man and the occasion are deserving of more attention. John Law has been called the father of modern stock jobbing. He may also be called the father of commercial banking—at least as it is practiced today. He may perhaps be regarded as the foster father of modern paper money. With John Law and his bank, his Mississippi Company, and his System, we see adumbrated the modern system of complex inter-relationships among industry, commerce, capital and the money mechanism, the system in which money derives its validity from the state of trade, and the state of trade is intricately and precariously balanced upon the state of money.

In the "boom" that in the wake of his audacious maneuvers developed simultaneously in Paris, in London, in Amsterdam, and in Italy, we may discern the culmination of the great revolution from medieval economy to Italian capitalism that had begun 500 years before, and the genesis of the modern era of bank money, security flotations, stock exchange manipulation and the general liquefaction of capital and wealth which is the characteristic of modern money economy.

More precisely, we find, in the era of John Law, the first widespread use of paper money in Europe. Beginning with Law and his bank, we note the rise of "bank money" as the chief element of the money mechanism, and the gradual submergence of coinage and the problems of coinage as the chief problems of monetary practice. Though the question of the ratio was to constitute a perplexing problem and to play a dominant rôle in monetary policy until late in the nineteenth century, henceforth it was the complex, baffling and deceptive subjects of central banking, reserve ratios, and credit control that were to entangle the understanding of men and vitiate control of the money mechanism.

൶ ൠ

Paper money was not, of course, something new to the world when John Law flooded France with his bank issues. It was well known in China, where it had been in use since the tenth century at least, and possibly as early as the ninth. There the phenomenon of inflation, with its consequences, had been repeatedly experienced, and Ma-Twan-lin, the Chinese historian, writing from personal experience in the thirteenth century, has described its manifestations in terms which make his account seem of contemporary times.[1] Marco Polo had brought back a racy description of the "means whereby the Great Khan may have, and in fact has, more treasure than all the Kings of the World," and if Marco were disbelieved, at least five other well recognized European travelers and writers from the thirteenth century to the fifteenth century independently described for their readers the Chinese device of paper money.*

* These writers are: William de Rubruquis (*ca.* 1215–1270); Roger Bacon (1214–1294); Hayton (1307); Pegollotti (*ca.* 1340); and Josafat Barbara (*ca.* 1436). Paper money was mentioned also by a number of Arabic writers, including Ibn Batuta (*ca.* 1348) and Ahmed Shibab Eddi (died 1338). Hayton is included among European writers, because his writing was done in France and in the French language. His book is an account of the visit of his relative, the King of Armenia, to the court of the Great Khan. Thomas Francis Carter, *The Invention of Printing in China and its Spread Westward* (New York, 1925), Notes, chap. xi.

In Europe, "leather," or parchment, money appears in the history of the feudal princes. Del Mar mentions several instances of its use, the earliest being the issue of stamped leather money in 862–879 by Ruric the Goth at Novgorod. In England, Edgar, King of Wessex, issued leather money in 959–975, and another case is recorded in the time of Edward I in 1285. In France, record appears of issues by Philip I in 1060–1103, by Louis IX in 1226, and by John II in 1346. Other instances appear in Norway, by Olaf I in 998, in Sicily in the twelfth century, and by Frederick II at Milan in 1235.[2] At the siege of Tyre, 1112, occurred the first issue of bank or promissory notes by the Venetians. The Doge Michieli, who conducted the siege in person, found it necessary, in order to satisfy the clamor of his troops for pay, to issue certain leather money, struck by his private order, and stamped with the arms of his own family. The issue was accompanied by a declaration and a promise that, on the return of the fleet to Venice, it should be redeemed at once at its full nominal value.[3]

Paper money, strictly speaking, could hardly have appeared in Europe before the end of the thirteenth century, for the art of paper-making was until that time a mystery of the Chinese and the Arabs. The first recorded paper mill in Christendom was set up in 1189 at Hérault on the French side of the Pyrenees, but for still another century Europe's needs were largely supplied by paper from the Saracen mills of Damascus and Spain. The first Italian paper factory had been set up at Montefano, in 1276,[4] and among the first paper of European manufacture of which we have specimens is that bearing the watermark of the mills at Fabriano, Italy, in 1293.[5]

In the *giro* banking that grew up in Italy, in the *Banco della Piazza* of Venice, in the Bank of St. George at Genoa, and later, in the case of the Bank of Amsterdam, a form of bank money was of course finding a wide use among financiers as a substitute for coin, and in the circulation of the "promises" or bonds of the various governments, another form of money substitute was beginning to be used. Toward the end of the seventeenth century, as we shall have occasion to notice in more detail, state issues of paper money were being undertaken in France, and achieved a considerable total outstanding.

◄§ §►

In England, the first paper money is attributed to the goldsmiths, with whom, because of the insecurity attendant upon the Puritan Revolution in the seventeenth century, many of the merchants and nobility became accustomed to leave their plate and money for safekeeping, receiving in exchange the goldsmiths' receipts. These receipts, or notes, being—originally at least—warehouse certificates for actual money or precious metal, were generally circulated and accepted in payment of services or obligations or goods. The goldsmith notes were not, however, endowed with legal tender quality, and were not, strictly speaking, money. The first English paper money which was endowed with the quality of legal tender was the exchequer order, which originated early in the reign of Charles II in 1665, during the period of Charles' first Dutch war. An exchequer order was an order to the Teller of the Receipt of the Exchequer to pay such and such a person so much out of the fund arising from this or that parliamentary supply. Whenever it represented the repayment of a loan, the exchequer order bore interest reckoned from the date of the loan. From that time on the exchequer order was made frequent use of by Charles II and his successors as a convenient way of anticipating revenue receipts. But the exchequer order was far from being true paper money. Though made transferable from hand to hand by parliamentary enactment, and full tender for the payment of public and private dues, the orders were transferable only by endorsement, and whenever the order represented the payment of a loan, it bore interest from the date of the loan.[6] The mere fact that the order bore interest deprived it of the first requisite of money, the quality of freely circulating, for paper which bears interest is regarded as a form of investment rather than as a species of currency. It tends to be kept or stored away until maturity, and if it is disposed of at any time before maturity the calculation of interest is troublesome.

৵৽ ৾৶

In the American colonies, the greatest invention was required to meet the scarcity of coin arising from the restrictions and prohibitions on the export of metal and coin by the European states, and the expanding requirements of the economic life developing on this continent. Numerous makeshifts, from wampum to beaver skins and tobacco and rice, served as media of exchange. Wampum, or *wampum peage*, consisted of beads from the inner whorls of the *Pirula carica* or *canaliculata* periwinkle shells so common on all the south coast of New England. Color was the basis of the nomenclature, as well as the difference in value. The Indians strung the beads on fibres of hemp or tendon, and the strings were embroidered on strips of deerskin, as many as four thousand beads being wrought into a belt four inches wide. Such belts were highly regarded as ornaments, and commanded a value of ten pounds sterling or more. This quality gave it the attributes of currency in the growing intercourse of the colonies. Various colonial enactments set values upon the wampum in exchange. In 1640, the colony of Massachusetts set a value of four pence for the white, and two for the blue. In 1641, this was changed to six pence, and the beads were made lawful money for any sum under £10. By 1645, the inventories of deceased colonists commonly contained items of *wampum peage*, and frequently there was no other money.[7]

The use of wampum extended as far southward as Virginia. There, and elsewhere in the South, tobacco was given a legal tender quality, and the first law passed by the first General Assembly of Virginia at Jamestown, July 31, 1619, was one fixing the price of tobacco. The various attempts made to stabilize the price of tobacco in terms of English money led to warehousing it under public authority, and the warehouse receipts were generally current at the sterling equivalent of the tobacco represented.[8] The demand for tobacco and its general acceptability and high price had made it universally valued, to such an extent that the quit rents of Virginia became payable in it, and in 1641 it was enacted that no debts contracted to be paid in coin could be sued in a court of law.[9]

The colony of Virginia authorized, about 1705 (although

we have no record of the enactment), the issuance of notes redeemable in tobacco, but they were not successful, and it was not until 1727 that tobacco notes were made legal tender.[10]

Although a mint had been established in 1652 in Massachusetts and continued for about thirty years, in 1690 the colony essayed an issue of paper money in order to meet the pay of soldiers on their return from the disastrous expedition against the French in Canada. The government had been utterly unprepared for their return, and seems to have presumed not only upon success but the capture of treasure. The soldiers being upon the point of mutiny for want of their wages, the government discharged the debt in paper notes, issued in denominations from two shillings to ten pounds, receivable for payment of taxes. The notes, however, were acceptable generally only at a discount, and were taken only by persons having payments to make to the exchequer.[11]

John Law is supposed by some to have traveled in the American colonies and to have come into first-hand contact with the colonial system of money substitutes. He undoubtedly drew upon the experience of the Bank of Amsterdam, which he studied closely while making his residence in the Netherlands. He spent some time also in Italy where he familiarized himself with the *giro* banking practiced there. In these various soils lay the seeds of his System, which, fertilized by the ingenuity of his own mind, germinated into his bank, and his system of bank money based upon evidences of commercial wealth which, in corrupted form, is the basic feature of the money mechanism in countries having a central banking system.

II. The Prepared Ground

THE financial situation of France at the close of the reign of Louis XIV in 1715 was prepared ground for fiat money and experiments with the money mechanism. During a long reign of seventy-two years, the Grand Monarque had elevated France to the foremost position in Europe, and in the process had re-

duced his subjects to poverty and the state to bankruptcy. At
the end of the reign of Louis XIV, in 1715, the consolidated
debt of the government totaled around two billion *livres*, and
the floating debt, an additional billion. The interest on this debt
was around 86,000,000 *livres*, against state revenues of
165,000,000 *livres*, leaving less than 70,000,000 *livres* to meet
a state budget of 150,000,000 *livres*. The debt had increased
twenty-fold in less than thirty years.

Just how much this amounted to in purchasing power is a
matter almost past determination because of the inflation of
values, the depreciation of the currency, the duality of the
coinage system, and the currency manipulation that had been
practiced unconscionably after the death of Colbert (1683),
beginning particularly in 1687. The *livre* had been successively
reduced from 362 to the gold *mark* (3777.5 English grains) in
1643 to 600 in 1709; and in terms of silver from 26.75 to the
mark to 41. These changes were made by the process of repeated
recoinages and new tariffs, ostensibly to adjust the changing
ratio of gold and silver. Between 1689 and 1715, we are informed by Despaux, the value of money was changed forty-
three times.[1]

"These money manipulations did not have the sole purpose
of furnishing revenue to the treasury or of following the fluctuations of parity in the ratio between the precious metals," says
Despaux. "They were employed for other and various ends. The
administration of the finances appears to have practiced a subtle
and ingenious monetary tactic, conceived in the eighteenth century, but almost forgotten until the twentieth when it was again
practiced by Germany. The financial administration, by modifications in the monetary unit, attempted to influence economic
phenomena much the same as central banks and governments
today manipulate foreign exchange. Changes in the specie were
made to prepare for the issue of loans, or to audit the circulation
of the treasury notes, or to regulate exchange, to modify the
balances of trade and accounts, to effect a redistribution of
wealth, to influence the price level of commodities, perhaps to
attentuate the economic crises and famines, since the currency

manipulation of 1693 to 1709 coincided with a period of bad harvests."

ᴤ ᴥ

The manipulation of the currency, the increase in public debt and the mismanagement of state finances had produced a state of chaos in France by 1709. "Gold and silver were hoarded or driven from the country," writes James Breck Perkins. "The lack of sufficient specie checked every branch of business. Bankers failed, the notes of merchants went to protest, there was no money with which to pay taxes. The king sent his plate to be melted down, and his example was followed by the rest of the nobility. Edicts were issued in order to improve the situation, but the laws of trade could not be controlled even by an absolute monarch. There is little doubt that the depreciation of the currency did more injury to France than the victories of Marlborough, and that it was an important factor in the desperate condition of that country in 1709. The Dutch claimed they might wisely continue the war when they could raise money at 5 per cent and the advances which the French obtained cost them 20 per cent."[2]

A series of successes on the field of battle in the latter days of Louis' reign saved that monarch from the humiliation of a complete collapse of public finance, and fortunately he died soon afterward. But on the death of Louis the true state of anarchy in the commerce and trade of France was fully revealed. The Duke of Noailles, the chief of the Council of Finance under the regency, wrote to Mme. de Maintenon, September 21, 1715: "We have found matters in a more terrible state than can be described; both the king and his subjects ruined; nothing paid for several years; confidence entirely gone. Hardly ever has the monarchy been in such a condition, though it has several times been near its ruin."

La Bruyère, who was also an eye witness of the day, described the countryside as follows: "One sees certain wild animals, male and female, scattered over the country, black, livid, burned by the sun, attached to the soil, which they cultivate with an invincible pertinacity. They have an articulate voice, and when they stand erect they show a human face, and in fact they are men. At night they retire into their dens; they live on water, black bread and roots."[3]

Such was the state of France when there appeared in Paris a Scotsman with a plan by which all of these misfortunes were to be repaired. This Scotsman was John Law.

III. Germination of the Seed

JOHN LAW was born in Edinburgh in 1671. His father was a goldsmith, and, as was customary at that period, combined with his trade the care of moneys entrusted to him, and many of the functions now discharged by bankers. John Law was educated at Edinburgh, where he showed an amazing apitude for mathematics, especially the intricacies of algebra, which was later to stand him in good stead while explaining the ramifications of his financial plans. On the death of his father, he went to London, where his prepossessing manner gained him friends, and he became known for his skill as a gambler and for his intrigues with women. He became involved in an affair, fought a duel with a Mr. Wilson and killed him on the spot. For this crime he was tried, convicted of murder, and sentenced to be hanged. He managed to obtain a commutation of sentence, and succeeded in escaping to the continent. Georges Oudard, in his *Amazing Life of John Law*, gives us a lively picture of the Scotsman's career as he wandered about Europe, increasing his financial knowledge, sharpening his wits, making friends among the highly placed, perfecting his ideas, and finally, achieving their execution in France during the regency of the Duke of Orleans.[1]

చక్ §చ

In the summer of 1700 John Law returned to his native land of Scotland, where he found a condition of affairs in which he thought to develop his growing financial ideas. In Scotland, as in England and throughout Europe, a spirit of gambling and speculation had been induced by the uncertainties of a long war, by the disturbances to trade which made some wealthy overnight and reduced others to poverty, by the inflated demand for war materials, by the depreciation of the currency that had been practiced not alone in France but elsewhere, by the sudden rise of banks, and by the discovery of the joint-stock mechanism.

A great many Scotsmen had been drawn into the scheme of William Paterson, founder of the Bank of England, for colonizing the Isthmus of Darien. This scheme was the Scottish Company of Africa and India. It had failed miserably and had created the utmost distress in Scotland, where the shares had been avidly taken up. Paper money issued by the company and profusely distributed in competition with bills of the Bank of Scotland had impaired the position of the bank. Conditions were heartbreaking. Manufacturers were no longer exporting their goods; land rents were not being paid; money was leaving the country; and two hundred thousand poor were crying out for bread.

❦ ❧

It was at this point that Law enunciated his great currency principle, of money based upon land values, rather than upon metallic values—what Henry Dunning MacLeod, whose theory it is that money consists of debt, denounces as the first "Lawism."[2]

Law recalled that there was not one poor person in Holland, and that the Venetian Republic had only about three hundred. Out of these conditions and the study he gave them Law began to write his famous treatise *Money and Trade Considered with a Proposal for Supplying the Nation with Money.*

"Wealth depends on commerce," he wrote, "and commerce depends on circulation." The Scotch had but little silver and gold, and therefore they were poor. To make them rich, they required banks which could pour forth a stream of currency. A proper bank and currency would make the valley of the Clyde and fields of Fife blossom with prosperity, and would transform the shopkeeper of Edinburgh into the merchant prince of Genoa and Amsterdam.

Law proceeded to attack the mercantilist theory then in

vogue, that a nation's wealth consisted of its stock of precious metals, and showed that the value of gold and silver fluctuated like pepper or corn. Land, on the other hand, was steady in value, intrinsically useful (whereas gold and silver were valuable chiefly in exchange) and always in demand.

"What I propose," Law announced boldly, "is to make a land currency equal to the value of the land and to the value of actual coined money without being subject, as is coined money, to a fall in value."

Law proposed, therefore, that commissioners should be authorized to issue paper money to all who required it, to be secured by mortgages to the value of two-thirds of the land, or issued for the entire value, upon the land's being turned over to the commission. Such a currency, he said, would necessarily be in proportion to the needs of the community. In other words, if any man wanted money, and had the land to secure it, he could get as much as he required; when no one needed money, there would be no demand, and none would be issued. Thus the currency would regulate itself, like a safety valve. So confident was he of the superiority of such a medium of exchange over gold and silver, that he advised a provision limiting the premium on paper to 10 per cent.

It is quite possible that had this scheme been adopted we would have witnessed a hundred years earlier the situation produced by the issuance of the *assignats* during the French Revolution. There was, however, little danger of the adoption of Law's proposals. The Scotch were smarting from the disastrous results of the Darien expedition, and they were not inclined to any new ventures.*

---

* If Law's theory of land money was rejected in Scotland, it still received its trial. In 1789 his tract, *Money and Trade Considered*, was translated into French. By that time all memory had elapsed of the great catastrophe with Law's System of sixty-nine years before. The revolutionary National Assembly had confiscated the property of the Church, and fascinated by the theory of land money began to put it into effect on a gigantic scale. The scheme resulted in disastrous collapse. The history of the *assignats* is but a repetition, under other circumstances, of all the great failures in Europe with managed currency. As it was based upon a theory which has no place in modern economics, it is more to our

IV. First Fruits

IF John Law was a prophet without honor in his own country, he found a ready ear in the Duke of Orleans, who had become Regent of France upon the death of Louis XIV. Orleans was anxious to be a popular ruler, and he had no stomach either for economy or for a debt repudiation—the alternatives offered by his ministers to meet the haggard state of the finances. The Regent was a notorious roué. Some years earlier he had met Law in a gambling den and had been impressed with the Scotsman's financial genius. When Law now presented himself at court, Orleans received him with open arms.

Law offered to assist France in her distress; to render her debt light by making her people rich; to restore her commerce, build up her industries; and make the regency of Orleans memorable as the beginning of an era of larger enterprise, increasing wealth, and abundant prosperity.

"What is needed," he said, in words which have a curiously modern ring, "is credit. The credit that I propose to establish will be different in its nature from the kinds of credit now in general use; it will be suited to this monarchy and the present state of affairs."

❧

The means of furnishing this requirement for enlarged trade would be a bank, and Law dwelt upon the advantages which such institutions had rendered wherever established, and could render in France. Banks (now in need of no advocates) were at that time unknown in France, and for that matter little known anywhere. The Bank of Amsterdam was regarded as a mystery; the Bank of England had been established but a few years, and its creation had been opposed by a large portion of those who were considered the practical, hard-headed men of the day.

Law urged the advantages of his bank. By the very act of

present purpose to trace the development of Law's System based on commercial and public securities, doctrines of Law which are still firmly embedded in modern theory, rather than to discuss the devolution of the "land money" doctrine.

issuing currency, he declared that he could make the country richer; that plenty of banknotes would not only aid a commerce that existed, but could create one that had no existence; that an abundant currency would of itself bring prosperity to the land.

"A state," he wrote, "must have a certain quantity of money proportioned to the number of its people," thus giving utterance to a belief that still has many adherents.

The idea of currency based upon land, which he had proposed to the Scotch, was, however, conspicuously absent in the plans he outlined to the regency. The theory of money which Law now advocated was that of money created on the security of commercial credit. This was not an original idea, rather an outgrowth of the English goldsmiths' practices, but Law was the first to propose and apply the theory on a national scale.

The plan which Law suggested was subject to little criticism. He advised that, in order to relieve business from the paralysis caused by the frequent depreciations of the currency of the government, the bills of the bank should be made payable in coin of a fixed weight and amount. He recognized also the necessity of measures by which the bills could always be promptly redeemed in coin.

✑ ৯

When the question of a charter came before the Council of Finance, however, it met with unfriendly reception. Saint-Simon, hidebound old member of the aristocracy and a member of the Council of the Regency, gives us in his memoirs an account of the deliberations. He himself, with naïve and frank appreciation of the weaknesses of his class, voiced the most pertinent and penetrating objections. The first objection, he said, was the difficulty of directing the bank with sufficient foresight and wisdom to avoid the dangers of over-issue of notes. A second disadvantage was that a bank under the control of the government might be safe in a republic or a limited monarchy, but it would be sure to be abused where the king was absolute. An unfortunate war, the prodigality of a sovereign, the avidity of a minister, a favorite, or a mistress, a craving for luxury, foolish expenditure, would very soon exhaust the bank and ruin those holding its notes—in other words, ruin the whole nation. Law's answers to such objections showed the hopefulness of a promoter rather than the sagacity of a man of affairs. A bank, he insisted, would so increase the wealth of the nation, and therefore the revenues of the king, that it was incredible to suppose that any monarch would destroy the usefulness of an institution from the existence of which he would be the chief gainer.[1]

The deliberations of the council and Law's astute arguments are of interest to us today because they present the same conflict and divergence of viewpoint over the proper sphere of banking, its limitations, and its mischievous possibilities which still appear and which will not be resolved until the money mechanism is treated not as the creator but as the safeguard of wealth.

≈§ §≈

Because of the objections of the council, the best Law could obtain was a charter for a private bank, which was granted May 2, 1716. The bank's powers were, however, ample. It could receive money on deposit, discount commercial paper, and issue notes. In the following month the bank (known as *Banque Générale*) modestly began its career in the house where Law lived, Place Louis le Grand.

The institution was immediately prosperous. The fact alone that its notes, under the terms of its charter, were redeemed in coin of a fixed weight gave new life to commerce. The money had been subjected by the government to so many modifications that the specie value of a *louis* or a *livre* fluctuated like the price of shares in the market. The notes of Law's bank furnished a currency safe and convenient in use, of which the value could not be modified by any royal edict. As a result, business relations abroad were renewed, interest rates on good paper dropped from 30 per cent to 6 per cent and then to 4 per cent. Bewildered money lenders closed their shops. Law's management seems to have been judicious and conservative. In October, 1716, tax collectors were ordered to make their remittances payable in Paris by notes of the bank and to pay these notes on sight when they were presented. This in effect made the bank notes legal tender.

For two and a half years the bank remained a private institution. During that time Law's success was gradually being acknowledged, and it is reported that Peter the Great of Russia sought Law's assistance in reorganizing the finances of his empire. The Regent began to urge new miracles from this financial wizard, and to offer Law new powers. In 1718 the *Banque Générale* was converted into a state bank with increased powers. From that moment Law's undoing began and he moved on, like a figure in a tragedy, into heights of power and renown that only made the more precipitate and tragic his eventual fall.

V. The Mississippi Bubble

WE now approach the flowering of Law's "System," the emergence and devolution of his great scheme for unifying the whole diverse substance of French economy into one grandiose whole, a great economic system conceived, delivered and nurtured by credit. The great speculative inflorescence which followed in its wake—the Mississippi Bubble—is usually exhibited in economic history as the product of financial hysteria, without reference to the solid bases upon which it was founded. As a speculative inflorescence it indeed deserves our closest attention, for it was the first great "boom" of modern times, and in it we may trace the pattern of all subsequent booms; but not alone for this reason will it be treated in some detail, but also because, involved in it, as we shall have occasion to note, was the great misconception over which in the modern world "the whole financial order, big and little"—to quote Frank A. Vanderlip—"came a cropper." This was the misconception over the possibility of giving currency liquidity to all forms of wealth.

⇜ ৪⇝

In 1717 fortune was smiling upon Law, and he now gave rein to his imagination in the audacious project of developing the colonial possessions of France. He drew up and presented to the Regent his scheme for his Mississippi Company (the

Compagnie d'Occident) which should enjoy extensive and monopolistic privileges in Louisiana. Louisiana was then but a name, an unknown territory of unknown extent in which the claims of the French government were staked out by a few scattered forts and trading posts.

When the extent and the present wealth of this territory is considered, we cannot but admire the audacity of imagination of the man who could conceive the gigantic enterprise of colonizing it, or fail to excuse the enthusiasm to which he succumbed, or the wild speculation which arose over the prospects for the development of this area. Certainly the speculative enthusiasm of France of 1718 to 1720 was founded on a far stronger basis than the speculative enthusiasm of the twenties of the twentieth century.

The capital of the company was set at 100,000,000 *livres*, but Law, either against his judgment or carried away by his enthusiasm, agreed that subscriptions could be made in state obligations, instead of coin. Thus the capital of the company, instead of being represented by ships, stores, forts and warehouses, was invested in obligations of a government whose credit was exceedingly poor. Only the interest on this sum would be available for the actual work of commerce, and this at most was 4,000,000 *livres* a year. The *Compagnie d'Occident*, founded with such extravagant hopes, thus became at the outset a vast machine which would swallow worthless state paper.

Nevertheless, Law was supported loyally by the Duke of Orleans and shortly afterward he added to the powers of his company the tobacco monopoly of France. Next, the East India Company and the *Compagnie de Chine* were absorbed, and in July, 1719, the privilege of coinage was granted the company. The following month, Law obtained the monopoly of the tax farm, and in doing so incurred the bitter enmity of the financial interests that had previously held the privilege.

Finally, Law proposed a vast conversion of the national debt, offering to advance the state some 1,500,000,000 *livres* at 3 per cent, intending to raise this enormous sum by sale of shares in the company. Thus, by a series of operations, Law had brought under his personal control most of the organized capital and enterprise of France. He had created an enormous trust under the aegis of the state, and if ever an opportunity for "planned economy" existed, it was now.

＊§ §＊

To float such an enterprise as Law had conceived was, however, an operation that would have taxed the ingenuity of our most inventive modern financiers. Law was equal to the occasion. All the methods of stock jobbery and promotion that are still so successfully practiced were used. Attempts at colonization were made in a manner to attract and delight the public. Large tracts of land were taken by prominent persons, Law himself taking a reservation in the Arkansas wilderness. Dealings in futures—equivalent to the "puts" and "calls" of Wall Street—were introduced. Law publicly took an option on shares of the company at a price 200 *livres* above the market and deposited 40,000 *livres* as security. Such a transaction filled the public with amazement, and as a stock jobbing operation it may rank as one of the major *coups* of history. The price of the shares at once advanced, and the public bought eagerly.

Prospectuses, of the most extravagant sort, were issued. In them, Law quoted freely, without acknowledgments, from Walter Raleigh's description of the Eldorado, which had delighted him in childhood. He had a plan of New Orleans published in the *Mercure* according to which this settlement on the mud banks of the Mississippi was a metropolis equal to many in Europe.

Another of Law's devices—one which was freely used during the 1920–1929 era—was that of issuing "rights to subscribe." He required subscribers to his new issues to be holders of a certain number of old shares, under the pretext of favoring early buyers of the shares, and as the new shares were always issued at a discount under the market price of the old, and consequently represented an immediate profit to their holders, there was always a headlong rush to obtain the shares of the old series, called "mothers" (*meres*), in order to be able to subscribe to the new, called "daughters" (*filles*). This demand naturally increased the price of the old and added to the general enthusiasm. Finally, there were shares of "mothers," "daughters" and "granddaughters" in circulation.

Still another device was that of allowing subscriptions to be paid in instalments. Shares were issued against 5 per cent paid in; the balance being payable in nineteen monthly instalments. This increased enormously the leverage of speculators, and was equivalent to trading on margin. As the shares rose by 100 per cent in less than two months time, profits of 450 per cent to 600 per cent were made by subscribers.

The most dangerous of his devices which have been aped in modern times was the declaration of dividends which had not been earned. At the first general meeting of the company, July 26, 1719, before there had been any earnings, he proposed and carried a dividend declaration of 12 per cent on the par value of the shares.

⋅৭ ৡ৹

Under these and similar measures, the price of the shares had risen in the space of forty days, between June 20, 1719, and July 27, by 100 per cent, a feat which recalls the 100 per cent stock dividend declared by the Goldman Sachs Trading Corporation within six weeks after the original public offering of its shares in the summer of 1929.

In July, 1719, the original shares of 500 *livres* par were quoted at 1,000. In September they sold at 5,000. As the market rose, additional issues were fed out to avid buyers. By October issues totaling 1,500,000,000 *livres* had been sold.

To support this tremendous security speculation, vast reserves of credit had to be opened, and they were obtained by the free use of the printing press. In the spring of 1719 the amount of bank notes outstanding was about 100,000,000 *livres*. By June and July 300,000,000 *livres* more were uttered. In the last six months of 1719, notes were issued by the Royal Bank to the amount of 800,000,000 *livres*. In July, to stem an incipient run on the bank, Law had taken the audacious step of lowering the value of gold! Instead of redeeming its paper with *louis* at 35 to the *livre*, the bank offered to pay out *louis* at the rate of 34 *livres* paper.

❧ ❦

The scene presented by the speculation which grew apace in the fall and winter of 1719 was one which had no parallel in previous history and has had few since. The Rue Quincampoix had been the resort for men dealing in government obligations, and the speculation in the securities of Law's companies centered there. In the days of the highest excitement it presented a scene such as could be witnessed nowhere else in the world, with the possible exception of the Exchange Alley of London, where the speculation in the South Sea shares was concurrently taking place. There were no brokers' offices, and persons dealing in the shares met and trafficked in the highway. Here could be found those of every rank and occupation. Princes and priests, doctors of the Sorbonne and shaven friars, mingled with money-shavers, shopkeepers, valets and coachmen. Women jostled for shares with men. Ladies of fashion went there, as they went to the opera. The cafés were full of gentlemen and ladies, who sipped their wine, played quadrille, and sent out servants to execute their orders. The owners of the houses on the street grew rich from the enormous rents which they obtained. Money was gained with such rapidity that those plying the humblest trades received exorbitant compensation.

The fortunes made in the Rue Quincampoix drew speculators from every part of Europe. A more cosmopolitan crowd was never seen than that which here jostled, shouted, bargained. Thirty thousand foreigners were in Paris during the autumn of 1719 in search of fortune, besides the hosts that came from all parts of France. So great was the eagerness to reach the city that seats in the coaches from such towns as Lyons, Bordeaux, and Brussels were engaged long in advance. Fabulous prices were given for a place, and those who could not go to Paris and buy shares speculated on seats in the stagecoach.

❧ ❦

For eight months there continued what would now be called a wild and rampant bull market, and the quotations on the shares gained on the average over ten points a day. Everyone was crazy with excitement long before the culmination of the speculation. The shares, which had sold at 500 *livres* in May were being quoted in November at 10,000. They soon rose to 12,000 and 15,000; there were many sales at those figures, even higher. It is said that as much as 20,000 *livres* was paid for a share of which the par value was 500. The highest prices were obtained in December and January, but though the market ceased to advance there was no rapid decline. From November, 1719, until February, 1720, the shares fluctuated between 10,000 and 15,000 *livres*.

Such a rise made for fabulous gains. A purchaser of the original shares, paying for them in bills of the state at 60 per cent discount, could get 15,000 *livres* for what cost him 200. Twenty thousand *livres* placed in shares in the latter part of 1718 would have realized nearly 2,000,000 a year later. A speculator who subscribed for a share in October, 1719, and sold in November, made 100 per cent on his investment in a month. A valet was said to have made fifty millions, a bootblack forty, and a restaurant waiter thirty. The word "millionaire," which has since become so familiar both in French and English, was first used to describe the Mississippian who had suddenly grown wealthy.

−§ §›

All France, all Europe, was deceived by this sudden vision of untold riches. The overburdened country of Louis XIV seemed transformed into a fairyland. The notes of the bank, of which a billion were now in circulation, the shares of the company, at the absurd prices at which they were now selling, were thought to be so much added to the national wealth. A grave writer estimated that in November, 1719, the country was richer by five billion *livres* than it had been a year before. And yet this fabulous increase was represented only by a few settlements in Louisiana, and a few more ships trading with the East.

Law, meantime, was working at a furious rate remodeling everything in the kingdom. He was not content with printing notes with dangerous obstinacy; he was also busy concerning matters of trade and agriculture. He had in mind the idea of depriving the clergy of their uncultivated lands and giving them to the peasants. He wanted asylums for the poor built in all parts of the country. He encouraged fisheries, and helped manufactures with substantial loans. He took an interest in large undertakings and furnished funds for building the bridge at Blois and for digging the canal at Briare. He wanted to have barracks built in the provinces in order to spare the inhabitants from having to house the troops. He was taking steps towards making Paris a seaport. He was effecting economies in the tax collections, amounting to 2,000,000 *livres* annually. He was on the point of abolishing tolls throughout the country in order to make the grain trade free. He was not only hastening to bring into force this much needed reform, but he was also reducing the import duties on oil, leather, tallow and wines. He abolished the offices connected with the ports, harbors and markets of all kinds in Paris, and this lowered by as much as 40 per cent the price of wood, coal, hay, bread, game, poultry, butter, eggs and cheese. Most of these reforms were abandoned after his fall.

The latter part of 1719 saw Law at the height of his greatness. He was the most prominent figure in Europe. He visited the street where millions were made daily out of his enterprises, and was received with an enthusiasm such as could hardly have been accorded a sovereign. His native town of Edinburgh sent the freedom of the city in a gold box to the Right Honorable John Law. The Chevalier of St. George, the head of the house of Stuart, pretender to the English throne, wrote to ask his favor and his bounty. The English ambassador in France was recalled because he was on unfriendly terms with the new financial autocrat. Law was declared to be a minister whose merits exceeded anything that the past had known, the present could conceive or the future would believe.

‎⋙ ⋘

On January 5, 1720, Law was made Comptroller General of France. He and his System had reached the zenith of their fortunes. Law surveyed a world inflated in an enormous bubble, as delicate and insubstantial as froth, a world gone mad in speculation, everywhere feverish activity, but activity of an unhealthy sort, concerned with the making of money rather than the creation of wealth, concerned with stocks and shares rather than ships and goods. Law must have been perplexed, dismayed at what he saw. He had conceived a "state within a state," an edifice of commerce and trade and industrial activity within the political state, a structure which would support and strengthen the degenerate and enfeebled state without; enterprise which would absorb the energies and interests of the people rather than the hollow and hectic life of the court.

Somewhere his plans had gone astray. Instead of creating a condition of industry and trade, geared and lubricated by the device of commercial credit, he found the same old interests and pursuits, but heightened and intensified by a spirit of gambling and speculation. A financial revolution had occurred which, like the political revolution of 1789, levelled all distinctions of rank. The greatest nobles shared an avidity for gain which was not surpassed by any lackey or coachman who became rich on the Rue Quincampoix. Royalty had lost something of its sanctity from its connection with banks and trading companies, which was a relationship inconsistent with the majesty of the throne as it had been personified by Louis XIV. The unconcealed greed of the nobility to share in the profits of Law's enterprises revealed the general spirit of commercialism that had suddenly been awakened. A feudal nobleman, living on his ancient estates, ruling his tenantry, despising trade and the vulgar interests of plebians, might command respect, but a duke dabbling in shares on the Rue Quincampoix put himself on the same level as the widow Chaumont, or André the Mississippian. . . . .

VI. The Final Experiment

IT is at this point in the story of Law's System, when the great speculative structure he had created was beginning to topple, that we note the development in all its theoretical perfection of the last great "Lawism": the attempt to give currency liquidity to wealth, the same disastrous attempt which the modern world has made with its heterogeneous and conflicting instrumentalities of credit and banking and money.

The speculative character of Law's edifice had become nowhere more evident than in the fact that the success of his whole
scheme depended upon the maintenance of the price level to
which the shares had risen, just as in 1933–1934 it was the
general conception that to restore prosperity prices must be restored to the 1926 level. Doubtless, at an earlier stage the prices
of the shares would have been an immaterial factor. With the
monopoly of foreign trade, together with the power over coinage
and tax collections in his hands, Law could have contented
himself with paying what the company could earn and disregard-
ing quotations. But this foresight Law lacked, as have also many
promoters and financiers since then who have been sincere and
honest in their intentions.

But six months later was too late. Prices had risen so rapidly
and exorbitantly, public interest had so focused on the share
market, that any action tending to disturb quotations would
have been fatal.

Moreover, inflation had spread to commodities, and a great
rise in prices had followed. Land was especially in demand.
Houses, chateaux and farms sold at three or four times their
former value. A property which had brought 700,000 *livres* a
few months before was now sold for over 2,000,000. A loaf of
bread, usually sold at from one to two *sous* a pound, now
brought three *sous*. The cost of other provisions had advanced
in the same proportion.

A collapse was inevitable, sooner or later; but Law, fascinated
by the thing he had set in motion, was lacking in the will to
throw on the brakes. Law feared the effect of a fall upon the
bank and the company, as well as upon his own popularity.

Early in November, however, large blocks of stock began to
be thrown on the market. Efforts to sustain prices led to further
inflation of the currency, and the continuing drop in the value
of the bank notes led to new measures to support their value. In
December, the bank notes were given an official premium of 5
per cent over coin. In February, the hoarding of gold or silver
was prohibited on severe penalties, and the act was enforced by
bounties to informers and summary search and inquisitorial
measures. These measures were without effect, and on March

11 the use of gold or silver for the payment of any debt was forbidden. Thus, for a short time, France had the distinction of being the one civilized country where a man could not pay his debts with gold or silver.

◄§ §►

To prohibit the use of gold and silver was a departure from the principles on which Law's bank had been organized; it was not, perhaps, at variance with the theories of a "managed currency" he had frequently announced. He had often argued against the use of the precious metals for currency, because of the fluctuations in their value, and had proposed, in their stead, a currency which would possess no intrinsic value, and of which the quantity would be fixed by the state in accordance with the needs of trade. Paper was most fit for this use, and therefore it had been adopted in France; gold and silver, like wool and silk, could now be put to some useful purpose. As the new money would have no intrinsic value, no one would be tempted to export it or convert it or melt it down. It would serve for one purpose only: that of circulation as a medium of exchange.[1]

◄§ §►

We come now to Law's final and revolutionary attempt to salvage his System. Law had proposed to the Scotch a system of money based on land; he now effectuated a system based completely on evidences of commercial wealth, an adumbration of the modern system of money based on commercial credit. In an effort to check the market decline in the shares of the company, and to put intrinsic value behind his bank paper, the Royal Bank and the company were consolidated, and two weeks later the value of the shares was fixed at 9,000 *livres*. A bureau of conversion was established, where the shares were purchased at that price, paid for in notes of the bank, or, conversely, sold at the same price. By making interchangeable the shares in his company, in which was absorbed most of the commercial activity of the country, and the paper of the bank, Law achieved a perfect assimilation, in theory, between money and wealth, and achieved the ideal still so eagerly sought of making capital wealth perfectly liquid and money perfectly representative of commercial activity.

The actual results were, of course, quite the contrary. The share market continued to fall, and shares were converted into bank money in enormous quantities. The shares which had been issued at from 500 to 5,000 *livres*, were now repurchased at 9,000. More than the wealth of the West and the East Indies would have been required to sustain such an operation. Over 2,000,000,000 *livres* were paid out, without effect, in an effort to sustain the market, and the currency was inflated to an extent far exceeding the issues of the year before. By the close of the era the amount of bank issues outstanding totaled 3,000,000,000 *livres*.

The general eagerness of holders to convert their shares into money was tempered only by the fact that the notes which they received in payment were rapidly becoming as worthless as the shares. Investors had to choose between an investment that would yield nothing, and notes that would buy nothing. The attempt to make money and commercial wealth synonymous was a fiasco. This perhaps most audacious attempt in history at managed currency overlooked one vital fact: when trade is bad good money is more than ever necessary. The state of money cannot be made to depend on the state of the market.

◅§ §▻

The continued drop in the price of shares and the corresponding rise in the price of bread and other necessities led to further frantic and desperate measures. The value of the bank money was officially lowered by 50 per cent.

This was, of course, a mere juggling of words, which made no man either richer or poorer, but to such a degree were wealth and money confused in the public mind that the effect of the decree was cataclysmic. The man who had a hundred *livre* note saw it worth, in six months, but fifty *livres*. The operator who had lulled himself with the belief that he was worth a million saw his property to be only five hundred thousand. The wealth represented by billions of shares and notes had been, indeed, but a dream, but it was a stern awakening to have a royal edict proclaim the fact that it was worth only half what it professed to be.

✌ ੬✒

The edict was repealed after having been in effect but six days, but the damage had been done past repair. From then on there remained only the ghastly work of gathering together the broken and shattered bits of the System, and the thankless task of reconciling a disillusioned public that for a year had been living in a fool's paradise.

The depreciation of the currency had caused such serious disturbances as, later in the century, might have ripened into revolution. Butchers, bakers, grocers, and other tradespeople were unwilling to receive paper money at all. Specie had been driven out of circulation. There arose a fierce demand for something with which one could buy bread to eat, wood to burn, clothes to wear. What had been a condition of physical need bade fair to become a condition of physical distress. Toward the end of May the prohibition of the use of the precious metals as currency was repealed, but as the metallic reserve of the bank was not 2 per cent of the amount of its circulation, the effort to restore convertibility resulted in a series of new disasters. The value of gold and silver was alternately raised and lowered. From September, 1719, to December, 1720, the value of gold was changed twenty-eight times, and that of silver thirty-five. This was a record surpassing the worst of the old régime. A *louis* ranged in value from thirty to seventy-two *livres* within six months. The weight of gold was the same, but the sum for which the government would issue or receive it fluctuated with startling rapidity. Such measures had no effect. In a condition of panic the only desire was to lay hold of a piece of gold, whether it was called ten *livres* or fifty. It would buy something for daily needs, or it could be put aside with the assurance that ultimately it would command its real value.

✌ ੬✒

The formal close of the System was marked by a decree of October 10, 1720, declaring the notes of the bank no longer

currency, and requiring contracts to be discharged and payments to be made in gold and silver. The paper currency of the
state, after an experience of less than two years, was extinguished. The experiment of a managed currency, of a currency
that should expand with the needs of trade, was abandoned. In
December, 1720, Law was forced to flee the country which he
had dominated as financial dictator for the space of two years.
In January, 1721, a gold *louis*, worth forty-five *livres*, purchased
a share of stock that had sold a year before for 20,000 *livres*.

VII. Appraisal of the System

THE manner in which the System was finally liquidated—the
guaranteeing of the notes of the bank by the state, the *visa*, or
examination of accounts and the fines that were levied on speculative profits, the final winding-up when all the papers, notes,
shares, and other records, were consumed in a great bonfire—
need not detain us here. It remains for us only to assay the System and analyze its general results.

For the first time in its history, Western civilization was presented with an experiment in paper money, pure and simple. For
the first time an effort was made to establish a money system
without the use of the precious metals. For the first time an
essay, on a national scale, was made at a "managed currency."
For the first time the intelligence of man grappled with the
abstrusities and perplexities of money. For the first time, the
attempt was made to bring under control the system of exchanges which had previously been only the tool of financial
statecraft, the subject of political practice and the object of
manipulation by the arbitragist, the bullionist and the speculator.

This attempt was not always conscious, nor was the experiment everywhere purposive, the objectives clearly defined, the
movement direct and to the point. It was subject, as most
rational activity, to emotional stimuli. Concretely, it was be-
clouded by the weakness in the character of the man Law, and

overthrown by the speculative mood of the masses. As an attempt to control the money mechanism, it was an abject failure.

୶ৡ ঽ঵

Nevertheless, there were positive results both in the development of theory and the evolution of practice. For good or evil, paper money, as a substitute for coined metal, became thereafter the common and acceptable medium of exchange. In both theory and practice, paper money possesses admitted advantages over a metal which is weighty and solid. In circulation, it is free from depreciation; that is, its value cannot be reduced by the process of wear or the sweating, clipping and abrasion of the money dealer. Its legal tender value remains constant at the rate determined by the state. To this degree it simplifies the control of the money mechanism by transferring it from the hands of the masses to the hands of the central authority.

In practice, it possesses great advantages over metallic money in the ease of its transportation. If money is a medium of exchange, that form of money which performs this service with the least expenditure of human labor is, on the simplest principles, the best. Gold has generally supplanted silver, at least for large payments and payments made in distant places, because of the greater value concentrated in a given weight or volume. Precisely in the same manner, paper money possesses advantages over gold. As Marco Polo observed of the paper money of the Great Khan, "They are so light that ten *bezants'* worth does not weigh one golden *bezant*. . . . . And with this paper money the merchants can buy what they like anywhere over the Empire whilst it is also vastly lighter to carry about on their journeys."

Ideally—though the point is gravely contestable—paper money is not subject, like the precious metals, to fluctuations in the supply arising from causes unconnected with its monetary functions. It is not in demand for use in the arts and industry, or for ornamentation; its supply may not be increased by developments in metallurgical skill or unforeseen discoveries of new lodes, nor is it reduced by the exhaustion of natural deposits, nor by abrasion, nor by hoarding. The monetary circulation may—

theoretically—be made to conform to the requirements of trade and commerce, the facilitation of which, by providing a medium of exchange, is its principal function.

In paper money we have, in fact, a mechanism of exchange superior to any that has heretofore been devised, and its expanding use in the monetary function may be regarded as an inevitable accompaniment of an increase in civilized commerce. Like all refinements of mechanism, however, it is accompanied by a delicacy of adjustment, an increase in leverage, a concentration of energy, that untutored hands may make of it a perfect engine of destruction, an explosive of easy catalysis; and it is to be seriously doubted whether the intelligence and the morals of mankind have yet attained the character necessary to cope with it.

୧ ୨

The experience of France under the tutelage of Law is not, of course, decisive, and the era of Law is not to be cited as an example of paper money failure. Probably more progress was made by Law in developing the true theory and nature of paper money than has been made at any time since. In fact, the truth probably is that in our modern attempts to deal with paper money we are still wallowing around in the same errors which engulfed the System.

When we examine Law's System stripped of all the complexities in which it was enmeshed, of all the modifications which were introduced as the result of the exigencies of the immediate situation, and reduced to the rational principles which Law pursued, with certain deviations, from the moment he first proclaimed them to the world, it is evident that what Law aimed at was the liquefaction of the wealth of France. The heavy and solid substance of French capital, unadventurous, conservative, concerned only with local exploitation, he sought to loosen and to cause to flow into the commercial channels that were then opening before the world. In a large measure he achieved his objective. The Revolution is said to have opened the field of politics for talent. Law opened the field of business for talent. He broke down the aristocracy of wealth. The fortunes realized from the System showed opportunities which an enlarged commerce could furnish for all. "The gates of wealth," he wrote to those who complained that vulgar adventurers had become suddenly wealthy, "are now open to all the world. It is that which distinguishes the fortunes of the old administration from those of the present."[1] If commercialism is bad, it is doubly so when its privileges for gain and exploitation are limited to a few. Bad as the price system is, it is perhaps better that it be universal rather than the tool of entrenched and predatory interests. Notwithstanding all the harm occasioned by the System, and all the misery it caused, it must be reckoned among the influences which made France at the close of the eighteenth century so far removed from France at its beginning.* Law, probably more than any other individual, was responsible for that loosening of the social strata that made possible the political eruptions seventy years later.

⨳ ⨴

The means by which Law developed his objective was, naturally, the manipulation of the money mechanism. By the Midas touch of his bank, he sought to convert into liquid wealth the greater part of the capital wealth of France, or at least that part of the capital wealth which was under his control. In giving the shares of the company a fixed value, negotiable for that sum at the bank, he merely exchanged one form of evidence of wealth for another. The bank note was only evidence, one step removed from the share certificate, of the assets represented by the System. If this was unsound, if it only hastened the general collapse of his System, it is well to consider that this is exactly what was done, only under greater camouflage and sophistry, by the enactments liberalizing the rediscount privileges of the American banking system in 1933. In one bold stroke Law achieved the perfect liquidity of banking and commercial capital which is the constant object of modern banking, pursued by a devious system of security exchanges, call loans, commercial banking,

---

* The commercial marine of France increased, for instance, by some six times between 1716 and 1738.

rediscounting and central banking. The essential difference is this:

Law attempted to build a money system based upon evidences of commercial wealth; modern banking attempts to build a money system upon evidences of debt. Law sought by the Midas touch of banking to convert tangible wealth, produced and above ground, into money; modern banking seeks to convert our debts, our lack of wealth, our promises to pay from proceeds of wealth which is still unproduced and still in the future, into money.

Book Eight. BIMETALLISM AND THE RISE OF THE GOLD STANDARD

THE appearance of the single gold standard in the currency systems of the modern world, the exotic quality of the standard and the tender substance of its growth, easily bruised by every wind of casuistry and political unrest, require, for their understanding, some reference to the question of the ratio and the unhealthy soil of bimetallism in which the gold standard is rooted.

I. The Question of the Ratio

THE development of gold coinage, or rather the reintroduction of gold in the coinage of Europe on a widespread scale in the thirteenth century, created a factor of extreme disturbance in the reviving money economy of Christendom. The maintenance of a stable relationship, or parity, between two precious metals, both of which were struck with the seal of the sovereign authority, and both of which were of equal validity in the discharge of obligations, now became the perplexing problem of honest governments, and at the same time the opportunity of dishonest ones. Nothing is more vocal of the incapacity of European philosophy and practice to deal with the money mechanism than the absorption of attention for the better part of five hundred years in the question of the ratio, the pages devoted to it in European currency history, the shifts and changes in business activity to accommodate itself to the disturbances it created, the orientation of statecraft around monetary policy connected with it, and the growth of parasitic financial activity feeding upon the opportunities it presented.

Though bimetallism was present in the ancient world, and undoubtedly offered the same problems as it did in modern Europe, it does not appear to have been, in general, a vital factor in monetary policy. While there are some who think that Roman money difficulties were the result of the imperial effort to establish a fixed ratio among the coinages of different metals, the real explanation of Roman money trouble was the dishonesty of the state, and the policy of manipulating the coinage in the interest of the treasury rather than for the benefit of commerce. The comparative immunity of the Empire to the ratio question was no doubt due to the fact that all Mediterranean civilization was embraced within the Empire frontiers, and foreign trade was negligible in relation to the domestic trade. Civilization centered in Rome, and commercial relations between Rome and the other centers of civilization such as China and India, were physical rather than financial. Much Roman gold and silver flowed out in payment for the silk of China and the spices and perfumes of India, but there were no spasmodic convulsions and sudden reversals in the flow of the metals which are characteristic of arbitrage operations. Commerce in the precious metals was unknown as a factor producing their drainage from the Empire.

In the previous period of history, before the Mediterranean was dominated by Rome, and when the trade of this area centered in the Greek commercial cities, arbitrage must have been an important factor in foreign trade. Every Greek city state had its own coinage, and the confusion, the diversity in weights and standards among these various coinages, offered fertile opportunity for the money changer and the dealer in precious metals. Yet so far as a factor influencing state policy, the variations in value between the metals appear to have been negligible. Certainly debasement of the coinage for the purpose of readjusting the ratio, which we find so frequently offered as an excuse for European monetary manipulations, does not appear to have been a necessity of the day. Debasement of the currency either for state profit or for the accommodation of changes in the ratio was rare in Greek history, and such debasements as occurred arose from the necessity of adjusting the standard to the worn and abraded state of the coinage in circulation. On the contrary, there are cases of actually raising the standard of the coinage for the greater prestige which a coinage of high intrinsic value seemed to offer. In the sixth century B.C., the Euboean unit was increased in a number of cities by about five grains, in emulation of an increase introduced by Pisistratus in Athens.

During the long period of Byzantine history, foreign trade was an important source of social income: Byzantium was, as we have seen, a commercial civilization whose contacts extended to the farthest outposts of the known world. Yet the problem of the ratio does not seem to have been a disturbing one in state economy. An undervaluation of silver in the monetary scheme may have been a factor in its disappearance from coinage; at any rate, we know that the money of Byzantium was exclusively gold and copper; but the fluctuations in the relative value of the metals was not, in the course of a thousand years, a sufficient factor to disturb either the gold basis of the money, or the actual quantity or quality of the standard. Though Byzantine gold moved out to the most distant corners of the earth and served as the measure of value to feudatories in England and to Persian merchants in India, there was no apparent diminution of supplies at Constantinople, no scarcity of metal that would provoke an alteration of the standard.

The fact is that Byzantium did not concern itself with "mercantilism." In both the early and later Greek civilization an economic structure was built upon money, but money was kept as a means rather than as an object of commercial activity. Property arose from the growth of natural rather than monetary wealth, and financial activity was concerned with the acquisition and movement of physical rather than monetary values.

◦§ ഉ◦

In Europe, however, hardly did gold reappear in the money system when the problem of the ratio became acute and crucial. It is in Italy that its manifestations first develop. Because of the financial organization that developed here, the growth of the financial-capitalist spirit, and the superior astuteness of the Italian commercialist, the ratio soon became a subject of state policy and the opportunity for the bullionist.

A rise in the value of silver against gold, which occurred in the second quarter of the fourteenth century, told immediately upon Florence, because of her mint rates. The ratio in Florence had been fixed at 13.62 while in France the ratio had been fixed at 12.6. The result on Florence was immediate, and silver disappeared from circulation. In 1345, says the historian Villani, there was a great scarcity. No silver money was seen with the exception of the *quattrini*. It was all melted down and transported. Great discontent arose among the wool merchants, who feared that the gold *florin*, in which they received their foreign payments, might fall too much. Being powerful in the state, their agitation was effective and in 1345 a recoinage was instituted. This was not successful, due apparently to an error in calculation, and within a short time a second recoinage was decreed. This likewise proved ineffectual and a third and finally a fourth followed within the space of the year. Yet, even so, the effort was only temporarily successful, and within two years the price of silver was again out of line, and a fifth recoinage was undertaken, in which a price was put upon silver so far removed from the market price that it really constituted a state subsidy to surrender silver, and was in effect a debasement of the money of account. Whether by way of effect or cause it is hard to say, but certainly silver in the middle of the succeeding century had so far disappeared in the Italian peninsula, or gold had so far increased, that the commercial ratio during the fifteenth century remained persistently low—9.25 both in Milan and Florence.[1]

⊷§ §⊷

Thus the main outlines of the effect of bimetallism become apparent. Starting out with a given ratio between the two metals, a difference in the ratio set by a neighboring state forces the ratio out of line. To restore the balance a debasement of the more valuable coinage is undertaken. Subsequent changes in the ratio force a debasement of the coins of the other metal. It is the familiar story of the monkey dividing the cheese for the cats. By a process of nibbling at one piece and then the other in order to restore the balance, the monkey ends by having swallowed the whole cheese.

The actual process in Florence was as follows: The first recoinage reduced the number of coins struck to a *mark* of silver from 167 to 132, but increased the value of each coin in terms of money of account (the *lire di piccioli*) from 2 *soldi* 6 *denari di piccioli* to 4 *soldi*. The net result was an actual depreciation both of the coinage and of the money of account. Subsequent recoinages increased the number of pieces coined from a *mark* of silver to 140, but retained the same value for them expressed in the money of account. This was, in effect, a debasement of the coinage. The recoinage of 1347 abolished the former coinages, and introduced a new coin struck at 111.6 to the *mark* of silver, but raised its value in terms of money of account to 5 *soldi*, thus again depreciating the money of account. From this period down to 1503 subsequent recoinages occurred during which the coinage was debased by increasing the number of *grossi* struck to the *mark* of silver from 111.6 to 166.666, while at the same time the money of account was depreciated by increasing the value of the *grossi* from 5 *soldi* to 7 *soldi*.

Tribute is generally paid to Florentine monetary probity because the gold *florin*, struck at 53 grains fine, was not altered in weight or fineness for 175 years of Florentine history; but this overlooks the fact that its stated value was constantly raised. Between 1252 and 1534 the gold *florin* was successively increased in value from 20 *soldi* of account to 150 *soldi* of account. If alterations were necessary in the silver coinage to take care of changes in the ratio it is hard to explain on this ground the frequent reductions in the value of the money of account in relation to the gold coinage.

◦§ §◦

In France during the same period the ratio of gold to silver was changed in a single century more than a hundred and fifty times, and with a roughness that is quite inconceivable to the modern mind. During a period of ten years, for example, the ratio fluctuated as follows:

1303	10.26	1310	15.64
1305	15.90	1311	19.55
1308	14.46	1313	14.37

Such changes can hardly be explained on grounds of trade

balances or differences in the production or supply of the two metals. They arose from the perpetual change in the composition and the alloy, debasements practiced as financial statecraft, and the international struggle for the precious metals under the theory that national wealth consisted of a large stock of gold and silver. A single instance will serve to show the arbitrary character of the changes made on the obviously specious pretext of adjusting the ratio. In 1342 the *mark* of gold, which in normal times just preceding was valued at 41 *livres* 13 *sols*, was proclaimed equal to 117 *livres*, and in 1360 the *mark* of silver, valued normally at 5 *livres*, rose to 102 *livres*.

These violent changes were largely the product of the rising capitalist philosophy which we have noted earlier. The idea that national wealth consisted of money stock dominated the political and commercial policies of Europe until well in the eighteenth century, when Adam Smith put it in its rightful place by emphasizing the importance of human labor as a source of wealth.

II. Emergence of the Single Standard

IT was not until 1663 that a definitive solution of the question of bimetallism was resolved. In that year, in England, by the Act of 15 Charles II (c. 7, sec. 12) the statutes forbidding the exportation of bullion were removed at one blow of astounding boldness. "Forasmuch," says the act, "as several considerable and advantageous trades cannot be conveniently driven and carried on without the species of money or bullion, and that it is founded by experience that they are carried in the greatest abundance (as to a common market) to such places as give free liberty for exporting the same, and the better to keep in and increase the current coin of this kingdom, be it enacted that from and after the 1st day of August 1663 it shall and may be lawful to and for any person or persons whatsoever to export out of any port of England and Wales in which there is a customer or collector, or out of the town of Berwick, all sorts of foreign coin or bullion of gold or silver, first making an entry thereof in such customhouse respectively, without paying any duty, custom, poundage, or fee for the same, any law, statute, or usage to the contrary notwithstanding."

୶ଽ ଽ୶

The importance of this enactment lies in its abandonment of the attempt to control, by means of mint rates of metal purchase and metal coinage, the working of the money mechanism and the flow of the precious metals. It was a step in the direction of *laissez faire* so far as the financial system was concerned. Shaw hails it as "a revolution as signal as that produced in the relations of labor to capital by the disuse of the old labor laws," and as a change from "a medieval state-bound, merely legislative system to the modern system, in which the flow of precious metals is determined by the perfectly natural and automatic action of international trade—is indeed the index and safety valve of it, and of the whole present commercial world-circle."[1] In Shaw's view, the change was the result of an intellectual attack upon the mercantilist theory, in which the monetary policies followed by the governments of Europe—the advantage of the process of altering the coinage—was impugned upon theoretic grounds. This attack arose from the general growth of the body of doctrinaire opinion embraced under the name Physiocratic.

Del Mar, on the other hand, regards the Act of 1663, and the subsequent Act of 1666, opening the English mints to the free coinage of the metals, as the greatest calamity which has occurred in the whole history of money, going so far as to characterize the latter act in several of his works as "The Crime of 1666." Though we cannot agree with his great thesis that the system of money suffered its greatest catastrophe when government surrendered its control of the money mechanism by the process—which became almost universal after the English enactment—of opening the mints to the free coinage of the metals for anyone who presented them, his caustic explanation of the Acts of 1663 and 1666 are probably nearer the truth than Shaw's.

In Del Mar's view, the abandonment of government control

over the movement and coinage of the metals was due directly and primarily to the pressure of the East India Company for freedom to export metal in unlimited quantities to the Indies, and the enactment was secured by influence put upon Charles by the intermediary of his mistress, Barbara Villiers. Such an explanation certainly accords with our experience in the methods of political bodies, which have always shown themselves more pliant and amenable before the pressure of entrenched interests than of intellectual doctrine.

꧁ ꧂

The prime importance of the Acts of 1663 and 1666 was that they paved the way for the establishment of the single gold standard. During the eighteenth century the mint ratio was, on the whole, in favor of silver in France, and conversely, in favor of gold in England and Spain. The result was that gold became almost the only constituent of the currency of England and Spain for the greater part of the century. What silver appeared in England was drawn off for the Indian trade, where the ratio of silver to gold was very low, possibly one to four. There can be little doubt that this fact had a great influence in actually determining the great currency legislation which closed the century and finally decided England upon gold, and France and the United States upon bimetallism strongly favoring silver.

The transition in England from the bimetallic to the gold standard may be traced briefly: Concurrent with the Act of Charles II freeing the precious metals from import and export restrictions, a new gold coin, the *guinea*, was introduced, and no attempt was made to give this coin a fixed value as against silver coins. The fixing of the value of the coin was left to the open market, and the treasury was allowed to accept the guinea in payment at the rate of exchange of the day.

This system which England now adopted, and which is known as the "parallel standard" or "alternative standard," did not prove satisfactory. Traders found it inconvenient to have to calculate continually in two different kinds of money which stood to each other in a fluctuating ratio, and under the pressure of this inconvenience the experiment had to be dropped.

Towards the end of the seventeenth century the English silver coinage, as a result of fraudulent abrasion and clipping, had lost a large part (a sampling showed an average of 48 per cent) of its original metallic content. As a result of the influence of the free market in the metals, the new and relatively full weight guineas rose in value to 30 shillings or more. The government of William and Mary, intending at the time to reform the debased silver currency, viewed these quotations with dismay. In order to put a stop to any further rise, it prohibited the treasury in August, 1695, from accepting the guinea at a rate of exchange higher than 30 shillings, and upon the reformation of the silver coinage the maximum rate for the guinea was in the first months of the following year reduced step by step to 22 shillings.

This process was consolidated by the Act of 1717 which fixed the legal tender value of the guinea at 21 shillings, at which rate it was coined until 1813.

❧ ☙

As the maximum rates fixed for the guinea were higher than the market ratio—that is, gold was more valuable as legal tender than as bullion, while silver was less valuable—the effect was to drive silver out of circulation.

In consequence of the low value of silver set by the statutory ratio, silver did not find its way to the English mint, and it became profitable to melt down for sale as metal the silver coins which had been recoined between 1695 and 1698 and had been brought up to their full statutory weight. Silver coins of full standard value disappeared entirely from circulation, and those remaining were so worn that their melting down was not a profitable proposition, notwithstanding the high price of silver.

The solution to this problem of preserving the advantages of the preponderating gold currency while retaining a silver circulation was found by the Act of 1774. This act provided that for sums exceeding £25 silver would be legal tender only by weight, the coins being calculated on the basis of 5 shillings 2 pence per ounce. The final abolition of the double standard did not come about until the end of the eighteenth century, and was occasioned by a new rise in the value of gold as against silver, which made it profitable to export gold and tender silver for minting. The English government, faced with the dilemma of accepting silver for minting and allowing gold to disappear, and unwilling to adopt the ineffective historical device of forbidding the export of gold, adopted the solution of forbidding the free coinage of silver which had prevailed by right since the Act of 1666. With the abolition of the free right of silver coinage in 1798, England forsook the system of bimetallism and passed into the stage of the single gold standard.

ৰ্৪ ৪৯

The actual formal and legal establishment of the gold standard did not take place, however, until 1816, following the currency disorder introduced by the Napoleonic wars. The legislation of 1816 supplanted the guinea of 21 shillings value by a new gold coin, the sovereign, worth 20 shillings. The silver coins were reduced in content to a point that brought their metallic value well under their legal tender value, and prevented their disappearance by melting or export. Gold coins alone were given full legal tender value, and the legal tender value of silver coins was limited to amounts not exceeding 40 shillings. The guinea survived only in nomenclature, today used mainly by British tailors.

III. Momentary Equilibrium

IN England the problem of the ratio was solved by the adoption of the single metal standard, the metal being gold, and the reduction of the other metals, copper and silver, to the status of satellites, with restricted orbit and function, and deriving their limited validity by reflection of their golden luminary. This solution was not the result of conscious effort directed by intelligence and governed by far-sighted objectives, but rather the chance outcome of the play and interplay of mercantile and financial interests in which the state was sometimes participant, sometimes helpless spectator. In Europe the history of the ratio is filled with even more blindness, and groping, undirected effort.

◆§ ◈◆

In Germany, where the chaos of coinage and currency had been most profound, a momentary solution to the ratio question had been devised in the so-called "alternative system," introduced about the middle of the eighteenth century. Frederick the Great issued an ordinance which, though nominally fixing a ratio, provided in effect that gold and silver coins could not be substituted for each other in making payments. The fixed ratio between the coins therefore lost its principal significance. In 1787 the fixed ratio was definitely abolished, the relative value of gold and silver being "left simply to competition." The preponderance of silver coins in the circulation gradually established silver as the standard of transactions, the gold coins being regarded more and more merely as "trade coins."[1]

◆§ ◈◆

In France the manipulations of the coinage by the Grand Monarque, Louis XIV, ostensibly to restore a parity between gold and silver, but actually to finance his extravagant court and wars, had led to the utmost confusion in the currency. Between 1696 and 1715 the *livre* of account had been depreciated, in terms of gold, by 50 per cent, through the process of calling in the outstanding coins and reissuing them at a higher value. By 1720, after the collapse of Law's System, some forty different gold *louis* and ten different silver *louis* were in circulation. In 1726, in an effort to restore some order to this chaotic system, a general recoinage was instituted on the basis of a ratio of 14.625 to 1. This ratio was subsequently adjusted (in 1785) to 15.5 to 1, but meantime the effect had been to draw off gold and leave the circulation predominantly silver.

This was the situation on the occasion of the currency reforms introduced by the French Revolution. In 1803, the monetary system was reorganized on the basis of the *franc*, with decimal divisions, and the familiar accounting by *livre*, *sol* (*sou*), and *denier*, so dear to readers of Dumas, officially ceased, though many of the old coins remained in circulation as late of 1852, and the *sou* in common speech until much later.

The Act of 7th Germinal of the year XI (March 28, 1803)

156

established the *franc* as a coin of silver weighing 5 grams, .900 fine, and retained a bimetallic standard in the provision that "gold coins of twenty and fifty *francs* are to be struck." The ratio adopted was 15.5 to 1, or the same as in monarchical France, so that aside from the adoption of the decimal system of accounting, the Revolution marked no decided change in the French currency system.

The bimetallic system, and the course of the ratio, tended to place France, and those countries which, following the Revolution, adopted the French system of *francs* (namely, Belgium, Switzerland, and Italy) largely upon a silver basis. The Belgian law of June 5, 1832, for instance, adopted the silver *franc* as a unit of coinage without ordering or permitting the coining of gold *francs*.

◄§ §►

Thus the course of the ratio and the currency provisions of the various states had brought about a general use of silver as the main or principal standard of value throughout Europe except the Netherlands. Of all the European states the Netherlands stood alone in the first part of the nineteenth century as a country with any considerable circulation of gold. By a law passed in 1816 (September 28), the same year in which the gold standard was formally established in England, the Netherlands had adopted a double standard based upon a ratio of 1 to 15.873. At this ratio gold was overvalued as compared with the actual market ratio, with the result that Holland coined gold coins exclusively. Notwithstanding the large coinages of gold, however, silver became the standard. The constant outflow of gold in foreign trade, and the fact that silver ranked in the public mind as the real currency, led to the currency law of November 26, 1847, which substituted a silver standard pure and simple for the actually existing double standard.

◄§ §►

In the United States, the currency system had been founded on a bimetallic basis on a scheme that was at once simple and direct, but the course of the ratio made it impossible to maintain two metals in circulation, and after a long period of trial and error, gold became predominant. By the Act of 1792 establishing the first mint, it was provided that gold and silver both should be legal tender for all payments at the ratio of 15 to 1, and that the coinage should be free for both metals. The relative values of the two metals had been fairly steady for some time at the ratio established, and on the face, circumstances never seemed more propitious for the working of the double standard.[2]

The establishment of a double standard had been due to Alexander Hamilton. Hamilton himself was an advocate of the single metallic standard, preferably gold, but his prime object was to secure an abundance of metallic money. Silver, being in use, must of course be retained, and gold brought in also, if possible, by the bimetallic system.[3]

Hardly had the act been passed, however, when silver began a steady fall relative to gold, and the standard began to "limp" and then to walk on one leg. The ratio never again touched the low figure of 15 to 1; and the relative decline in silver which had led in England to the substitution of the gold standard, led to the disappearance of gold coinage in the United States. In the twenties of the nineteenth century, gold went to a premium of 5 per cent. The greater part of the American circulation consisted of foreign silver coins, especially of Spanish *piasters*— the Spanish "milled dollar," which circulated at a rate of exchange fixed by law. The attempt to maintain a parity between the *piaster* and the American dollar led to the disappearance of the latter, at the same time keeping the mint busy to the profit of the money-brokers. The coinage of dollar pieces was consequently suspended in 1805 by the President, and none was coined until 1836.[4]

As early as 1818 the United States began to recognize that Hamilton's ratio of 15 to 1 differed so much from the market ratio that if it were still designed to maintain a double standard, a new adjustment of the legal relations between the two metals was necessary. While nominally possessing a double standard, the country really had a single standard, and that, silver. A committee of Congress recommended in 1832 the establishment of a single silver standard, but the close commercial and financial relations with England implied the necessity of a gold coinage. This was achieved by the Acts of June 28, 1834, and January 18, 1837, which established a ratio of 16 to 1.[5] To bring the coinage into this ratio, the familiar device of lowering the content of the more valuable coin, which we have noted elsewhere, was adopted.

The amount of pure silver in the dollar was left unchanged at 371.25 grains, but the fine gold content of the gold dollar was reduced from 24.75 grains to 23.22 grains, a debasement of 6.26 per cent. The ratio taken was higher than the market (then about 15.6 to 1) so that now it was cheaper to pay debts in gold than silver. In consequence, no more silver was tendered to the mints, and upwards of $50,000,000 at once disappeared, being sent abroad in payment of obligations, or melted down for other uses at home. Within three months after the passage of the Act of 1834 gold began to move toward the United States in such quantities that for a time alarm was created in London over the reserve position of the Bank of England.[6] From 1834 on the United States was, for all practical purposes, on a gold standard.

Thus, about the middle of the nineteenth century we find silver fairly well established as the standard of value on the European continent and in the Middle and Far East, and gold as the standard of value only in England, the United States and a few smaller states, such as Portugal, and the English colonies.

It was at this point that the discovery of the Californian and Australian gold fields, and the immense increase of the supplies of gold metal that followed upon these discoveries, introduced a new disturbance in the ratio. The effect was immediate upon the fragile mechanism of money, and a new revolution occurred in the currency systems of the world.

IV. Dethroning of a Monarch

THE opening of great gold areas almost simultaneously in both

Australia and California had an effect upon the price and money systems of the world as pronounced in effect as the earlier flood of precious metal that followed the discovery of the Americas. The effect upon the ratio was immediate. Gold now began to depreciate in value in relation to silver, and, in countries on a bimetallic standard, to force silver out of circulation into export or into hoarding.

The movement was first felt in the United States. With a market ratio of around 15.7 to 1 and a legal ratio of 16 to 1, the effect had been to drive out the silver dollars from circulation. The drop in the ratio toward 15.5 to 1 now made it profitable to the money brokers to melt down or export the smaller coins: half dollars, quarters and dimes. To protect this subsidiary coinage, which was necessary for change and small transactions, the inevitable debasement was adopted. By the Currency Act of February 21, 1853, the silver content of the subsidiary coinage was reduced by 6.91 per cent, to correspond to a ratio of 14.88 to 1 (from 371.25 grains to the dollar to 345.6 grains). This made silver more valuable as coin than as bullion, and to prevent the money brokers from tendering silver for minting, coinage was restricted to government account. In effect, this was a demonetization of silver as subsidiary money. The content of the one-dollar piece was not changed, and it remained formally the "standard dollar," a full legal tender coin, with unlimited coinage privilege; but as none was in circulation, none could disappear, and it was not profitable to tender silver for coinage into dollars. The total effect of the Currency Act of 1853 and the trend of the ratio was to place the money of the United States more firmly upon the gold basis.

◄§ §►

The countries dominated by the French system and legal ratio of 15.5 had not been immediately affected, although the ratio crossed this line in 1851. But by the sixties these states found it necessary to take steps similar to those used in the United States. The first defensive step to prevent the outflow of silver was taken by Switzerland in 1860, which began to coin its subsidiary silver as token money with a content below its face value, by reducing

the fineness from .900 to .800. Two years later Italy followed
suit, by reducing its small silver coins to .835 fine.[1]

France, bound by commercial and political ties to these
smaller countries, and unwilling to see her dominance threatened, called a monetary convention in 1865 for the purpose of
evolving common action to meet the threat of the ratio. The
result of this conference was the formation of the Latin Monetary Union among France, Italy, Switzerland and Belgium,
under the terms of which the signatories agreed to coin their
silver pieces of 2 *francs* or less on a basis of .835 fine, to restrict
silver coinage exclusively for the account of the issuing state,
and to accept in public payments the coins of each state irre-
spective of origin. The effect of these provisions was to abandon
the free silver standard, by reducing the small coins to the status
of token money, which, however, might circulate freely as legal
tender within the four countries which were members of the
Union. It was an approach to the gold standard, but it was not
yet a gold standard. It was still a fictitious double standard.

Thus, within two generations after Holland had abandoned
the double standard for silver, the new position acquired by
gold, and the consequent course of the ratio, was rapidly bringing Europe to gold as the standard of value.

❧ ❧

It is quite likely that the conference that produced the Latin
Monetary Union would have adopted the free gold standard
had it not been for the opposition of the Bank of France and the
money interest in France headed by the Rothschilds. To them,
bimetallism afforded a lucrative opportunity for profitable arbitrage operations, and it was only when the bank found itself
obliged to pay gold and receive silver that it could bring itself to
depart from bimetallic policy.[2]

Hardly had the hermaphroditic system created by the union
been fairly established when fresh troubles arose. On May 1,
1866, Italy was forced to suspend specie payments, which
meant that small silver was no longer redeemable in Italy. As
the Union required this token money to be accepted freely by all
the signatories, a profit arose in exporting Italian silver to the

other three countries. The money interest was not slow to seize its opportunity, and the commerce assumed enormous proportions. Soon most of the Italian small coin was in circulation in the territory of the allies, where it produced a plethora of silver circulation, at the same time further weakening the Italian financial position. It was obvious that new measures had to be devised.

❦ ❧

The Paris Exposition of 1867 afforded the French government an opportunity to retire gracefully from its opposition to the gold standard by calling a new conference. This was an international monetary conference attended by representatives of nineteen European governments and the United States. The idea behind the call to conference was a hope still entertained in France of inducing the world to adopt a universal money system on the double standard, but the overwhelming sentiment was in favor of the gold standard.

Although the attempt to retain the double standard was a mistake, there was much to recommend a greater world uniformity of money based upon a single metal, and conditions were favorable for such an agreement. The day was fortunately one of international agreements and freer international intercourse, and it was hoped that the principles of the Latin union might be extended to form the basis of a world union. But the principal states, such as England, the German states, and Holland, declared themselves satisfied with their traditional standards, and this opportunity for a concerted intellectual attack upon the problem of the ratio and the standard went for naught. The principal contribution of the conference was the recommendation of the gold standard.

❦ ❧

The solution of the ratio problem in Europe was not to be the achievement of well intentioned conferences, or the intelligent action of statecraft, but the by-product of the Franco-Prussian War and a new turn in the market for the metals.

In Germany the condition of the currency had been one of the greatest chaos prior to the establishment of the gold standard. Six different systems were legally in force, and in addition an uncounted number and variety of coins were to be found in circulation. The currency muddle can hardly be more clearly described than was done in a document which Ludwig Bamberger, at the time a leading authority in the Reichstag on matters of finance and economics, placed before the Customs Parliament on May 5, 1870, on the occasion of a speech delivered on the question of the necessity of unifying the German currency. He is quoted by Helfferich as follows:

"I have here a so-called 'bordereau,' namely, a table setting forth specifically the types of money which a trader enclosed with a draft to his bankers. The 'bordereau' is dated the 19th December, 1869. It relates to a sum of 15,834 *gulden*. I have extracted it from the correspondence of a bank. It contains the coins of which these 15,834 *gulden* were composed, and in order that you might understand its true meaning, I must add that the draft came from a small town in the province of Rhenish Hessen. The town is small, 3,000 to 4,000 inhabitants, and has but a single inn—not sufficiently attractive to be frequented by strangers. It is a payment composed of receipts from rents, purchase agreements, and from sales of wheat, barley, fruit, and similar products, brought from the various surrounding villages to this small town to be sold through the agency of a merchant. What was thus collected from the pockets of the peasants is as follows: The sum of 15,834 *gulden* consisted of *double talers, crown talers*, pieces of two and one-half *gulden*, of two *gulden*, one *gulden*, one-half *gulden*, one-third, one-sixth and one-twelfth Imperial *talers*, five-*franc* pieces, two-*franc* pieces, one-*franc* pieces. Then we have gold coins such as *pistoles*, double and single *Friedrichsdor*, half-sovereigns, Russian *Imperials*, dollars, *Napoleons*, Dutch *Wilhelmsdor*, Austrian and Württemberg *ducats*, Hessian ten-*gulden* pieces, and last of all a piece of Danish gold."[3]

Under the terms of the Treaty of Frankfort, an indemnity of five billion *francs* was levied upon the defeated French. This indemnity made all considerations of monetary reform in France impossible for the moment, and threw the currency of

Germany into further confusion. At a time when the government was considering the establishment of the gold standard, the French indemnity payments caused a strong demand on all international money markets for German currencies, and large amounts of silver were sent to Germany for the satisfaction of payments due and were delivered to the German mints for coinage. The strong flow of silver is explained by the fact that by reason of the indemnity which France was required to pay, Germany became, in a sense, a creditor of the whole world. As Germany had at that time a silver standard, silver became the more important metal for the purpose of covering drafts on Germany. Finally, the Berlin mint was authorized by the Prussian government on July 3, 1871, not to buy further silver from private persons.

⋖§ §⋗

The actual establishment of the gold standard in Germany was made by Act of December 4, 1871, which defined the *mark* as 1/1395 of a pound weight of fine gold (5.532 English grains), and was completed by the Act of July 9, 1873, which proclaimed in its first article the formal acceptance of the gold standard. The act permitted coinage for individuals, or free coinage, within certain restrictions, and subject to seignorage to be determined by the Chancellor of the Reich, but not to exceed seven *marks* a pound of fine gold.

In 1872 the Scandinavian kingdoms of Sweden, Norway and Denmark followed Germany in establishing a gold standard. The Netherlands reluctantly followed, half-heartedly, by receding from a silver to a double standard. By 1873, however, it became imperative to suspend the free coinage of silver. The gold standard was definitely adopted as the result of two acts, the first, in 1875, establishing a gold 10-*gulden* piece and permitting its coinage on private account, the second, in 1877, definitely suspending the free coinage of silver.

⋖§ §⋗

In the United States, the predominant position of gold had been given further recognition by the Act of 1873. Since the

Act of 1853, which reduced fractional silver currency to a token basis, as we have noted, the country had been, to all purposes, on a gold standard. By the Act of 1873, the free coinage of the silver dollar piece was suspended, thus leaving the field free to gold. As there were no silver dollars in circulation, and no silver was being tendered for minting (because of the ratio), the act occasioned little notice at the time. In 1875 and 1876, however, when the trend of the ratio was reversed, and silver began to depreciate rapidly, the right of silver coinage again presented a profitable possibility to the mining interests, and agitation began for silver coinage. The Act of 1873 was denounced as "The Crime of 1873" and agitation was brought to such a pitch that, as a compromise, the various silver purchase acts were passed with their threat to the American monetary system. Under these acts, the mints were indeed not reopened to the free coinage of silver, but the government relieved the mining interests by purchasing some 300,000,000 ounces of silver on the open market over a period of years (1870–1893) and coining it into silver dollars. When this process threatened to bankrupt the government in 1893, these attempts to give a forced circulation to silver were abandoned, and in 1900 the gold standard was definitely and formally adopted by act of Congress.

꽃 꽃

In Europe, the final settlement of the ratio question, at least for the nineteenth century, occurred when the rush of the world to gold, and the closing of the mints to the coinage of silver, combined with a slower demand for the metal from the East, began to push the ratio in the other direction. Silver had begun to decline relatively, and from the high point of 15.19 achieved in the year 1859[4] dropped until, within a few years, it became again profitable in France, where the ratio was still legally 15.5 to 1, to present silver for coinage. The drop became precipitate from 1873 on, and would have produced collapse of the whole coinage system in France had not the government, by a series of steps, gradually restricted the amounts of silver that might be presented at the mints. In the middle of 1876 France and Belgium at last definitely suspended the coinage of silver legal tender money, and in 1878 the suspension of the free coinage of silver was at last ordered for the whole area covered by the Latin Union. The cessation of silver coinage in the Latin Union sealed the fate of silver throughout Europe. Austria-Hungary turned away from silver in 1878–1879, and at the same period Russia did likewise.

"Thus," in the words of Helfferich, "within a few years a radical change in the international currency machinery had taken place. When, after being drawn off in large masses by Asia in the fifties and sixties, silver began in the seventies again to force its way into European circulation, it found the door banged, barred, and bolted against it by one country after another, even by countries on a paper basis. Ludwig Bamberger, at the time, aptly described this historical and worldwide phenomenon as the 'dethroning of a world-monarch.' All important civilized European states ostracized the metal which for thousands of years had enjoyed equal privileges with gold. Only Asia, Mexico, and a few Central and South American countries remained open to silver."[5]

If however the problem of the ratio was at last definitely solved for the money systems of the modern world, it only opened the way to vaster and more imponderable problems of money control. The driving out of silver from the money systems of the Western world, and the basing of these systems upon a metal so much more precious, so much more limited in quantity, revived, inevitably, the age-old cry of a scarcity of money to which Adam Smith called attention, and provided the specious excuse for the unlimited issues of paper money, based, theoretically, upon gold, but, practically, upon nothing more than the pious hopes of mankind. It is that development, which began to mount upon the world stage like the climax in a Greek tragedy, to which we now turn our attention.

Book Nine. THE RISE OF BANK MONEY

B Y the nineteenth century there had begun to appear out of the confusion of European monetary history, like timid faces in a storm, certain practices upon which might be fixed some hope for a more ordered régime of money. Unfortunately, these embryos of principle never gestated; the trend taken by monetary developments of the past hundred years has been such as to destroy all the accumulated wisdom of the thousand years preceding, and to set loose new monsters of destruction for a dazed and harassed world to combat. We shall attempt in this chapter to set forth briefly the main advances in monetary science and to indicate how they have been nullified.

I. The Retreat from Achievement

ONE of the most hopeful of the achievements of the seventeenth and eighteenth centuries was the formal abandonment by government of its prerogative to control the minting of money. In perfect theory, and under ideal conditions, it is the state alone, as the agency of society, which can exercise that plenary and permeant control of the money mechanism which is necessary for its highest functioning in the economic order. Nevertheless, so abused had been this sovereign prerogative that as a practical measure its surrender had the most salutary results. The surrender of the coinage privilege was first accomplished, as we have observed, in England by the Act of 1666 (Act of Free Coinage of 18 Car. II, c. 5) which opened the mint to coinage by individuals.

Under a régime of free coinage, the state exercises no more than its police power. In coinage for private account the state merely converts the raw metal presented by individuals into pieces of uniform size, and impresses its insignia on the pieces as certification of their weight and fineness. The state's function is no more and no less than that which it performs in inspecting the scales of green-grocers and setting official standards of weights and measures.

The principle of free coinage has proved its practical worth as a deterrent to debasement and depreciation. Where coinage is on private account there is no profit to the state in tampering with the standard, and there is no opportunity for such practice by the individual. The circulation of coins of similar appearance and denomination but of uncertain standard, the arbitrary and unpredictable modifications in the standard by autocratic government, the temptations to profit which were constantly dangled before despotic rulers—these were evils which had perplexed and harassed society and hindered the natural growth of economy since the days when coined money first appeared. By a stroke they were swept away. At the same time, the institution of free coinage, by giving stability and character to one of the chief instruments of organized economy, made possible a more vigorous and healthy commercial life and gave prestige and increased substance to the government adopting it.

The importance of free coinage has been generally overlooked. Indeed, the temptations offered by the central bank mechanism, the necessities of war, and public pressure for abundance of money, all aided by a "managed-money" school of economists, have succeeded in suppressing free coinage everywhere and for many years coinage altogether. The monopoly of the state has become an iron hand, under which the value of money has become a matter not of the standard but of the fiat of the state. The development and dénouement of this process we shall examine further on.

Under the Gold Standard Act of Great Britain, of 1925, the right to present metal to the English mints for coinage has been withdrawn from individuals, and restricted to the Bank of England. The French monetary reforms of 1928 accomplished the same effect by permitting the Bank of France to redeem its notes either in coin or in gold bars, and elsewhere in Europe the coinage was restricted to the state. In the United States, by the Gold Reserve Act of 1934, not only was free coinage suspended, but the monopoly of gold was vested in the Treasury and citizens were forbidden to acquire, hold, or trade in the metal except at the pleasure of the Secretary. The value of the dollar domestically became one of official fiat, while its international value was maintained by freely buying and selling gold at $35 an ounce, a price fixed by Presidential proclamation of January 31, 1934.

≤§ §≥

Another advance toward a more intelligent control of money was the single metal standard. During the centuries of disastrous attempts to give to metals a currency at a fixed relationship to each other, the money system had been the prey of the bullionist, the arbitragist and the speculator, who made their profit by taking advantage of the fluctuating market of the two metals, circumventing the fiat of the state, and draining the country of its undervalued metal in order to sell it at a profit elsewhere.

The establishment of the single metal standard at once destroyed the opportunity for these speculative profits and to that extent removed the money mechanism as an object of commerce, and allowed the economy of the country to concern itself in greater safety and assurance with its primary purpose of the production of physical wealth for the satisfaction of human needs, rather than in the specious pursuit of money profit.

The actually great advantage of the single standard has likewise been generally lost. This is partly because of the strength of bimetallic tradition, partly because it involved the demonetization of a historic metal, partly because gold, though the more precious metal, is less capable of sustaining a universal monetary standard—less capable because its greater scarcity and value renders its coinage into hand to hand currency impracticable and hence unfamiliar to the commonalty.

There are good arguments for silver as a universal standard. It is more abundant—mine production being five times that of gold (252 million ounces in 1970, compared with 46 million ounces of gold). It is cheap enough to be coined in small denominations—though the price would probably rise if it were remonetized. However, silver is becoming so important industrially that current production and more is all consumed, for

such uses as photography, brazing, and the electronics industries. Such heavy demand, unless balanced by increased production, might cause complications in maintaining an adequate
money supply. On the other hand, nearly half of the gold mined
since the discovery of America exists today in central bank
vaults, and industrial consumption takes less than half of current output.

The chief reason that the advantage of the single standard has
never been fully recognized is that—theory to the contrary—
nowhere in the world has a monetary system rested upon a one-
metal basis. Since the rise of central banking, which was almost
coincident with the establishment of the theoretical single (gold)
standard, the money system has remained dual. Instead of
money consisting of gold, or gold and silver and copper, as
previously, it has consisted of gold and paper. Theoretically, the
paper is representative of gold, but actually it is representative
of something less than either silver or copper—that is, debt, the
debts of industry and the debts of government. Upon this fact—
the diversity of items which make up the paper, and hence the
money system—has been built a new system of money speculation, arbitrage operations and financial manipulation which
throws into the shade all the antisocial practices that grew up in
monetary practice during the seven hundred years following the
commercial renascence.

Perhaps the real solution to the problem of the single standard
would be the adoption of a theoretical measure of value—some
form of the "commodity dollar" that is advocated by proponents
of managed currency. The actual standard used may not be so
important as is generally believed, but it is necessary that the
standard be fully understood by those using it. Our present
money system, in which gold constitutes merely a portion, and
an insignificant portion, of the security behind the paper money
outstanding, is a hermaphrodite. It is neither gold nor commercial paper, but a deceptive combination of both. To the
engineers of the system, its composition is fully understod, but
the public long believed that its money was gold, and implicitly
relied upon that fact, while the money traders recognized it for
what it was, and made their profit by playing upon these dif-

ferences, now draining one country of its gold, now another, and in the process forcing the central bank authorities into recurrent chills and sweats over the fear that the public would discover the imposture that was being played upon them.

&ह ६ॐ

The third advance in practice was the use of paper money representative of actual coin or metal warehoused in banks under authority of the state. This practice, in its simplest and purest form, appeared in the history of the Bank of Venice, the Bank of Amsterdam, and the Bank of Hamburg. The use of paper billets, or receipts, of the bank, in preference to good yellow or white metal, arose, as we have seen, because of the confusion of the coinage and the variety of pieces with which the merchant had to deal. The bank became an assayer, sorting out the good coins, weighing and testing them, and giving the client a warehouse receipt entitling him to their equivalent in good money of the realm. The superscription of the bank upon a piece of paper became a better certificate of valid money than the seal of the state upon the coin, and because it was not, like coin, subject to wear and abrasion, it became a more acceptable medium of payment than the actual metal.

The actual and theoretical advantages of paper money over actual metal in circulation have already been touched upon. The superiority of paper for making large payments, or payments in distant places, is unquestionable. It is true economy in the use of the precious metals in that it saves them from abrasion and loss. It removes a source of profit by "sweating," filing, shaving, clipping, and other practices of the bullionist where coined money is the principal medium of exchange. By means of representative paper, a piece of metal can be infinitely subdivided, so that the question of scarcity of a metal for circulation is not important. Except for small change, where metal coins are more convenient, paper money is, in fact, an ideal money for the use of a perfectly intelligent people.

The reason for the failure of paper money to function properly is the inability of human nature, as at present constituted, to withstand its temptations. Paper money was subjected by governments to abuses of the most distressing character, until the power of the state to issue it was restricted by an outraged society. The power passed for a generation to the commercial banking system, where it was similarly abused; the result was a new brood of Loki's offspring—panics, concentration of wealth, poverty in the midst of plenty, political revolution, and economic stagnation.

In the twentieth century, sovereignties began to reassert their monopoly of money, and under the pretext of assuring full employment through the manipulation of the interest rate, have used their power for the spread of statism, the socialization of activity, the annihilation of private property, and the extinction of individual liberty.

II. Beginnings of Paper Money in England

WE have already traced the first great experiment in the use of paper money in Europe, when it appeared in France at the beginning of the eighteenth century as a cloud no bigger than a man's hand. It is now necessary to observe its spread—in its extension in the money systems of Europe and America—until it filled the economic sky and covered the world with its dark and ominous shadow.

In England, the first paper money enjoying a legal tender status by the authority of the state was the exchequer order of Charles II, which we have noted in an earlier chapter. The exchequer order did not prove popular as a medium of exchange. In 1696 it was supplanted by the exchequer bill, an invention mothered by the necessities of William III's wars. The order differed from the bill in that it was convertible on demand into cash. An elaborate scheme was set up to provide for the convertibility of the bills, and funds were provided for this purpose by making the bills a charge upon the proceeds of certain state revenues. The bill was always fully covered, and the amount outstanding at any one time was strictly limited. It was good money, but it remained, in effect, a form of investment, a short-term government loan, which it is today. In 1707, the Bank of England, which had been called into being thirteen years earlier and which was struggling to keep its head above water, was entrusted with the guarantee and redemption of the bills; and from then on they gradually passed out of use as currency. There was more profit to the bank in fostering the use of its own notes, and paper money issued by government was effectively superseded by the banker's bill or note. From the middle of the eighteenth century to 1844, when the note issue function was centralized in the Bank of England, the privately issued bank note became the only form of hand to hand paper money in England.

Bank notes, including those of the Bank of England, were, however, private paper, accepted only by custom, unrecognized by the state, and devoid of any quality of legal tender. The right to issue such paper was conferred by act of Parliament or by charter on lines that were not uniform. In certain parts of the country a monopoly was granted to the Bank of England, in other parts paper issues were authorized with or without regulation. It was not until the Act of 3-4 William IV in 1833 that a limited legal tender quality was given by Parliament to the Bank of England note.

❧ ❧

The bank note had been a logical development of the goldsmith's note, which had become popular during the political disturbances incident to the Puritan Revolution. English merchants had been in the custom of depositing their cash in the London Tower, until Charles I seized £120,000 of the treasure in 1640, and repaid it only after long delay and much protest. As a result merchants and nobles began to leave their coin and valuables with the goldsmiths, receiving in exchange the goldsmith's receipts or notes. Because it represented the actual deposit of money, it came to be freely received in private transactions as money. Though the goldsmith's note was never legal tender, it served to accustom the commercial community with the use of paper equivalents of money.

As gold and silver are fungible, it was not necessary to retain the actual coin or plate deposited if an equivalent of value could always be returned upon demand. It was only a step to the discovery by the more unprincipled goldsmiths that funds of clients might be lent out so long as the goldsmith retained on hand sufficient amounts to meet anticipated calls for the return of deposits.

≈§ §≈

The practice of the goldsmiths, of using deposited funds to their own interest and profit, was essentially unsound, if not actually dishonest and fraudulent. A warehouseman, taking goods deposited with him and devoting them to his own profit, either by use or by loan to another, is guilty of a tort, a conversion of goods for which he is liable in civil, if not in criminal, law. By a casuistry which is now elevated into an economic principle, but which has no defenders outside the realm of banking, a warehouseman who deals in money is subject to a diviner law: the banker is free to use for his private interest and profit the money left in trust.

The practice of the goldsmiths was in harmony with the financial ethics of the times, but it is to be noted that with the warehouseman the only deviation from the code was the practice of the factors in pledging the property of their principals left with them on consignment for the purpose of sale. The factors frequently had been compelled by the financial needs of their overseas clients to advance them money before the sale of the goods consigned to them had been consummated; to meet the drafts they began, in turn, to pledge the goods for advances from their own bankers. This pledging of property left in trust or on consignment was nothing more than a conversion, but during the sixteenth century it had become so common that the custom was finally legalized by parliamentary enactment. Such hypothecations were permitted, however, only in the case of goods whose owner had received advances from the factor, and only to the extent of such advances.

Today, it is a well defined principle, sanctified by experience and enshrined in the statutory and common law, that a warehouseman shall not engage in trade and, that, while receiving goods in safekeeping, he shall neither store nor own goods of his own of the same character which he stores.

Yet at such a distance from this well-established principle is that followed by the banker that he may not only deal in his own capital, but may also lend out the funds entrusted him by his depositors. He may go even further. He may create fictitious deposits on his books, which shall rank equally and ratably with actual deposits in any division of assets in case of liquidation.*

ঙ৷ ৶

The goldsmiths had lent freely to Charles II and he had spent the money in the support of a profligate court, set up in imitation of Versailles. The result was a royal default. On January 2, 1672, Charles II issued a proclamation repudiating his debts, and sequestrating to his own use some £1,328,526 lent by the goldsmiths. As this money was the property of some 10,000 depositors the loss spread ruin and suffering throughout London.†

In spite of this early experience in the viciousness of the goldsmith system, it evidently met a commercial need of the day, for it continued to expand. After the rise of joint-stock companies toward the end of the century, the goldsmiths' business passed into the hands of the chartered banks. Under the régime of corporate banking the same practices were followed, extended and even sanctioned by the terms of the charter or by act of Parliament.

There seems to have been no conception on the part of government of the unsoundness and impropriety of this system of private money, and no awareness of the threat to the safety and well-being of the state through the exercise of such tremendous and ungoverned power of note issue. Thus, the Bank of Australasia, chartered March 28, 1835, was privileged by its

---

* It is true that Roman jurisprudence recognized the right of the banker to use deposited funds to his own profit, but English concepts are an outgrowth of common law, to which Roman law made, at most, a negligible contribution.

† These effects of Charles' default are disputed by R. D. Richards, "The 'Stop of the Exchequer,'" *Economic History*, Vol. II (1930), No. 5, pp. 45–62.

charter to issue circulating notes of one pound denomination and upward to an amount of three times the paid-in capital plus the total of deposits. The charter of the Colonial Bank, issued in the following year, limited note issues merely by a provision restricting the discounts of the bank's own paper to one-third of the total discounts of the bank.

"As the most decisive proof of the indifference of the state to these mere private paper tokens," says Shaw, "no attempt was made to safeguard the public against the dangers of unregulated paper. Disaster after disaster had to come upon the country before the British government realized the necessity of insisting upon some form of cover as a guarantee of the financial soundness of the private issue of paper. And when at last the necessity was realized, there was the greatest diversity in the means which were adopted in order to cope with the danger."[1]

III. Revival of a Principle

THE Bank of England, which is the parent of modern banks of issue, and around which the English banking and money system is built, was created not with the object of bringing the money mechanism under more intelligent control, but to provide means outside the onerous sources of taxes and public loans for the financial requirements of an impecunious government.

Such has been the motivating force leading to the establishment of all the great banks of issue of modern times. Such had been the purpose in founding the first Bank of North America, which financed the Revolution in this country; such had been the purpose in forming the first and the second Bank of the United States, and in operating the present national banking system of this country. Such had been the lure which induced the Regency to grant the charter for the *Banque Générale* to John Law. Banking became, in the eyes of the nineteenth century, the magic wand, the Midas-touch, with which to turn the solid substance of capital into the glistening and fluid thing of money. The idea of using banking as a means to a more intelligent control of the money mechanism did not appear until later, and for 150 years banking in England was a precarious business, a reed bent by every wind of political or commercial disturbance. The story of the Bank of England is no different from the story of others.

ᛏᚷ ᚷᛏ

In the case of the Bank of England, the necessities that called it into existence had been the War of the Palatinate, embarked upon against France after the deposition of James II, his flight to the court of Louis XIV and the accession of William of Orange to the English throne. The high-handed policies of the Stuart kings toward their obligations, and the unsettled state of England as a result of the Bloodless Revolution, had made investors wary of entrusting their funds to the government.

To finance the war with France the government accepted a proposal of a bank presented by William Paterson, a Scots promoter, whose antecedents apparently did not bear too close scrutiny. It was this same Paterson whose notorious Darien scheme had ruined half of Scotland. His proposal was that, in return for an advance of £1,000,000 to the government, the government should accord to him and his associates £65,000 a year as interest and the costs of management, and, in addition, authority to issue bills which should be legal tender. The proposal to give the bills a legal tender was unacceptable to the government, and the whole idea was repugnant to many of the Lords. The pressing need of money, however, finally overcame the prejudices of the upper body of Parliament, and a charter was granted authorizing the bank to issue notes (without legal tender quality, however), to deal in bullion and commercial bills, and to make advances upon merchandise. It enjoyed, in addition, the privilege of limited liability for its shareholders, the advantage of holding the government deposits, and the power of lending money in excess of deposits by reason of the circulating notes it was allowed to issue against government debt. These privileges gave the bank an immense advantage over the goldsmiths.

ᛏᚷ ᚷᛏ

The bank had hardly been in existence two years when it was forced to suspend payments. Created as a financial tool of the Whigs, it had to support the government without any regard to the economic or financial soundness of its operations, or its obligations to the commercial community which trusted in its paper. The suspension of specie payments, which lasted from July 13, 1695, to the autumn of 1697, was followed by a depreciation of the bank notes, which fell to a discount of 17 per cent. This was hardly unnatural, since the account submitted to the House of Commons on December 4, 1696, showed notes outstanding to be £764,196, supported by cash of only £35,664.

Specie payments were resumed in 1698, but in 1720, after the collapse of the South Sea Bubble, in which the bank was not entirely a passive observer or agent, a run occurred which was met only by making payments in light six-pences and shillings, by engaging men to fill up the line, draw money and redeposit it at another window, and by the fortunate intervention of the festival of Michaelmas, during which the bank remained closed while public alarm subsided.[1] A similar crisis occurred in 1745 following the success of the Pretender in Scotland, and was met by the same tactics.

The next collapse of the Bank of England occurred in 1797. Thirty years of fairly successful operation of the bank had produced a flood of note-issuing institutions in imitation, and by 1793 there were nearly four hundred note-issuing banks in business. The wars with France and the struggle with the American colonists, combined with a currency chaos produced by an immense, various, and unregulated note issue, led to a general collapse of credit in 1793, and one-third of all the English banks of issue suspended payment. The Bank of England followed suit by suspending payments in 1797.

The suspension of 1797 continued throughout the period of the Napoleonic wars. In 1816, partial resumption was attempted, and then postponed. Final resumption of specie payments did not occur until 1821, when the bank commenced to redeem its own issue at discount. During this period, 1797 to 1821, practically every bank of issue in Europe had suspended specie payments.

ৰৎ ৡৡ

It was not until 1844, when Sir Robert Peel's Bank Act was passed, that the first real attack was made against lax banking and unsound paper money. The country had gone through a severe crisis in 1825, which had arisen from a frenzy of speculation and foreign lending, particularly to the newly formed states of South America. Stock companies had been formed with objects as indefinite and impracticable as in the time of the South Sea Bubble—one, for instance, for the purpose of draining the Red Sea to recover gold lost by the Egyptians when pursuing the Israelites. Some £150,000,000 of British money, it is estimated, was sunk in government loans and corporate investments in Mexico and South America alone. This speculation, it was generally believed, had grown out of the excessive extension of country banks, without any legal regulation, and by the unwarranted expansion of loans both by these banks and by the Bank of England. The reserves of the Bank of England had been gradually whittled down from £13,800,000 in March, 1824, to £3,012,150 in November, 1825, and the country banks had been brought up short by the failure of Sir Peter Cole and Company. Collapse followed, sixty-three banks were forced to suspend, and the consequences were so severe, says Walter Bagehot, that they were remembered after nearly fifty years.

The debacle of 1825 had forced attention upon the necessity of reform, and in 1833 restrictions were placed upon the issue of notes by country banks, and the Bank of England was given a wider monopoly of the note-issue power. It was not, however, until a second crisis occurred, that of 1839, that thoroughgoing reform was undertaken, and the banking and note system of England was given the foundations upon which, with some modifications, it rested until 1945, when it was taken over by the government.

Sir Robert Peel, who sponsored the Act of 1844, was dominated by the purpose of making the notes of the Bank of England as "good as gold." The declared purpose of the act was "to cause our mixed circulation of coin and bank notes to expand and contract, as it would have expanded and contracted under similar circumstances had it consisted exclusively of coin." In other words, the paper circulation of England was to be made to represent as nearly as possible warehouse receipts for actual metallic money.

With this object the note-issue department of the Bank of England was separated from the banking department, so that the gold held against the note issue would be clearly set forth, and not confounded with the reserves held against deposits. The act, however, allowed a maximum amount of £14,000,000 uncovered notes, that is, notes not supported by gold, but provided that they should be backed by government bonds. For this purpose £14,000,000 government securities were transferred from the banking to the note-issue department.

The limit of £14,000,000 for the uncovered circulation was determined upon by having regard to the minimum amount of notes that could be counted to remain always in circulation. It was found that the net circulation in December, 1839, during the worst of the run, had not fallen below £14,732,000, and it was argued that at least £2,000,000 must be kept in the banking reserve of the bank. It was considered safe, therefore, to fix the uncovered circulation at £14,000,000; and it was left to the play of the foreign exchanges to control fluctuations above that amount.

The country banks were still permitted to retain the note-issuing powers conferred by their charters, but a great many of these banks had become insolvent, and it was expected that the privilege would be gradually withdrawn as the charters expired, with eventual concentration of all the note-issue function in the Bank of England. In order to take up the vacuum caused by such note retirements the act provided that the Bank of England might increase its fiduciary issue against securities by an amount equivalent to two-thirds the amount of such other notes retired.

"The Act of 1844," says Conant, "proposed substantially to destroy the bank note as an instrument of credit and make it a mere certificate of coin, leaving to other forms of commercial paper the functions which the bank note had in part performed."[2]

❧ ❧

Sir Robert Peel's Act is criticized by modern economists on

the ground that it fixed upon England a rigid, inelastic money system. The theory upon which Peel worked is in sharp contrast to that which later found widespread acceptance, that note issue should expand and contract with the needs of trade, and still further from the currently prevailing view that the money supply should conform to the requirement of full employment on a steady price level, or from the view advocated by the so-called Chicago school, that the money supply should increase at a mathematically determined pace. Peel's concept of the function of central banking was that the notes of a central bank should be always convertible, and that this convertibility can be assured only by making them fully representative of money. In a word, he went on the theory that the capstone of an arch should not be made of rubber.

The actual results of Peel's legislation will be examined in a later chapter, while, meantime, we turn to developments of the paper money device in America.

IV. Groping Toward Control in America

MONETARY history in the United States during the first seventy-five years of its federal existence is the story of feeble and sporadic attempts to deal with the new engine of paper money. Despite an awareness of the dangers in paper money and the prohibitions against its use written into the Constitution, prohibitions that were systematically ignored, the actual management of monetary policy was marked by ignorance and political subservience. The federal government and the states each took their hand at dabbling with it, crossing each other and defeating their common objectives in the process, leaving it in the end the shuttlecock for the play of speculators, manipulators and financial parasites.

One thing stands out clearly in a survey of the period, perhaps more clearly in this country than in the case of England: the gradual merging of money and banking, and the confounding of the problems of credit with those of the media of exchange.

With the dawn of the nineteenth century, the study of money is no longer the study of coinage, of the ratio between the metals, of the coinage prerogative, or of the question of metallic supplies. The problem enlarges, as it has been gradually enlarging since the reëstablishment of interest as a formal institution of economy, until it becomes a study of commerce-debt relationships and the institutions which exercise authority over the body of commercial debt. Our story, therefore, must from now on concern itself largely with the money mechanism as it is affected and moulded by banking and credit.

◄§ §►

During the colonial days, the shortage of circulating media had been supplied, as we have observed, by the use of barter implements: wampum, beaver, tobacco and rice, and later by the use of colonial paper money. Paper money, representing warehoused tobacco or rice had been introduced in the southern colonies with some success, and in Massachusetts, the Land and Manufacturers Bank had, in 1740, begun to issue notes redeemable in goods. These forms of money, which possessed the one advantage of representing a quantity of tangible wealth, gave way to note issues backed by nothing more than the credit of the colonies, which was a very nebulous substance. During the Revolutionary War the Continental Congress had issued notes in such quantities that their value became characterized by a phrase that is still current in our speech as a synonym for worthlessness.

From the situation produced by the inability of the colonial governments or the Continental Congress to control money, the commercial community turned for relief to bank notes. Despite the successes of the Revolutionary army on the field, the problem of financing the war had become more and more pressing, and after the fall of Charleston in 1780, it became imperative to find new methods of raising money. As in England in 1694, a bank was proposed, and the Bank of Pennsylvania was called into existence.

The Bank of Pennsylvania was created with a capital subscription of £400 in coin and £103,360 in depreciated Continental currency, and its notes were nothing more than interest-bearing obligations payable at a future time. It lasted for a year, when its functions were taken over by the more stably organized Bank of North America, the creation of Robert Morris. This bank did much to restore order to the chaos of federation finances and continued in business for sixty-five years.

☚ ☛

The framers of the Constitution had inserted a provision forbidding the states to coin money; emit bills of credit (that is, circulating notes), or "make anything but gold and silver coin a tender in payment of debts" (Art. I, Sec. 10). The federal government was an instrument of delegated powers, that is, it enjoyed no powers not specifically conferred by the Constitution, all others being reserved to the states, except as limited, as in the case of money. It is noteworthy in connection with our present survey, that while the Constitution authorized the Congress "to coin money, regulate the value thereof, and of foreign coin" (Art. I, Sec. 8), nothing is said about emitting bills of credit, or declaring instruments of credit as legal tender.

Despite these explicit limitations, state after state continued to charter banks with the right of note issue, and even as quasi-legal tender. Even so strict a federalist as Alexander Hamilton, leading proponent of centralized authority and first Secretary of the Treasury, thought it proper for the federal government to create bank credit as a money mechanism. His fiscal plan for strengthening the federal government included a bank, the first Bank of the United States, which was chartered in 1791. Fortunately, it was managed with conservatism, a conservatism uncharacteristic of the times, and indeed Hamilton's effort to provide the country with a sound banking and money system antedated that of Sir Robert Peel by fifty years.

The Bank of the United States was organized with a capital of $10,000,000, of which one-fifth was subscribed by the government by way of loan, and note issues were limited by a provision restricting all the liabilities of the bank, except deposit liabilities, to an amount not exceeding the capital of the bank. Despite any specific Constitutional authority, but in reliance upon "implied" powers—a doctrine sanctified by the early decisions of the Supreme Court under its first chief justice John Marshall—the notes were declared legal tender for government dues so long as they were redeemable in coin. The bank did not enjoy a monopoly of the note issue, as the various states still chartered banks with this privilege, but its large capital and preeminent status were calculated to give it a commanding position in the banking system.

The bank followed a conservative policy so far as note issue was concerned. Its statement for January 24, 1811, showed $5,009,567 in coin against $5,037,125 circulating notes outstanding and $5,900,423 in individual deposits. Government deposits in the amount of $1,929,999 were offset by United States 6 per cent stock in the amount of $2,750,000.

Hamilton's concept of a strong centralized banking system, controlled by the federal government, was not due for realization. In 1811, the charter of the bank expired and Congress refused a renewal, largely on political and constitutional grounds. A second Bank of the United States was founded in 1816, but it became an object of political opportunism, and in 1836 it ceased to function as a state institution.

の 》

Meantime, despite the provisions of the Constitution, state banks were springing up like mushrooms, all issuing circulating notes and obtaining their acceptability as money despite their invalidity as legal tender, and in such number that, before long, conservative financiers began to grow alarmed. Oliver Wolcott, who succeeded Hamilton as Secretary of the Treasury, wrote in 1795: "These institutions have all been mismanaged. I look upon them with terror. They are at present the curse, and I fear they will prove the ruin, of the government. Immense operations depend on a trifling capital, fluctuating between the coffers of the different banks." John Adams, just elected to the presidency, also wrote of the growing evil of unregulated paper money. Because of the supposed immense advantage to agriculture, he said, the Massachusetts legislature was authhorizing a number of new banks, but credit could not be solid when a man was likely to be repaid for a loan in bank bills that were constantly depreciating.

But these were voices in the wilderness. Bank expansion continued at a heedless, unregulated pace. Little money was required to be paid on subscriptions, as the profits from the note issue were enough to take care of all. Says Hoggson, "The allowed emission of bank bills was so large that the question of profits depended simply upon whether the new bank could get its bills accepted first by borrowers, and then by the public in the surrounding district. In fact, the further from home the bank bills were distributed the better, as there was less chance of their returning at an inopportune time."[1]

❧

Panics and financial collapses followed as a matter of course, leading to various proposals of how to sustain confidence in the system. The main devices were four, each according to a particular theory of how to multiply loaves and fishes, or how to make candy wool. They were: note issues upon general assets; issues protected by a general safety fund; issues based upon public securities; and issues based upon the faith and credit of the states.[2]

It was in the New England states, and particularly in Massachusetts, that the theory developed of regulating note issue in relation to the general assets of the bank. No limitations were imposed upon note issues in the colonial enactments of Massachusetts, but an act of 1792 prohibited notes below $5 denomination, and note-issuing banks were directed to limit the amount of notes, together with "money loaned by them by a credit on their books or otherwise," to "twice the amount of their capital stock in gold and silver, actually deposited in the banks and held to answer the demands against the same." A general law passed in 1799 prohibited banking by unincorporated companies, or the issue, except by the Nantucket Bank, of notes of smaller than $5 denomination. In 1805 the restriction was modified so as to permit the issue of bills of $1, $2, and $3 denomination to the amount of 5 per cent of paid-up capital. In 1809 the limit was raised to 15 per cent, reduced to 10 per cent in 1812, and again increased in 1818 to 25 per cent, remaining at this figure down until state bank notes were finally extinguished by the passage of the National Bank Act amendment in 1864.[3]

The Massachusetts method of control was put to the test in 1814 when, incident to the war with England, and the extinction of the Bank of the United States, there occurred a widespread collapse of banking. The New England banks succeeded in maintaining payments in coin, and after the passage of the crisis, banking capital flocked to Massachusetts, and the organization of banks proceeded with alarming rapidity. At the end of 1836, seventy-eight new banks had been added to the sixty-two older banks. In spite of the enactment of 1829 limiting note circulation of banks to 125 per cent of capital, and total obligations, exclusive of deposits, to twice the capital, the crisis of 1837 was like a scythe over this crop, and thirty-two Massachusetts banks wound up between 1837 and 1844.

The crisis of 1837 brought greater state control into the banking system: the institution of bank examiners, and greater liability of stockholders for the redemption of notes. But even these were not enough. A new crop of banks arose, followed by a new speculative mania, which culminated in the crisis of 1857. In 1862, just before the establishment of the national banking system, the 183 banks in operation in Massachusetts had created a credit structure of $73,685,000 in notes and deposit liabilities supported by only $9,595,000 in cash, a ratio of 13 per cent.[4]

The continued issues of bank notes that circulated as money, but without legal tender quality, was supportable only by confidence that the notes would be redeemed on demand in gold or silver coin. To strengthen confidence the system of bank guaranty by a safety fund was first initiated in New York in 1829. By legislative act of that year banks were required to deposit annually with the treasurer of the state a sum equal to one-half of one per cent of their capital stock until the deposits should amount to 3 per cent, the sum so accumulated to be held to pay off liabilities of failed institutions. The panic of 1837 put the fund to its test, and it was kept intact only by allowing canal tolls to be paid in notes of defunct banks. Bank failures in the three years following proved how ineffective was deposit guaranty in the face of general banking overextension. The fund was exhausted, and the solvent banks had to be assessed to maintain the guaranty. Redemption of notes was finally suspended, temporarily, and in 1842 the act was modified by making the guaranty cover only notes, instead of all the liabilities. In 1857 the whole attempt at guaranty was abandoned.

Conant thought the safety fund system failed because it was to cover all liabilities instead of simply the liability for note issues, but this is a view, like so much taught in formal economics, that proceeds on logic rather than on understanding of human nature. The real reason for the failure, like the reason for the failure of all such schemes, is that bad apples will rot good apples, but good apples will not make bad apples sound. The safety fund system made the soundly operated institutions responsible for the mistakes and malfeasance of the recklessly operated, over the operations of which neither they nor the state exercised any control or responsibility.

So long as the opportunities for profit exist, with few or no questions asked as to how the institutions are managed, the speculative element is willing to pay assessments on the same basis that a racketeer buys protection from the police—by recouping itself through extending operations. Many of the shyster element—and banking attracted many of this kind—evaded the law by issuing notes in excess of the maximum limits, or by obtaining through political influence charters which gave them special privileges. The conservatively managed institutions, lending upon the safer risks, upon which naturally the margins of profit were smaller, found the assessments burdensome, and were compelled to embark upon the more speculative business in order to carry the charges.

◆§ §◆

The third form of control arose out of the campaign for "free banking," as it was called—that is, total liberty for individuals or associations to engage in banking merely on compliance with statutory requirements, and without the necessity of acquiring a charter by legislative act. The Free Banking Act of New York, passed April 18, 1838, authorized individuals or associations to issue notes against a reserve in coin of 12.5 per cent and the deposit with the state comptroller of an equivalent amount of federal and state securities approved by the comptroller.

The financial interest was prompt to take advantage of the free banking law, and by the end of 1839 seventy-six persons or associations were issuing notes, and applications from fifty-seven more were on file. Before the first of January, 1841, eight of these institutions had gone out of business, and eighteen more followed in the course of the year. Modifications of the system, however, improved the operations of the free banking system somewhat, and it was successful enough to attract attention in Canada in 1850. Later, it became the pattern for the national banking system established in 1863.

᭄ ᭄

Various states modeled their banking legislation after that of Massachusetts or New York. In Maine, for instance, banks were allowed to issue notes up to 50 per cent of capital, and up to the full amount of capital provided the excess were covered by a reserve in specie, that is, in coin, equivalent to one-third the amount of notes issued. Vermont patterned its legislation of 1831 after the New York safety fund act. But if the safety fund system proved salutary in the East, where more conservative traditions were beginning to gain strength, in the newer states of the West, the system only proved the opportunity for further abuse.

Hardly had a safety fund been enacted in Michigan, in 1836, when it was forgotten in a frenzy of paper inflation that in the following years swept over the West like a prairie wind. The panic of the following year became the occasion for lowering, rather than raising banking standards, and an act was passed permitting banks to begin business in a condition of suspension of specie payments. Thirty per cent of the capital was required to be paid up in coin, but this provision was evaded by borrowing the money for a few days when the bank commissioners made their tours of inspection. A bank could be organized by any twelve persons able to put up $50,000 consisting of $15,000 cash and the balance in bonds and mortgages that could meet the approval of the auditor general. After the resumption of specie payments, it became the practice to organize banks in the most inaccessible places in order to make it difficult to present the notes for redemption, and eastern speculators developed a profitable business of taking out Michigan charters and distributing the notes in other states where the standing of the bank could not be known. Fraudulent overissues were frequent and in many cases not even recorded.

Before long a million dollars in worthless bank notes were in circulation, a bewildering variety of issues each circulating at its own rate of discount with a confusion that required corps of bookkeepers to keep the accounts of a firm straight. Merchants kept couriers by whom they hurried off to the banks the notes they were compelled to take, in order to exchange them—if possible—for something which had more value. Misery and bankruptcy spread over the state, with the inevitable harvest of stay laws and laws fixing the value at which the property of debtors should be taken. The climax came in 1844 when, nearly all the "free banks" being in the hands of receivers, the state supreme court held that the general banking law had been passed in violation of the constitution and hence that even the receiverships had no legal existence!

The experience of Michigan was repeated elsewhere in the West. Banking laws basing note issues upon securities were adopted by Illinois in 1851, Indiana in 1852, Wisconsin in 1853, and other states soon afterward. The restrictions which had been developed in New York were ignored, and so rampant was the note-issue mania that the notes came to be called by the appropriate name of "red dog" and "wild cat" currency.The inflation that resulted presented patterns that were repeated in the decade 1920–1929, which we shall have occasion to examine later. The rising crop of banks created a fictitious demand and a rising market for securities (to be used as capital stock) and a consequent stimulus to the creation of public debt by the issue of securities. This was followed by more bank notes being issued against the securities, demand increasing and the market rising, more securities issues, more bank notes, and so on in an endless chain of debt creation and the inflation of paper wealth. The process was finally brought to a stop by the panic of 1857.

◄§ §►

The fourth method of control, that of note issues against the faith and credit of the state, developed chiefly in the southern states. As it was tried, it was a tragic failure—"one of the most dismal chapters in American banking," comments Conant.[5]

Kentucky, in 1820, had created a state bank with the power of note issue, but within two years the notes were quoted at 62.5 cents on the dollar, and the whole state was soon embroiled in a legal controversy over the bank, a controversy that almost ended in revolution. Alabama created a state bank with the naïve object of distributing its notes as evenly as possible throughout the state: to assure this, a directorate of between sixty and seventy persons was chosen annually by the state legislature; and various public funds were turned over and some $13,800,000 state bonds were issued to support the notes. A period rivaling that of the Mississippi Bubble followed. Political control of the bank and apparently unlimited supplies of money brought "good times" and cast a roseate flush over the state; so intoxicated with money did the state become that an act was passed (January 9, 1836) abolishing direct taxation and setting aside $100,000 of bank money to meet the state budget.

The inevitable end came with the panic of 1837. An investigation showed $6,000,000 of the bank's assets to be worthless. Confidence in paper money "supported by the faith and credit and wealth of the state"—to use the favorite phrase of champions of government paper money—suddenly collapsed, and with it the whole structure of business and credit in Alabama. The lesson of the experiment is indicated by the provision in the Constitution of 1867 that "the state shall not be a stockholder in any bank, nor shall the credit of the state ever be given or loaned to any banking company or association or corporation."

Not deterred by the experience of Alabama, however, Mississippi, in 1838, established a state bank with a capital of $15,000,000 provided by a state bond issue. Management was of the worst, and the bank ran its course within four years. When the bank collapsed, the state repudiated its obligations on the bonds, bringing wails of angered anguish particularly from British bond buyers who had invested heavily in the issues. The results are described by Henry V. Poor:

The $48,000,000 of the bank's loans were never paid; the $23,000,000 of notes and deposits were never redeemed. The whole system fell, a huge and shapeless wreck, leaving the people of the state very much as they came into the world. Their condition at the time beggars description. Society was broken up at its very foundations. Everybody was in debt, without any possible means of payment. Lands became worthless, for the reason that no one had any money to pay for them. The only personal property left was slaves, to save which, such numbers of people fled with them from the state that the common return upon legal processes against debtors was in the very abbreviated form 'G. T. T.'—*gone to Texas*—a state which in this way received a mighty accession of her population."[6]

◄§ §►

Several other southern and western states went through similar experiences. The Territory of Florida incorporated the Union Bank of Florida on February 12, 1833, with a capital of $1,000,000, assisted by an issue of territorial bonds of which half were sold in Europe. The state government, after the admission of Florida to the Union, refused to recognize the privileges of the bank and the Secretary of State in 1858 reported that its circulating notes were not worth twenty cents on the dollar. A real estate bank was one of the features of the Arkansas system, towards which the subscribers were required to pay nothing in but merely to secure their subscriptions by mortgaging their real estate. Incorporated in 1838, its career was four short years. In 1842 the directors made an assignment, and the notes afterward passed for about 25 per cent of their face value in specie.

Illinois tried several experiments at issuing circulating notes "on the credit of the state," and the circulation of the State Bank of Illinois, incorporated in 1821, did not exceed $300,000, but even this moderate limit did not keep the notes from falling within three years to twenty-five cents on the dollar. In 1825 the bank was ended by collecting all the notes in its possession and publicly burning them at Vandalia, in the public square. Another bank formed in 1835 collapsed in 1842, and the Constitution of 1848 provided that no state bank should thereafter be created nor should the state own any banking stock. A state bank in Tennessee, formed in 1820 stood up for twelve years, but failed in 1832. Louisiana incorporated the Union Bank of Louisiana in 1832 on lines similar to those of the Union Bank of Florida, and issued some $17,000,000 in bonds to provide the capital for it and two other institutions, all three of which succumbed in 1842.

Georgia, Vermont, Missouri, Delaware and the Carolinas all tried state ownership and management of banks, but the first two early abandoned the experiment, and the others ceased to be banks of issue upon the establishment of the national banking system.

۞ ۞

Throughout this period neither Congress nor the courts came face to face with the Constitutional prohibitions upon the issuance of paper money—or indeed what was money. The term "money" (derived from *moneta*) properly refers only to minted coins, while the term "currency" embraces whatever is generally circulated and accepted. Meantime, three usages had grown up to describe the different forms of circulation—lawful money, standard money, and legal tender.

Lawful money, of distinctly American usage, originally meant only coined gold and silver. Since 1837, other forms of circulation have at times been treated as "lawful money," but the term has never been defined by statutes or courts. Legal tender implies what can be lawfully offered in payment of debts and dues, although in certain cases this quality may be limited to payment of government dues—and in the case of state authorized bank notes, only state dues. National bank notes (discussed *infra*) were never legal tender until 1933, while Federal Reserve notes, first authorized in 1913, were legal tender but never lawful money, and the Federal Reserve Act declared that the notes should be redeemed on demand "in lawful money." In 1933, all forms of federal circulation were declared legal tender, with disastrous confusion as to the actual legal qualities of money.[7]

In 1974, a suit was brought in the District Court of California by Mobley M. Milam, an attorney of San Diego, to require the Federal Reserve to redeem its notes in lawful money. To do so would create havoc in the monetary system, since Federal Reserve notes comprise (1974) some $66 billion of total circulation of some $75 billion, the balance being mostly fractional coin. The purpose of the suit was to face the courts with the Constitutional inconsistencies involved in the present monetary system; the suit was dismissed by the court, and also by the Circuit Court of Appeals, and subsequently by the Supreme Court.

The establishment of the national banking system in 1863–1864 removed note issues of the state banking systems, and introduced a new régime in the control of private money. By the National Bank Act of 1863, as amended in 1864, the privilege of note issue was restricted to nationally chartered banks (by the process of taxing state note issues out of existence) and the notes themselves were required to be secured by the deposit with the Treasurer of the United States of an equivalent amount of United States Government securities.

The act had been passed as a war measure, sponsored by the Secretary of the Treasury, Salmon P. Chase, to aid in financing the federal government, and had been a part of his policy of carrying on the war by means of loans rather than by taxes. Irredeemable fiat money (greenbacks) had been issued by the federal government to such an amount that they had fallen to a discount of 65 per cent in terms of gold, and it had become imperative, as in 1780, as in 1694, to bolster the credit of government by calling in the aid of the banking mechanism. The prime purpose in basing the bank note issue upon government credit was thus to strengthen the government by providing a market for federal securities rather than to strengthen society by means of sound money.

By placing paper money solely upon the back of federal

credit, however, the act achieved for the note issue a security and uniformity which it had not hitherto possessed, and to that extent was a long forward step. The successful outcome of the war redeemed the hopes of the sponsors of this form of note issue, and as the wealth and power of the country expanded, the value of the national bank notes rose, and was re-established at par on the resumption of specie payments in 1879, with redemption of notes in coin.

But if the substitution of federal credit for state and private credit behind the bank note issue was to introduce uniformity and a greater degree of security, it also introduced a new problem of major import in the control of the money mechanism. This problem, which is still so little understood, because it is so elusive and has so little appearance of actual money, is that of deposit credit. Before taking up this manifestation of the money mechanism, it is necessary once more to advert to the English experience with money following the passage of the Act of 1844.

V. Extension of Central Banking

It had taken Europe four hundred years to learn how to deal with the problem of bimetallism; perhaps two hundred years is not too long for man to learn how to deal with the problem of bank money. By the Act of 1844, which made the English note issue almost synonymous with gold, Sir Robert Peel thought he had achieved the sought-for solution. The principal finance ministers of Europe evidently thought so too, for the Bank of England became the model for European central banking.

Events proved otherwise. Neither limits on the note issue, nor requirements as to cover, were sufficient to forestall panics and breakdowns in the money mechanism. Within three years after the passage of the act, that is, in 1847, the banking reserve of the bank had been reduced to such an extent as to threaten suspension of discounting. In order to support the banking function of the institution, the issue department was sacrificed. The government intervened, authorizing the bank, in effect, to disregard the legal reserve restrictions upon the note issue. Fortunately, this recourse did not become a necessity.

◄§ §►

The great mistake of the Act of 1844 was the mistake that has been made in the commercial banking legislation of this country. The doctrine upon which the act had been built was that bank notes are a form of currency entirely distinct from other commercial paper and forms of credit. The law was framed to arrest commercial expansion by limiting the power of note issue; it failed absolutely in this object because such operations can be carried on, and usually are carried on, by other means than banknotes.

The problem was thus not one of the control of actual money, but the control of the entire money mechanism, and the control of the system which has in its power the creation of money. By 1844 the money mechanism had passed beyond the control of government and into that of the banking system. The crisis of 1847 early demonstrated the futility of note-issue control without a concomitant control of credit. The actual situation that developed, as John Stuart Mill wrote,[1] was that the bank, safe so far as its circulation was concerned, had actually over-extended itself on the banking side, and that, faced with a panic, it was caught without banking reserves and had to contract its credit, with acute results on the commercial and banking community which relied upon the central institution for aid. Conant explains what happened, as follows:

"It was the theory of the supporters of the act that the currency would fluctuate in exact accordance with the fluctuations of a metallic currency by the self-acting provision for the issue of notes only in exchange for gold and the issue of gold in exchange for notes. Both sides in the discussion of the bill, when it was pending in Parliament, seem to have made the incredible blunder of overlooking the fact that gold could be obtained (through the banking department) by the presentation of checks. This was exactly what happened in 1847. The bank saw its bullion decreasing on the one hand and its banking reserve decreasing on the other hand, while gold and notes poured out of the banking department in the discharge of its obligations. The banking reserve was chiefly in notes which had been obtained by the surrender to the issue department of such gold as was received on deposit, but the payment of these notes to customers either swelled the note circulation or reduced the gold in the bank by just the amount of the payment."[2]

ঙ৶ ৶৶

Ten years later, in 1857, another crisis occurred, due to excessive and unwise lending as a result of over-optimism regarding foreign trade prospects. The bank found itself in the same position as in 1847, and similar measures were taken. On this occasion the bank was forced to use the authority to increase its fiduciary issue beyond the limit imposed by the Bank Charter Act, although the excess issue at no time reached £1,000,000, and the infringement of the act lasted only eighteen days.

Again in 1866, the growth of banking without sufficient attention to liquidity, and the use of bank credit to support a speculative craze in which within a few years nearly three hundred companies, with a total nominal capital of £504,000,000, had been organized, prepared the way for a crash which was finally precipitated by the failure of the famous house of Overend, Gurney and Co. The Act of 1844 was once more suspended.

ঙ৶ ৶৶

The financial storms of 1873–1879 and 1882–1884 were outridden by the Bank of England, largely as a result of more conservative management and the happy circumstance of an increasing world gold production for which the Bank of England, as a result of its world importance and discount policy, became the chief depository. Elsewhere in Europe and America these periods of depression were occasioned or accompanied by widespread bank failures and breakdowns in the money mechanism.

In 1890, the Bank of England once again faced crisis, again the result of widespread and excessive speculation in foreign securities, particularly American and Argentine. This time it was the failure of Baring Brothers that precipitated the crash. The bank was saved, as it had been in 1839, by a loan of £10,000,000 from France, the proceeds of which were imported in gold.

◄§ §►

Yet in spite of these periods of strain and near breakdown, such was the general prestige of English institutions and the power of the Bank of England—a prestige and power derived from the English steel and coal industry and an overseas commerce that constantly refilled the depleted coffers of the bank— that the bank became the accepted model in Europe, as English tailoring the model for male attire. Central banking, as it expanded throughout Europe, was ostensibly patterned after English practices, especially in regard to concentrating the banking reserves in one institution. The one redeeming feature of the bank, the principle of making the notes practically synonymous with gold, which Sir Robert Peel had laid down as a basic principle, was, however, generally disregarded.

Thus, the *Reichsbank*, which was established in 1875, was entrusted with the note issue of the German Empire, and in order to enable it to unify the currency it was empowered to absorb the issues of the local banks just as the Bank of England had been authorized to do by Peel's act. A fixed limit was set to the circulation. Notes issued within this limit required a cover of only one-third; beyond this limit notes could be issued but only against a full cover. The "cover," however, could consist not only of gold bullion, foreign gold coin, or other money having currency in Germany, but also of imperial treasury bonds. This concept of "cover" of course vitiated the whole idea of a gold backed currency. Moreover, the "contingent" note issue, i.e., that portion required to be covered only one-third, which had been set in 1875 at 250,000,000 *marks* was subsequently raised to 550,000,000 *marks* and in 1910 had reached 750,000,000 *marks*. This bank disappeared in the World War I inflation, and the later *Bundesbank* was under no restrictions as to note issue reserves except public policy and convenience.

In France, the note issue was concentrated in 1848 in the *Banque de France*, in imitation of Peel's act, but the control was regulated by legislation, with limits nominally fixed by legislation but conveniently enlarged from time to time, from 350 million *francs* to 12 billion *francs* by the outbreak of World War I. In 1928 the *franc* was devalued to one fifth its former value, and a new law, *à la* the Federal Reserve act, required gold equivalent to 35 per cent of total note and deposit liabilities. This did not prevent further devaluations in the *franc* in 1936, in 1937, and again in 1938. The following year the gold reserve requirement was suspended and has not been restored (1974). Further devaluations followed, in 1940, in 1945, in 1948, and in 1958, when the gold value was reduced to .0018 grams of fine gold to the *franc*. The existing *franc* was now abandoned for a new *franc* equivalent to 100 of the old, thereby establishing a new *franc* nominally containing .18 grams fine gold, but no *francs* were coined and the content was again reduced on August 10, 1969, to .16 grams fine gold.[3]

The experience of other countries of Europe paralleled that of France. In Italy notes are issued by the Bank of Italy, under a reserve requirement of 40 per cent in gold or foreign exchange, suspended however since 1935. Only two European countries currently maintain a gold reserve requirement for the note issue —The Netherlands and Switzerland. For The Netherlands the requirement, since 1956, has been 50 per cent, but this may be in gold or foreign exchange. In Switzerland, the requirement, in effect since 1905, is 40 per cent in gold. In neither case, however, are the notes presently (1976) redeemable in gold.

The tendency everywhere has been to eliminate gold reserve requirements, either at minimum amounts or at fixed minimum ratios, and to leave the question in the hands of the monetary authorities. In the United States this was accomplished by legislation in 1965, removing the gold reserve against deposits, and in 1968, against notes. The result has been, since the reform of currencies following World War II, the appearance of stability but the actual continuance of inflation and the deepening erosion of monetary values.

VI. Seed of the New Inflation

THE theory behind the founding of the first great banks of modern times—the Venetian *Banco della Piazza del Rialto*, the Bank of Amsterdam, and the Bank of Hamburg—had been that their function should be one of strict deposit. The continental banks, with the exception indeed of the Bank of St. George, accepted from the merchants coins of all countries of repute and held them as reserve against the bills issued by the bank. The notes of these earlier banks were, as J. E. Thorold Rogers points out, "of the nature of dock warrants, entitling the holder to claim not only the sum which they expressed, but, theoretically at least, the very coins which were deposited against them."[1]

We have noted how scrupulously this principle was regarded at Hamburg, and at Amsterdam, at least as late as 1672. Elsewhere, as the banks were made to serve the financial requirements of their governments by means of loans of the deposits entrusted to them, this principle was gradually lost sight of, if it was ever recognized. In England, as a result of the practices developed by the goldsmiths, an opposite concept grew up. The Bank of England was founded on a totally different idea from that upon which the continental banks were established. "It purported to give in its bills the equivalent of what it had received," says Thorold Rogers, "but it never pretended to take the deposit for any other purpose than that of trading with it."[2]

Thus, the conception of responsibility to depositors for the safekeeping of deposited money as the prime and paramount duty of banks never appeared in English theory. While the idea that the deposit and discount function may have something to do with the money mechanism received some consideration in the debates on the bank reform of 1844, Andréadès correctly points out, in his history of the Bank of England, that the currency doctrine developed left out of sight the operation of other instruments of credit under the control of the banker, such as bills of exchange, private promissory notes, checks, bonds, stocks, etc., which do in fact perform, though sluggishly, the functions of a circulating medium, and are equally effective, in their way, as bank notes, on prices and the movements of commodities.[3]

We have already examined the breakdown of the money system in 1844 as a result of the failure of the Bank of England to protect its banking reserves, but from that day to this neither the Bank of England nor the English joint-stocks banks have been under any reserve requirements for banking liabilities.

꿱 ꙮ

In this country, banking has been frankly regarded as a system for the creation of private money rather than for the safeguarding of money already created. Miller says, in the opening of his work *Banking Theories in the United States Before 1860:* "The colonists saw in a bank little more than the source of a form of currency. They complained frequently of a scarcity of circulating medium, and urged the issue of paper money to supply the want. With the exception of some reference to the service rendered by banks as safe depositories for the precious metals and other valuables, virtually the whole discussion of banks turned upon the matter of securing an adequate currency."[4]

When the first banks were organized it was taken for granted that their chief function would be the issue of a circulating medium for the communities in which they were located, and that their real value would arise from this service. Confusion of note-issue functions with banking were widespread. In spite of the clarity with which Alexander Hamilton explained the nature of deposit credit in his report on the Bank of the United States in 1800, there was such confusion in the public mind that the Professor of Political Economy at the University of Pennsylvania could write, as late as 1838, that "the furnishing of a paper circulation was the essential feature of the banking system."[5]

In 1833, the New York State Bank Commissioner declared: "The legitimate use of banks is not for the purpose of loaning capital, but for the purpose of furnishing a currency to be used instead of specie."[6] Daniel Webster declared, in 1839, "What is that, then, without which any institution is not a bank, and with which it is a bank? It is a power to issue promissory notes with a view to their circulation."[7]

The general banking law of 1838 of New York, which substituted for the safety fund the requirement that banks keep a
reserve of 12.5 per cent in specie against notes in circulation
made no mention of reserves against deposits, and apparently
the subject did not even appear in the debates. And we have
already noted, in the comments of the great monetary authority
of the nineteenth century, Charles Conant, written as late as
1896, his error in presuming that the mistake of the New York
safety fund was in making the guarantee cover deposits as well
as notes.

"It is remarkable that the similarity of notes and deposits as
parallel forms of bank credit was so long unrecognized in New
York," says Miss Myers, "for the banks in that city seem always
to have had a larger proportion of deposit currency than of
circulating notes. The Bank of New York in 1791, when it was
still the only bank in the city, reported nearly 50 per cent more
deposits than notes outstanding."[8] In 1839 the ratio of notes to
deposits of New York City banks was 41.7 per cent, in 1849,
27.1 per cent, and in 1859, 9.3 per cent. The reverse was true
for the country banks of New York, where the ratio of notes to
deposits was as high as 319 per cent in 1839, but by 1859, notes
of country banks had dropped to only 78.3 per cent of deposits.

ª§ §ª

Although banking theory, as it developed in this country,
never embraced the idea that the banker's responsibility in regard to deposited funds was primarily an obligation toward
those depositing these funds, and a duty for keeping these funds
secure, there was some recognition of the importance of deposits
as an aspect of the money mechanism. Hamilton perceived the
dual nature of deposits in his *Report on a National Bank* in
1790. After explaining that banks can put a far greater sum into
circulation than they have on hand in gold and silver, he pointed
out that every loan which a bank makes is, in its first shape, a
book credit, and in many cases is merely transferred to different
creditors, circulating as such and performing the office of money
until someone, into whose possession it has come, decides to use

it in cancellation of his debt to the bank, or to call for its conversion into coin or notes.[9]

Gallatin wrote in 1831:

"The credits in account current or 'deposits' of our banks are also, in their origin and effect, perfectly assimilated to bank notes. Any person depositing money in the bank, or having any demand whatever upon it, may at his option be paid in notes, or have the amount entered to his credit on the books of the bank. The bank notes and the deposits rest precisely on the same basis. . . . . We can in no respect whatever perceive the slightest difference between the two."[10]

In England, Professor Miller points out, the principle does not seem to have received any consideration until 1829, when James Pennington insisted that deposits be given a coördinate importance with notes as part of the currency.[11] His theories were ignored, as we have seen, in the reformation of the banking system by the Act of 1844.

◆§ ﬞ◆

In this country, toward the fifties, the banking community itself began to recognize the importance of deposits as an instrument of money, and along with this awakening to the dangerous power in their hands, began to show some attention to the needs of stricter reserve standards. New York banks, which were beginning to exercise their hegemony over American finance, began about this time to carry more substantial reserves against deposits than was customary for the country as a whole.

It was not until the creation of the national banking system in 1863 and 1864, however, that banks were compelled by law to carry minimum cash reserves against deposits. The National Bank Act required banks in the larger cities (reserve city banks) to keep in their vaults at all times a reserve in lawful money equivalent to 25 per cent of aggregate note and deposit liabilities. Banks outside these reserve cities were required to maintain similar reserves of at least 15 per cent, but they were permitted to include as reserves, up to three-fifths of the requirements, their deposits in reserve city banks. In 1874, the requirement for vault reserves against notes was repealed, vault cash being held thereafter solely as a reserve against deposits, while notes were protected by the government bonds and a 5 per cent redemption fund held by the Treasurer of the United States at Washington for the account of the bank and for the redemption of the notes.

No legal requirements for reserves against deposits in state banks existed, however, until 1892. The state of New York in that year enacted that banks in cities of more than 800,000 population (which included only New York City) must keep a vault reserve of 15 per cent of aggregate deposits, and banks in other cities, a reserve of 10 per cent. Banks might include as reserves, up to one-half the requirements, their deposits in banks or trust companies of capital of $200,000 or more approved by the state superintendent of banks.

ক্ষ ৪৯

The significance of this unconcern toward deposits, or the tremendous inflationary possibilities that lay in the manipulation of the deposit mechanism, becomes apparent when the tenor of the times is remarked.

The Midas complex, the desire to turn everything into money, to get a higher and higher money equivalent for the production of farm and factory, to make money cheaper and easier to acquire, either by loan or exchange, had become in the second half of the nineteenth century the dominant theme in the symphony of American civilization. After the Civil War era, which marked the final defeat of agrarian economy and the submergence of American life into mercantilism and industrialism, the manna of cheap money became the universal cry, and as with the Israelites, the easier the manna was acquired, the louder became the complaint, the less willing the people to struggle for it. The deposit mechanism, in the hands of unregulated commercial banking, became the means of satisfying the demands of the commercial community for easier credit and cheaper money, while at the same time providing a harvest in profits to the banking interests that catered to the public demand.

It shall be our task, in the pages that follow, to trace the gradual expansion of the deposit mechanism until it became, in the twentieth century, the agency for the unprecedented monetary inflation of the modern age.

Book Ten. THE INFLATIONARY AGE

No more trenchant commentary on the monetary problem in modern times can be offered than the coincident increase in the supply of monetary metal and the insatiable demand for money. In these latter years nature has burgeoned gold, but a money famine has become chronic, and the more bountiful the supplies of metal, the greater the want.

I. The Open Sesame

In the fifth decade of the nineteenth century world production of gold suddenly leaped to new and unprecedented levels. From an average annual production of 650,000 ounces, for the decade 1831–1840, production was lifted to over 1,760,000 annually for the decade 1841–1850, and then to over 6,000,000 ounces annually during the succeeding decades. Such a wealth of precious metal had not bedazzled the eyes of men since the days of the Spanish treasure ships. In the twenty-five years from 1850 to 1875, the markets of the world were flooded with the extraordinary amount of over 150,000,000 ounces of gold, or more, according to the estimates of Dr. Adolph Soetbeer, than had been won from the mines since the discovery of America.[1] Production was to be held at very nearly these high levels down to 1900, when—following the discovery of the Rand gold fields of South Africa—it was to mount still higher. Since 1900 annual world gold production has increased from around 15 million ounces annually to 41 million by 1970. Silver production reached 300 million ounces annually by 1970 compared with 150 million at the turn of the century.

What is significant is the amount of these metals that remains in use. Of the estimated 2.6 billion ounces of gold produced since the discovery of America, in 1970 some 45 per cent was known to be in existence in the vaults of central banks throughout the world. At the outbreak of World War II, some 12.7 billion ounces of silver, of an estimated 16.8 billion ounces produced since 1492, were visible in monetary and non-monetary stocks: however, due to subsequent demonetizations and rising industrial consumption, visible stocks have been reduced to around 700 million ounces (1975).[2]

◄§ §►

Despite the fact that by 1873 over a billion dollars of gold had been drawn out of the California mines alone since their opening in 1849, and in the same period an additional quarter billion from other American mines, the cry for cheaper money was reverberating throughout the nation. In 1874 the echo resounded in the halls of Congress in the passage of the inflation act of that year, vetoed by President Grant, and from that time on American monetary history has been an intensified struggle between the advocates of "sound" money and "cheap" money.

The Civil War had been financed by both the Union and Confederate governments by bonds and paper issues rather than by taxes; business was buoyed by this increase in government purchasing power unaccompanied by any reduction of private purchasing power which would have resulted from corresponding taxation, and prices were forced to inflationary levels. The release of the national energies on the conclusion of peace, combined with the leverage of a fiat money mechanism, had induced a febrile internal expansion in commerce, industry and agriculture. The country went heavily into debt, borrowing in both the domestic and foreign markets, and began to overbuild. From 1860 to 1867 the railway mileage of the country had been increased at the rate of 1,311 miles a year. Nearly 5,000 miles of track were laid in 1864 and in the three years, 1870 through 1872, over 19,500 miles. Other activity was on similar though less grandiloquent scale: farmers, particularly, were going into debt. Abroad, a similar boom was in progress, financed largely by the inflationary and speculative stimulus of the Austro-Italian War of 1866 and the Franco-Prussian War of 1870.

Meantime, the money system had begun to creak under the

strain, and prices had been falling. The restriction upon state note issues, imposed by the National Bank Act amendment of 1864, the redemption of the public debt which served as the basis for the national bank notes, the crystallized structure of the federal note issue (greenbacks), which had of course ceased to expand after the close of the war, and the gradual demonetization of silver by legislation and by market action of the ratio, all tended to offset the influences of larger gold supplies and to produce an actual as well as relative contraction of the circulation.* Abroad, similar influences, particularly that of the demonetization of silver, which we have traced, were at work. And in 1873 the effects cumulated in a concussion that was worldwide.

The crisis of 1873 was but one of a series that have occurred at startlingly regular intervals since the rise of commercial banking, and which have grown with the increasing penetration of money economy into every pore of productive activity. Others occurred in 1879, and 1890 and 1893, in 1907 and 1929. At each crisis, the principal remedy advocated was a further expansion of the money system, a stronger dose of the tonic of cheap money and cheap credit. The only difference was one of method. Not since the days when the world was intoxicated with the elixir of John Law's system had there risen from industrialist and agriculturist, banker and merchant, from political forum and pulpit, such a paean to cheap and still cheaper money.

The decline in prices following the end of the Civil War had been met by a series of quasi-inflationary measures. Despite an earlier pledge to the contrary, Congress in 1868 forbade further redemption of the greenbacks. At that time $356,000,000 were still outstanding. An act of July 12, 1870, authorized an increase in the bank note issue from a maximum of $300,000,000 to $354,000,000. An inflation act passed in 1874 provided for

* Money in circulation dropped from $1,083,541,000 in 1865 to $774,966,000 in 1870. (Annual Reports of the Secretary of the Treasury.)

an increase in the greenbacks until the outstanding total reached
$400,000,000, but this act was vetoed by President Grant. The
pressure for cheaper money became the opportunity of the silver
interests, to whom the drop in the price of the metal after 1873
was proving disastrous, and in 1876 a crop of silver bills came
up in Congress. On February 28, 1878, the Bland-Allison Silver
Purchase Act was passed over presidential veto, directing the
Secretary of the Treasury to purchase silver to the amount not
less than $2,000,000 and not more than $4,000,000 monthly,
and to cause it to be coined into money as fast as purchased.
This measure failed to satisfy, and by the Act of July 14, 1890,
the monthly silver purchases were raised to 4,500,000 ounces.

When it finally became clear that the effect of forcing silver
into circulation was only to drive gold into hoarding, and the
policy of silver purchases was abandoned in 1893, the monetary
stock of silver had been increased from $82,000,000 to
$624,000,000.

Between 1870 and 1892, as a result of these various measures,
the total money in circulation had increased from $774,966,000
to $1,601,347,000.

Meantime, while the representatives of the people were at-
tempting to quiet the cry for cheap money by the various seda-
tives we have outlined, the commercial and banking community
itself was devising its own remedy. This was the use of the bank
check and deposit credit.

&

In deposit credit was the answer to the insistent demand from
agriculture and industry for cheaper money which the coinage
of metal or the issuance of bank notes within the rigid limits of
the National Bank Act failed to provide. In deposit credit was
an instrument for the creation of purchasing power almost unlimited. Under the cloak of the commercial banker, King Midas
again appeared. John Law had attempted to convert the commercial wealth of France into money, but the commercial
banker, eclipsing Law, began, on a magnificent scale, to turn
debt into money, and very poverty into wealth.

&

In spite of its importance in every phase of modern commercial civilization, the true nature of deposit credit is not generally understood beyond the circle of bankers and professional economists. A deposit credit may be defined as an obligation of a bank to pay a certain sum on demand, the obligation being indicated by an entry on the books of the bank rather than in the form of a transferable document. It is usually thought of as the bank's receipt, set up on its books, for money actually deposited in the bank. While deposits were originally created in this fashion, the larger part of commercial bank deposits arise from loans made in favor of customers by the bank, and indicated by the deposit entry. As long as the proceeds of the loan are left on deposit, or merely transferred to another customer of the bank by means of a check, no money or very little money is involved. It is a fictitious loan, in the money or goods sense, and made possible by the universal use of the bank check in effecting payments. So long as customers do not draw down the resulting deposits in actual cash, but transfer them from one to another by check, it appears to be something real and tangible, so real that many people are dumfounded when they are informed that there may be over 750 billion dollars of commercial bank deposits in all the banks, yet the total sum of money in circulation may be less than 70 billion dollars (1975).

◆§ §◆

Although the check came into fairly wide use in making larger business payments in the cities after the Revolutionary War, the great expansion in its use for ordinary payments dates, in this country, from the establishment of the national banking system in 1863–1864. Prior to that time credit expansion had been by means of the bank note. A borrower at a bank commonly received the proceeds of a loan in cash or bank notes, and except for larger sums, which might be transferred by check, made his payments in cash. The system is common throughout Europe, where the use of the bank check is still limited.

With the privilege of note issue cut off for state banks, and drastically limited in the case of national banks, bankers began to turn to deposit credit and the check as a means of expanding their credit operations. They discovered that they could do just as well by inducing their customers to take down their loans in the form of deposit credit at the bank, and by urging their depositors to use the bank check for local payments instead of filling up their pockets with silver cart wheels and paper money.

There was tremendous convenience in the bank check. As paper money had been a vast improvement, physically speaking, over the use of coin, so the bank check was a great advance over the use of paper money. The individual could execute with a single piece of paper a payment for any amount within his capacity. He was not compelled to carry about a bundle of notes of different denomination, and small change in his pocket as well. It was a form of money not subject to theft, for it was not valid without the depositor's signature on its face. Every man, in fact, became his own mint, issuing money in amounts limited only by his ability to command credit at his bank.

The bank check quickly exercised its fascinating possibilities, and within fifty years approximately 85 per cent of the payments of the country were being made by check rather than by cash.[3] There was tremendous leverage in this. In deposit credit and the bank check lay the machinery for the creation of a vast inflation, the actual measure of which we shall now detail.

II. The Progress of Inflation

THE progress of bank credit inflation from the Civil War to the Great Crash of 1933 may be traced as follows:

In 1865, the year after the amendment to the National Bank Act had definitely restricted the note-issue privilege to national banks, commercial bank credit outstanding amounted to $747,-400,000, consisting of $289,000,000 in national and residual state bank notes, and $457,400,000 deposit liabilities. The year 1865 was one of post-war inflation, when specie payments were suspended and government issues were at a distressing discount, and the gold stock amounted to only $189,000,000. Yet this gold stock constituted a reserve of over 25 per cent of bank liabilities—a figure to be borne in mind in considering the course of this ratio.*

In 1880, the year after the resumption of specie payments, bank notes outstanding amounted to $344,000,000 but deposit liabilities had grown to $1,132,000,000. The gold stock at this time was $351,841,000 or 23.9 per cent of commercial bank liabilities outstanding. Following the resumption of specie payments, gold was attracted to this country and by 1890 the gold stock amounted to $695,563,000. During the ten-year period, there had occurred a gradual reduction of bank notes outstanding. Due to debt redemption by the Federal Government and consequent higher prices for government bonds, which were required as reserve against bank notes, bankers were finding it more profitable to extend their operations via the deposit route rather than by issuing notes. In 1890 bank note issues amounted to only $186,000,000, while deposit liabilities had risen to $2,606,800,000. Against these total deposit liabilities the gold stock stood at a relationship of 26.7 per cent.

Bank notes thereafter ceased to be any considerable proportion of total bank credit. The increase in the public debt incident to the depression of 1893–1896, and the Spanish-American War, rendered it profitable to increase the note issue, but the great expansion occurred in the form of deposits. These amounted to $4,753,000,000 in 1900, $10,772,000,000 in 1910, $30,560,000,000 in 1920 and $42,996,000,000 in 1930. Bank notes in this last named year amounted to only $698,000,000.

ఆర్ ోు

In the forty years 1890 to 1930, the population of the country doubled, the value of farm property increased three and a half times, pig iron production four and a half times, exports five

---

* Gold is taken rather than cash holdings because in a gold standard country, all the instruments of money (government notes, bank notes, and deposits) are, in final analysis, demands upon gold. In an individual bank, of course, a variety of items may be regarded as prime reserves against deposits—government currency, bank notes (of other banks) and deposits with other banks.

times, coal production five times, and freight traffic five and a half times, but commercial bank deposits increased over seventeen and a half times.

Thus, while the gold stock had increased proportionally with the increase of industrial production, the expansion in bank credit had far outstripped both and had thus been at the expense of a thinning gold reserve. The monetary gold stock available to support and redeem this tremendous amount of bank liabilities that was being created, which had been 25.3 per cent of total note and deposit liabilities of banks in 1865, and 23.9 per cent in 1880, steadily dropped under the pressure of the public upon the banking interest for more and more credit, standing in 1900 at 20.4 per cent, in 1910 at 14.2 per cent and in 1930 at 10.4 per cent. Such had been the diminution of reserves that by the decade 1920–1930, banking was being conducted "on a shoestring."

The case has here been stated in terms of total note and deposit liabilities to total gold stock. It may be stated another way, in terms of the cash holdings of the banks to their deposit liabilities. In 1890, national and state commercial banks and trust companies held vault cash of only $434,325,000 to meet deposit liabilities of $2,420,800,000, or a reserve of slightly less than 18 per cent. The reserve percentage would be even less if deposits in savings banks were included, since savings deposits are usually paid out on demand, and their reserves are in still smaller ratio to their liabilities. The actual ratio of all bank cash to all bank deposit liabilities was 12 per cent. In 1900 the ratio of vault cash to deposit liabilities of commercial banks had dropped to 14.8 per cent, and in 1910 to 12.7 per cent—vault cash in those years being respectively $706,302,000 and $1,366,164,000.

From 1890 on, the banking system as a whole, and individual banks in particular, were pushing against reserve requirements. The system was rapidly reaching a stage in which any shock to banking confidence would set the whole structure toppling.

In 1893 the country was precipitated into a depression which was generally regarded prior to 1929 as the most severe which the country had ever experienced. It was a depression that was world wide. A variety of causes is assigned, but its genesis is dated from the collapse of Baring Brothers in London, which occurred as the result of an over-extension of credit in South America and a resulting Argentine default. To preserve the liquidity of English banking, the Bank of England was forced to obtain a gold loan from the Bank of France, and English banking houses began to withdraw their American credits.

In addition to these influences, there had been a febrile expansion of American business, with excessive purchases from abroad, financed by foreign credits, and a consequent decline in the American trade balance. The attempt to increase the currency via the bimetallic route—the silver purchases—had only resulted in a drain on gold and uneasiness over the soundness of the money system, and this uneasiness was intensified by the proposed demonetization of silver in India in 1893—which meant a further drop in the value of this metal. The national banks of the East, warned by the European crisis, began to scan their loans and to strengthen their gold holdings—at the expense, naturally, of their correspondent banks. All these forces came to a head in 1893. On May 9, the Chemical National Bank of Chicago closed its doors, and two days later, the Columbia National Bank of the same city. The infection spread rapidly, and by July the country was in the grip of a financial paralysis.

Banking institutions, national, state and private, were daily suspending, depositors were withdrawing their cash from the banks, and industrial enterprises were coming to a halt. Twenty-five national banks suspended in June—a number never before exceeded in an entire year—seventy-eight suspended in July, and thirty-eight in August. The collapse of private and state banks was even more alarming. An average of about seventy suspensions a year—a figure disturbing enough when the influence of banking on general business is considered—swelled to 415 during the first eight months of 1893. Though the New York banks had succeeded in increasing their reserves to 30 per cent of net deposits in June, it was hopeless to attempt to maintain a sound core surrounded by such rotten fruit. By August 5, their reserves were below the legal minimum, and the only alternative was to suspend specie payments.

President Cleveland had hastened, on June 30, to summon Congress into extraordinary session to repeal the silver purchase acts, but this did little to stay the progress of the panic. Banks all over the country were refusing to make payments in cash, offering instead certified or clearing-house checks. This was no more than exchanging one form of bank obligation for another. Currency went to a premium, and many factories were obliged to shut down for lack of money to pay their employees.

All varieties of devices were introduced as substitute money. Certificates and clearing-house checks were issued in scores of communities, the 10 per cent tax on state bank note issues was disregarded and state and private bank notes reappeared. Certificates and certified checks were issued by single banks where clearing houses did not exist; they were issued by railway companies and manufacturers when arrangements could not be made with banks. In a few cases they were issued with the guarantee of the local authorities. Thus, the whole fabric of money disintegrated under the strain of a vast weight of credit obligations payable on demand in money.

Conant, commenting upon the crisis of 1893, points out that the overissue of bank notes played little part in bringing on the debacle, and blames the extension of banking on deposits instead of on the capital and surplus of the banks. Bank capital, he recalls, had increased 70 per cent from 1870 to 1892, and the number of banks had more than doubled, but individual deposits had been multiplied three and a half times and had risen from one-third of total liabilities to more than one-half.[1]

The crisis of 1893 was met by the repeal of the silver purchase acts, which restored confidence in the official monetary system; by the use of government credit to buy gold from abroad, which fortified the foreign exchanges and diminished the strain on the banks from this direction; by a curtailment of foreign purchases, which redressed the foreign trade balances and assisted in strengthening monetary reserves of the country; and finally by the extinction of a large volume of inflated bank and investment credit by means of defaults, bankruptcies and foreclosures. Thus relieved, the banking system, in which no reform had been made, went again on its crisis-bestrewn way.

In 1907, the country again experienced a sharp money panic, fortunately of shorter duration, and again the familiar substitutes for money developed in 1893 were called into use. In two-thirds of the cities of more than 25,000 population the banks suspended cash payments to one degree or another, and in at least half the larger cities resort was made to clearing-house loan certificates, clearing-house checks, cashiers' checks payable only through the clearing house, or other substitutes for legal money. The necessity for banking reform finally became apparent, but such was the blindness of the age that the bank suspensions were taken as evidence of a need for laxer, rather than stricter, reserve requirements, and agitation centered upon a demand for a "more flexible currency." This thinly veiled cry for cheaper money was met in 1913 by the passage of the Federal Reserve Act.

III. The Federal Reserve System

THE common explanation for the institution of the Federal Reserve System is that the concentration of the banking reserves of the country into one institution permitted a greater mobility to these reserves; that is, by pooling the cash, it was possible to use it, like a central fire station, to put out incipient runs on banks and to meet seasonal demands for cash in certain localities. In the optimistic language of one of its chief sponsors, J. Laurence Laughlin, written in 1914, "The rigidity of credit-banking in the past, the destructive snatching of reserves, are displaced by a system which allows good commercial paper to be converted into lawful reserves. . . . . In time of panic—if any such arrives—there will be no reason for a run on cash reserves, or, if there is a semblance of it, there will be a quick and ready way by which reserves can be replenished. There can be no serious run on the cash by the public, because the member bank can furnish at will reserve notes by making request for them at the Reserve Bank."[1]

Following the panic of 1907 Congress had appointed a National Monetary Commission to study the whole question of improvements in the banking system, and so assiduously did it perform this task that twenty-four volumes were required to report its findings. Yet it is remarkable that one may find in these volumes exhaustive treatment of the banking and credit systems of the principal countries of the world, but no treatment of the essentials of a monetary system, such as a definition of the standard, the nature of coinage, and the integrity of the reserve.

The one thing demanded by the public and reflected in the ensuing legislation was a mechanism for making money and credit more plentiful. It was the "flexible currency" provisions of the Federal Reserve Act which obtained the enthusiastic endorsement of the commercial and banking community—the promise of cheaper and more plentiful money, and the prospect that credit-debt expansion on a vaster scale than had ever been dreamed of might now proceed. To the bankers, the Federal Reserve Act meant the employment of a larger proportion of total assets in the market, hence with greater profit on bank capital; to the commercial community, it meant easier credit, with money more freely available, if not at lower rates, at least for more speculative ventures. A realistic appreciation of these factors, written at the time, is that of the noted journalist, C. W. Barron:

"The 'motif' underlying the Federal Reserve Act is not that which is nominated in the bond. 'An elastic currency' could have been had by an enactment of twenty lines. The 'means of rediscounting commercial paper' are already at hand and such discounts exist to the extent of at least 100 millions in the national banking system. It is not 'to establish a more effective supervision of banking in the United States,' for that could be accomplished by increasing the appropriation and enlarging the salaries of the examiners, so that men with larger experience and breadth of vision would perform more effective supervision.

"The purpose of the act most largely in its inception was 'for other purposes,' and these 'purposes' can never be wisely or effectively carried out; if persisted in they spell disaster to the country. The hidden purpose or 'motif' which inaugurated this legislation, however in effect it may work out under wise administration, is to cheapen money.

"The whole primary discussion of this bank act was to make money easier, to cheapen it to the farmer and producer and manufacturer and merchant. Senators and representatives both proclaimed within and without Washington that what they were seeking was a financial system that would give us an average rate approaching that of the Bank of France, where interest over a series of years averages between 3 and 4 per cent. They frankly said they hoped for something under the 4 per cent rate."[2]

≈§ §≈

To understand how the Federal Reserve System gave a greater leverage to the inflation mechanism of deposit banking, it is necessary to outline the relative provisions of the act. The act created twelve Federal Reserve Banks, each serving a separate geographical region of the country, and made them depositories for the cash reserves of the national banking system. At the time of the creation of the System, much emphasis was placed on the note issue functions of the Reserve Banks (the banks being permitted, in effect, to issue legal tender notes against a combined security of gold and certain types of commercial instruments of debt, provided the gold proportion of the reserve constituted at least 40 per cent of the total).[3] Because of the growth of check-money and the expansion of deposit credit, however, the real leverage in the money system occurred in the banking reserve requirements of the System. The opportunity offered for bank credit inflation will be understood by setting forth the various reserve requirements, and the manner in which they were manipulated:

(1) The Federal Reserve System lowered the reserve requirements against deposits. The national banking system had classified banks according to the size of the city in which they were located, as Central Reserve City Banks, Reserve City Banks, and Country Banks. For Central Reserve City Banks a reserve of 25 per cent of total net deposits was required to be

held in cash in the bank's own vaults; for Reserve City Banks a reserve of 25 per cent of total net deposits, of which one-half might be held on deposit with designated correspondent banks; and for Country Banks, a reserve of 15 per cent of total net deposits, of which three-fifths might be held on deposit with designated correspondent banks.

The Federal Reserve Act classified deposits into two categories, demand and time, with separate reserve requirements for each category. For demand deposits the act reduced the reserve requirements to 18 per cent for Central Reserve City Banks, of which six-eighteenths (6 per cent of total net demand deposits) were to be held in the bank's own vault, seven-eighteenths to be held on deposit with the Federal Reserve Bank for its district, and five-eighteenths optional, either in the bank's own vault or on deposit with the Federal Reserve Bank. Reserve City Banks were required to maintain against demand deposits a reserve of 15 per cent, of which five-fifteenths (5 per cent of total net demand deposits) should be held in vault, six-fifteenths on deposit with the Federal Reserve Bank, and four-fifteenths optional. Country Banks were required to maintain reserves of 12 per cent against demand deposits, of which four-twelfths (4 per cent of total net demand deposits) should be held in vault, five-twelfths on deposit with the Federal Reserve Bank, and three-twelfths optional. For time deposits the reserve was only 5 per cent for all classes of banks.

(2) In 1917, as an aid in floating government war loans, the reserve requirements were further relaxed, the proportionate reserves being reduced to 13 per cent, 10 per cent and 7 per cent, according to the classification of the bank, with 3 per cent for time deposits for all classes. The amendment provided that all reserve cash should be held on deposit with the Federal Reserve Banks.

Although, under this amendment, till or vault cash could no longer be counted in as reserves, the amount of till cash required to meet daily withdrawals was small, so that the result was an actual reduction in reserve requirements.

The effect of the amendment was to cause the banks to maintain smaller and smaller amounts of vault cash, in order to expand their operations to the maximum, and to rely on the nearby Reserve Bank for accommodation to meet sudden cash withdrawals. For instance, between June, 1917, before the new reserve requirements went into effect, and June 30, 1930, net demand plus time deposits of member banks of the Federal Reserve System increased from $12,000,000,000 to $32,000,-000,000, but holdings of vault cash at the time time decreased from about $800,000,000 to less than $500,000,000. By making progressive economies in their use of vault cash at a time of rapid increase in their deposit liabilities, member banks were able to reduce their vault cash to less than 3 per cent of their net demand plus time deposits by 1919, to less than 2 per cent by 1924, and to less than 1.5 per cent by 1930. In New York City, for instance, member bank holdings of vault cash in June, 1930, averaged only three-fourths of 1 per cent of their net demand plus time deposits and less than 1 per cent of their net demand deposits alone. The practical effect of the 1917 amendment was, it was found, to reduce reserves against net demand deposits from 18 per cent to 14 per cent for Central Reserve City Banks, and from 15 per cent to 12 per cent for Reserve City Banks, with no change for Country Banks.[4]

(3) During the decade ending 1930, at a time when the banking power of the country was being strengthened inordinately by large accretions of gold from abroad, the banking system further diluted its reserves by a process of wholesale reclassification of demand deposits into time deposits in order to take advantage of the lower reserve requirements. A special investigation conducted in May, 1931, by the Federal Reserve System, revealed the fact that out of $13,000,000,000 of time deposits held by member banks at that time, $3,000,000,000 consisted of individual accounts with balances in excess of $25,000. Even though accounts of this size may consist of inactive deposits with a low turnover, the Committee on Member Bank Reserves concluded that they were not the typical small savings accounts for the accommodation of which the low reserve against time deposits was primarily instituted. In 1914, when national banks were required to maintain the same reserve against all of their deposits, they held only about $1,200,000,-

000 in time deposits. Following the lowering of the reserve requirements against these deposits, time deposits increased steadily and amounted to about $8,700,000,000 at national banks alone in 1930. During the same period, time deposits of non-national commercial banks, including both state member and non-member banks, increased from about $2,800,000,000 to $10,200,000,000 and savings deposits of mutual and stock savings banks from $4,800,000,000 to $10,500,000,000. The increase in time or savings deposits for national banks was over 600 per cent, for non-national commercial banks over 250 per cent, and for savings banks 120 per cent.

"With only a 3 per cent reserve required against time deposits," the committee found, "there is an inducement for member banks to persuade or permit commercial customers to classify a large part of their working accounts as time deposits and then to permit a very rapid turnover on that small part of these accounts that remain in the demand-deposit classification."

అఆ ఊ

As a result of these various provisions and subterfuges, the committee reported, between 1914 and 1931, the period covered by its survey, total net deposits of member banks increased from $7,500,000,000 to $32,000,000,000 or more than 300 per cent in less than two decades. Some of this increase reflected the accession of state banks to membership in the Federal Reserve System, but the greater part reflected the expansion of member bank credit. While war financing and the huge inflow of gold which followed the war constituted the immediate driving force back of much of this expansion, it was facilitated by a progressive reduction in effective member bank requirements for reserves. Thus member banks actually held (in 1931) about $2,900,000,000 of reserves against $32,000,000,000 of net deposits. These reserves were both the legal reserves which they held with the Federal Reserve Banks and cash which they held in their vaults. If the vault cash requirements of national banks prior to 1914 had been retained in the Federal Reserve Act, member banks would have been required to hold about $4,400,000,000 instead of $2,900,000,000. This means that, in the aggregate, total reserve requirements were about 34 per cent less in proportion to their deposits than they were before the Federal Reserve Act was passed. "It is clear, consequently," said the committee, "that the largest expansion of member bank credit since 1914 has been facilitated by a progressive diminution in reserve requirements as well as by large imports of gold."

ﬠ§ ﻉﻬ

(4) As the reserves held by member banks against their deposit liabilities are concentrated in the Federal Reserve Banks, so these reserves in turn constitute deposits with the Federal Reserve Banks. Against these deposits, which are the prime reserves of the commercial banks, the Federal Reserve Banks were required to hold, *as a minimum*, gold to the extent of only 35 per cent.[5] In other words, just as commercial banks could expand their liabilities on the basis of small amounts of cash, so the Federal Reserve Banks could expand their liabilities upon small amounts of gold. This was achieved by permitting member banks to strengthen their reserves with the Federal Reserve Banks by borrowing upon the security of government bonds and by discounting their commercial paper. If a bank wished to expand its operations, and did not have the cash for the minimum reserve requirements it could, in effect, create a fictitious reserve by borrowing the credit of the Federal Reserve Bank. The only limit was the legal restriction upon the Federal Reserve Bank against permitting its gold reserve to drop below the 35 per cent minimum ratio to its deposit liabilities. Thus, if the average reserves held by the commercial banks against their deposits were taken as 10 per cent, and the gold reserves held by the System against these reserves at 35 per cent, the actual gold held against the commercial deposits of the System could be reduced to as low as 3.5 per cent.

ﬠ§ ﻉﻬ

(5) A final mechanism by which deposits were inflated is that of "open market operations" by the Federal Reserve Banks themselves. Theoretically designed to enable the central banks to regulate the volume of bank credit, and hence to check, as

well as encourage, expansion, it has proved more effective as a spur than as a restraint to expansion. Under the Federal Reserve Act, a Federal Reserve Bank is authorized to invest not only in rediscounts and advances to member banks, but in a defined category of commercial obligations.[6] These items may be purchased and sold "in the open market, at home or abroad, either from or to domestic or foreign banks, firms, corporations, or individuals."[7] Such dealings in the money market directly with the public are called "open market operations."

A purchase of investments on the open market is paid for by the Federal Reserve Bank either in Federal Reserve notes or by check drawn on itself, depending on whether the bank wishes to increase the actual quantity of money in circulation, or the banking power of the System. If paid in notes, the money passes directly into circulation; if paid by check, the recipient of the check deposits it with his commercial bank, which in turn presents it to the Federal Reserve Bank for credit. This credit thus becomes a deposit to the account of the member bank, and as such deposits constitute banking reserves for the member bank, the lending power of the member bank is thereby multiplied. Conversely, of course, the effect of selling portfolio holdings by the Federal Reserve Banks is to reduce reserve credit outstanding, and to restrict the lending operations of member banks.

In 1924, with the object of creating money conditions in the international markets favorable to the efforts of Great Britain and a number of lesser European countries to return to the gold standard, the Federal Reserve System embarked on its famous "easy credit" policy, by reducing the rate at which it lent to member banks (the rediscount rate) and by forcing Reserve Bank credit into the banking system by heavy open market operations. As a result, between the end of 1923 and the end of 1927, $548,000,000 of Federal Reserve credit had been forced into the banking system by purchases of bills and securities. This amount must be multiplied many times to appreciate its effect on the credit power of the banking system.

During the early years of this policy, the effect of this leverage was nullified to some extent by the more cautious policy of the commercial banks themselves, which took occasion to reduce their own borrowings at the Reserve Banks from $857,000,000 to $314,000,000 during the year 1924. They soon got the idea, however, and encouraged by the reduction of the rediscount rate from 4.5 per cent to 3 per cent (in New York), they began again to borrow to increase their reserves, and their own lending power. By the end of 1927 they were again in debt by the amount of $609,000,000.

When the central bank authorities became alarmed in 1928 over the results of their easy credit policy, and attempted to halt the further expansion of credit, it was too late. As rapidly as the Reserve Banks drew credit out of the banking system by the process of selling bills and securities, it was siphoned back in by the banks increasing their own borrowing. By the end of July, 1929, the Reserve Banks had reduced the volume of their open market purchases to $222,000,000, but meantime member banks had increased their borrowings to $1,076,000,000, and when the Reserve authorities began to shake their fingers in warning the head of the largest American bank replied by thumbing his nose and announcing that his institution would continue to support the security markets, and had twenty-five million dollars to lend.

᭣ ᭢

The actual degree to which the gold reserves of the Federal Reserve System were thinned out behind the deposit liabilities at any one time cannot be precisely stated as the gold holdings of the System supported both deposit and note liabilities. On December 31, 1928, when the speculative frenzy was approaching a climax, the gold holdings of the System amounted to only $2,584,232,000 against note liabilities of $1,838,194,000 and total net deposit liabilities of member banks of $33,397,000,-000. As the Federal Reserve Act required, as a minimum metallic reserve against notes issued, gold in amount equivalent to 40 per cent of note liabilities, or $735,277,000 at this date, the remaining gold holdings represented a reserve of only slightly over 5.5 per cent of the total commercial deposit liabilities of the System. Actually, of the gold held by the Reserve Banks, $1,307,437,000 had been deposited as security against

notes issued, so that the remaining gold held by the Federal
Reserve Banks ($1,276,795,000) constituted a reserve of only
3.9 per cent against the total deposits of member banks.

Not all the gold reserves of the country were concentrated in
the Federal Reserve Banks, nor, on the other hand, did the
Federal Reserve System comprise the total banking power of
the country. The greater number of banks were outside the
System. In the same year the total demand and time deposit
liabilities of all commercial banks and trust companies (but not
private banks and savings banks) amounted to a total of
$42,900,000,000, and the total monetary gold of the country
amounted to $4,109,000,000, or a reserve of 9.6 per cent.

IV. The Gushing Rock

IT will prove useful to analyze the operations of the Federal
Reserve System, not only for an understanding of the Great
Crash of 1933, but as a guide to understanding the monetary
bankruptcy of the country, made visible in August, 1971, by
the suspension of all gold redemption by the United States
Treasury. An extraordinary change in the direction of credit
had been going on in the preceding decade. Between June 30,
1921, and June 30, 1929, total loans and investments of member banks increased from $24,121,000,000 to $35,711,000,-
000. Ordinary commercial loans, which traditionally should
form the major portion of the assets of deposit banks, fell from
one-half to one-third the total. It is a remarkable fact that these
loans were actually less in the boom year of 1929 than in the
depression year of 1921 in spite of a rise of nearly 80 per cent
in industrial production. These loans stood at $12,844,000,000
on June 30, 1921, and at $12,804,000,000, on June 30, 1929.

Meanwhile, during these eight years, the more speculative
and less liquid loans on securities and urban real estate together
rose nearly eight billion dollars, representing almost three-
fourths of the total increase in loans and investments during the
period. Diversion of credit into these markets had the two-fold

consequence of financing a prolonged and colossal speculation and of loading the banks with the kinds of assets which are particularly difficult to liquidate under conditions of declining prices. From 1922 to 1929, the ratio of loans on securities to total loans and investments of reporting member banks advanced from 25 per cent to somewhat more than 43 per cent; while from 1924 to 1929, the prices of industrial common stocks more than tripled, their index numbers, according to the compilations of the Standard Statistics Company, rising from 65.6 to 216.1 in September, 1929. On September 30, 1929, New York banks and trust companies alone had over seven billion dollars loaned to New York Stock Exchange brokers to finance security speculation.

Not only was bank credit poured freely into the security markets with the result of inflating security prices, but vast amounts of bank credit were used indirectly, through the investment banking system, in the flotation of new issues. During the five years ending 1924, the average annual volume of new capital issues, exclusive of refunding issues and United States Government issues, was $4,280,000,000. During the next five years the average annual volume mounted to $7,730,000,000, and in 1929 over ten billion dollars of new capital was subscribed. The total amount of new money made available to corporations, states and municipal bodies, and to foreign governments and corporations, either by way of shares or loans, was in excess of thirty-eight billion dollars in these five years.

In floating these issues the credit facilities of the commercial banks were called into active play. The commercial banker's aid appears at three stages:

(a) In periods of a rising or active capital market, corporations desiring to expand their plant or operations frequently obtain short-term loans from commercial banks against the security of inventory, receivables or other liquid assets, expecting to refund the loans by a capital issue. The bank generally understands the purpose of the short-term borrowing.

(b) The investment banker who provides the necessary long-term capital to the corporation does so by the purchase of the shares or bonds to be issued. As the investment banker is ordinarily possessed of relatively small capital, he calls upon the aid of his correspondent commercial bank. In assuming a commitment, the investment banker relies upon a quick sale of the securities to relieve him of his responsibility. There is, however, a short interval of time in which he must finance his commitment, and in doing so, the credit of the commercial bank is used. The bank advances, usually against the deposit of other securities held by the investment banker, the sum necessary to purchase the issue of stocks, and is repaid upon their sale.

(c) The investment banker relieves himself of his obligation by selling the securities to investors, using for this purpose a corps of salesmen and a group of smaller dealers in securities. In a rising market investors buy avidly, frequently beyond their means, and apply to their commercial banker for aid. They purchase the shares or bonds by means of a loan from their banker secured by the deposit of the purchased securities. If the investor buys through a broker "on margin" the broker, in turn, carries the securities through the aid of a bank loan. Thus the vicious circle.

⋙ ⋘

Not only did the commercial banks assist the process of security speculation by financing the investment banker and the pseudo-investor, but they purchased large blocks of bonds outright. The prospects of high yields and large profits from the turnover of investments filled the portfolios of banks with many high coupon bonds of foreign governments and corporations and with second, third and fourth grade bonds of American companies and municipalities. Between 1921 and 1929, member banks' holdings of securities, aside from United States Government securities, increased from $3,507,000,000 to $5,921,000,000. The result was to convert many a bank from the status of a commercial credit institution to that of an investment company. The unsoundness of this process became apparent later when banks had to liquidate these holdings on a falling market. It was a policy of borrowing at short term (using deposits which are payable on demand) and lending at long term (for bond holdings despite the fact that they are marketable, are loans at long term) which the banks would never have tolerated on the part of their commercial customers.

◄§ §►

A second outlet for the excessive credit created by the banking system was in financing an urban real estate boom. During the decade 1920–1930, people were moving in a constant stream into the cities; the population of the sixty-three metropolitan zones (cities of 100,000 or more plus adjacent counties) rose from 46,491,000 to 59,118,000, or from 44 per cent of total population to 48 per cent. Seventy-four per cent of the increase in total population during the decade occurred in the metropolitan areas.

A huge building boom followed, the Federal Reserve Board index of building contracts awarded, 1923–1925 taken as 100, rising from 63 in 1920 to 122 in 1925, and 135 in 1928. This boom occurred chiefly in skyscraper offices and expensive apartment house developments, whose notes were more readily marketable, rather than in the modest single family accommodations. The result was that when the era had passed the slums still existed, like rats' nests around the whitened skeletons of downtown mastodons.

Until 1927, national banks were limited in their real estate loans to amounts no greater than 25 per cent of their paid-in capital and unimpaired surplus or one-third of their time deposits; nor could they make loans on improved real estate for more than one year. In 1927, in response to demand for liberalization of these requirements, the MacFadden Act was passed permitting the making of real estate loans to 25 per cent of paid-in capital and unimpaired surplus or one-half of time deposits. In addition, banks could now extend loans to a maximum of five years.

By 1929, member bank loans against real estate, other than farm land, amounted to $2,760,000,000, against $875,000,000 in 1921, but the growth of bank credit on real estate is not fully indicated by these figures. There is reason to believe that a considerable and increasing proportion of the "commercial" loans made by banks in this period were directly or indirectly loans on real estate. The tremendous urban and suburban developments, begun and completed in this decade, and the continued rise in the assessed valuation of real property, coupled with the large real estate holdings of banks convinced the President's Research Committee on Social Trends "of the magnitude of speculative enterprise in real estate and of the important role which banking credit played in its unfolding."[1]

◄§ §►

Two other important groups of borrowers appeared at the sylvan pool of credit during this decade, ready to draw off purchasing power as rapidly as it was replenished from the copious springs of the banking system. From the end of World War I down to the end of 1929, over nine billion dollars was lent abroad, the movement reaching its peak in the four years 1925–1928, when nearly $4,80,000,000 in foreign government and corporation issues were floated in the New York market. This money was provided, through investment banking channels, by private investors, but the movement was stimulated greatly by the assistance of the commercial banks. While much of this money was invested more wisely than is generally thought, it is true that sums were provided for all sorts of unwise purposes, from financing reparations payments (in Germany) to building battleships (in Chile) and removing a mountain (in Rio de Janeiro). By 1931, a nominal amount of $2,383,000,000 invested in South America had suffered a market depreciation of over 80 per cent; $1,793,000,000 European government loans had declined 43 per cent[2]; and by March, 1934, approximately $2,930,000,000 foreign loans were in default.[3]

At home, consumers had discovered the ease of going into debt for automobiles, radios, furniture and groceries, but after the enactment of the Federal Reserve System, the use of credit grew at an astounding rate. In 1910, of total retail sales of twenty billion dollars, approximately 10 per cent are estimated to have been made on credit. By 1929, half the sixty billion dollars of retail sales in that year were credit transactions, and of the thirty billion dollars worth of goods sold on credit in that year, some seven billion dollars were sold on instalments.[4] Sales made on

open account were financed by the store itself, generally by resources supplied by the commercial banks; sales made on instalments were financed through instalment finance companies
which in turn discounted a large part of their paper at the banks.

Thus, so effective had been the smiting of the rock that by
1929 the United States was overwhelmed by a flood of credit.
It had covered the land. It was pouring into every nook and
cranny of the national economy. Flimsy structures of business—
the speculative and trading element—it carried away on the
crest of the wave, while those of a more substantial and conservative sort it either submerged or destroyed by undermining their
foundations.

V. Disintegration Abroad

ABROAD, as in America, money systems were being dissolved by
the new inflation. In England, where the use of the bank check
had undergone a similar, though perhaps not so extensive, expansion as here, the inflation occurred in the field of deposit
credit. In Europe, where the bank check was more restricted,
government money was watered by an infiltration of commercial
and government credit through the note issue device. Less developed countries, South American particularly, were taught by
American "money doctors" the use of commercial credit as a
means of note issue expansion, and "Federal Reserve" systems,
in imitation of the American, were grafted, in all their complexity, upon their rude and unprepared economy. Frequently,
loans were floated in the American market to hasten the process.
Everywhere, from the turn of the century on, banking and credit
became the fetish of statesmen, the manna of an errant civilization wandering in the desert of monetary illusion.

৺৶ ৡৱ

In England, the hegemony of credit gradually became centered in the Bank of England. Although it had never enjoyed
the preferred legal status conferred upon the Federal Reserve

Banks, it had become in fact the "bankers' bank" of England, and the final reserve for the banking power of the country, with more actual authority and influence than the Federal Reserve Banks ever achieved. Below it were the great joint-stock banks, eighteen in number, organized upon the basis of head offices and branches, which dominated the avenues of commercial credit. Of these eighteen, five controlled between 80 and 85 per cent of the deposit credit of the country.* The joint-stock banks carried their banking reserves as deposits with the Bank of England.

Up to the outbreak of World War I, the Bank of England note was almost the exclusive paper currency in circulation, and, as we have noted, it could be increased only by the deposit of equivalent amounts of gold. In July, 1914, Bank of England note and deposit liabilities amounted to £97,900,000 against which the gold reserve amounted to £38,600,000, a ratio slightly less than 40 per cent. Notes issued amounted to £29,700,000.[1] On the outbreak of war, a run occurred on the bank, and by August 5 the gold reserve had dropped to £26,000,000. Again convertibility was suspended.

The British government, like the other participants in the war, like the Federal Government during the Civil War, was reluctant to finance military expenditures by taxation—a method which would have brought the war home to the masses too quickly—and currency inflation was adopted. Instead of outright fiat money, however, which would have shaken confidence, the specious device was adopted of a quasi-independent authority, the Currency Redemption Fund, which issued notes secured by non-interest bearing government securities and a meager amount of gold. By the end of the war, there were £323,400,000 currency notes in issue as against £70,200,000 notes of the Bank of England. The gold behind the currency notes was never more than 10 per cent of the amount issued.[2] At the same time the note and deposit liabilities of the Bank of England rose to £311,400,000 against gold reserves of £80,-000,000, a ratio of less than 26 per cent.

* The "Big Five" (Midland Bank, Lloyds Bank, Barclays Bank, Westminster Bank, and National Provincial Bank).

Resumption of gold payments was undertaken in 1925, but the credit structure had become too inflated for the most heroic efforts to sustain, and in September, 1931, England went off the free gold standard. As W. A. Shaw pointed out in prophetic words a year before that event occurred, the banking system of England was working "to the full limit of its capacity." "For," he said, "the condition of British industry is so perilous, and has now been such for so long a time, that the banks are loaded up with worthless industrial securities, both paper and plant."[3]

The inability of England to support the gold standard, after resumption of gold payments in 1925, may be enlightened by an examination of the banking position in that year. Total demand liabilities of the Big Five joint-stock banks amounted to £1,513,935,000, supported by reserves of cash or balances with the Bank of England of only £198,824,000, a ratio of only 13.1 per cent. To support this amount of bank credit, the total gold stock of England at the same date was only £146,325,000, of which £142,764,000 was held by the Bank of England. This was a reserve of only 9.7 per cent gold against the commercial banking liabilities of the country on the books of the Big Five.

British banking is frequently held up for admiration because no internal runs have occurred on the banks, but this overlooks a vital point. A run *did occur*. Runs on banks, like plagues, are of uncertain origin. In the case of England in 1931, the run started from abroad—slow at first but panicky later, when the Bank of France began to call its London deposits. London, as the international banker, should have been prepared for an attack from this quarter, but when it appeared, it was found to be one of the foolish virgins. The trouble, of course, was that England had attempted to return to the pre-war parity of the pound, a gold unit of value upon which a vast, unmanageable structure of credit had been erected. The sterling value of this mass of debt should have been written down by a currency devaluation—a course which the English, very properly, regarded with horror—or it should have been reduced by an internal deflation. Neither was done.

◦§ ۞◦

In Europe, the methods of war finance adopted brought universal inflation. We need not recount its familiar history in Russia, in Germany, where the *mark* reached finally one-trillionth of its pre-war value, in France and elsewhere, for it is but the story of the Roman emperors and the medieval princes which we have already told. What is of more concern at the moment is the method taken to restore the gold standard. This was the deceptive "gold exchange standard"—one of the Class A exhibits of the delusion of credit, and the sophistry of the phrase "economy in the use of gold."

The gold exchange standard emerged as one of the recommendations of a European conference held in Genoa, Italy, in 1922. It was presented as a device to "economize gold." Under the gold exchange standard, in lieu of gold, central banks may count as reserves against notes or deposits current deposits in banks in countries on a free gold standard, or foreign exchange payable in gold currencies. Nominally, this achieved economy in the use of gold, since a given amount of credit could be supported by a smaller base of gold. Actually it meant a further pyramiding of credit. Let us see how it worked in the period 1925–1929, taking for illustration the system used in Austria.

An Austrian corporation has issued a long-term loan in New York, the net proceeds of which are $1,000,000. The corporation, which needs *schillings*, has sold the proceeds of the loan to a Viennese bank. The latter in turn has sold the credit with the banks in New York to the Austrian national bank. As the New York bank deposit is nominally convertible into gold, the process has increased the "metallic" reserve of the latter, and enabled it to increase its notes in circulation or demand deposits by about $3,000,000 or about 21,000,000 *schillings*, assuming a reserve ratio of 33.33 per cent (the legal requirement was actually lower). As these notes or deposits were in turn reserves for the commercial banks, commercial credit of three or four times this amount could be created.

The loan to the Austrian corporation of $1,000,000 resulted in an equal increase in deposits on the books of the New York bank with which the proceeds of the loan were deposited. Against this deposit the New York bank had to maintain a reserve with the Federal Reserve Bank of 13 per cent, or $130,-000. The latter in turn was required to maintain a reserve of 35 per cent against its deposits, or $45,500. Thus, under the gold exchange standard system, against an actual gold reserve of less than $50,000 in the Federal Reserve Bank of New York, a central bank operating on the gold exchange standard was able to increase its notes in circulation or demand deposits by about $3,000,000, upon which, in turn, the commercial banks could build a deposit credit structure of $10,000,000 to $12,000,000.[4]

Here, then, was inflation with a vengeance, all the more vicious because the mechanism was so complex that the ordinary man did not comprehend it, and consequently accepted it blindly. If money is intrinsic, and deposits are to be really representative of actual money left with bankers, then it is legerdemain and duplicity of the rankest sort continually to reduce the amount of money available to meet calls from depositors. If, however, money is purely conventional, then there is no need whatsoever of gold reserves, and it is fraud practiced upon the public to lead it to believe that money is intrinsic and supported by gold.

VI. Reaping the Whirlwind

THE events beginning in 1929 and culminating in the bank closures and economic debacle of 1933 revealed, for all to see, the consequences that can befall a country that allows itself to fall under captivation by the money mechanism: a collapse of enterprise; corrosive unemployment; want in the midst of plenty; and spread of idleness, misery, and despair—all leading to political innovation, acceptance of the totalitarian state, national paranoia, military venture, madness, and the holocaust of another world war.

During the interval between the two world wars, the course of inflation, temporarily halted, resumed through the use of bank credit, and in frantic efforts to support this expansive growth, a world scramble for gold reserves began.

Despite an extraordinary activity in gold mining, particularly in South Africa, that doubled annual production in two decades, from 20 million ounces annually to nearly 40 million annually in 1939, a gold famine prevailed. The trouble was that no amount of gold would have sufficed, for as rapidly as it was added to the stores of the central banks, new bank credit was created.

By the beginning of 1929, four countries—the United States, France, the United Kingdom, and Germany—had increased their gold holdings by 2.4 times over pre-war, and held 59 per cent of world gold reserves as against 49 per cent at the end of 1913. In 1929, the ratio of cash to total bank deposits in these countries stood as follows: United Kingdom, 11.3 per cent; France, 7.4 per cent; United States, 7.3 per cent; Germany 3.1 per cent.[1]

Thus, while lesser countries were trying to lay hold of gold by the deceptive device of borrowing it, or multiplying its effectiveness by the gold exchange standard, the greater, by the manipulation of discount rates and the application of tariff barriers, were effectively retaining, and adding to, their existing supplies.

When American investors began to grow wary of the tremendous amounts of foreign borrowing in New York, and the bond market suddenly broke in May, 1928, one stimulus to artificial gold movements was removed, and in the lesser countries the pinch of gold shortage began to grow acute. In England, in August of the following year, a group of speculative enterprises built up by a promoter by the name of Clarence Hatry suddenly collapsed when Mr. Hatry was caught in defalcations and sent to prison. Investors began to sell to realize cash, and American securities held in England began to be offered on the New York Stock Exchange. In New York, speculation had gone so far that it took only a pin prick to rupture the bubble, and in October a crash occurred which rocked the world. On October 24, no fewer than 12,894,650 shares were sold on the New York Stock Exchange amid scenes of wild panic. Values of prime stocks broke in half, and men, broken in spirit, committed suicide in the streets. Over a billion shares changed hands during that fateful year—a record not approached in the following thirty years. Leading banking houses formed an emergency pool to stem the tide, but in vain. On October 29, the market sank in a new collapse, with 16,410,030 shares being sold, a gigantic figure for that period. At the end of the first year of the crash, an aggregate deflation of $40,000,000,000 in the value of New York Stock Exchange securities had resulted.

ᐧᐧᕲ ᕲᐧᐧ

But the stock exchange collapse was but the splendid conflagration that marked the close of an era. A gnawing flame had for years been creeping through the withered dry grass of banking. Its toll is to be read in the record of bank failures during the dazzling decade of the twenties. Bank failures reached 900 a year compared with 85 a year the preceding decade. When it is realized that each bank represents a community of depositors, whose business and homes and personal security are often entirely dependent upon the safety of their funds, and that the effect of the bank failures represented, in effect, the destruction of the economic life of 5,642 separate communities, the bitter blight of suspensions can be more clearly visualized. It was a situation which not the strongest nation could long endure.

ᐧᐧᕲ ᕲᐧᐧ

The stock exchange collapse revealed to the world the whole flimsy character of the financial situation, and as the eyes of men widened in distrust and suspicion, the debacle spread. In the United States, banks began to suspend in increasing number— 1,352 in 1930 and 2,294 in 1931—trade dried up, and commercial failures increased. Huge industrial combinations began to disintegrate. Ivar Kreuger, whose Swedish Match Company had been banker to governments, committed suicide as his paper towers fell to pieces. Samuel Insull, czar of a utility empire, fled from his domain as the law cried vengeance.

Abroad, the gold standard was everywhere falling. In the spring of 1931, the principal commercial bank of Austria—the *Credit-Anstalt*—failed. This involved Germany, and in July President Hoover proposed his famous moratorium on reparations payments. This was extended to private payments, under

the "stand-still" agreements. But England was now involved, because of its inability to withdraw its German credits, and when a
run on British gold began from abroad, it was too weak to survive. The suspension of gold payments by the Bank of England
in September, 1931, was a world catastrophe, and by July, 1933,
of the major countries of the world only Belgium, Switzerland,
France, The Netherlands, Italy, and Poland could be classified
as on the gold standard.*

◦§ §◦

Efforts made in this country to deal with the situation that
had developed were futile for the simple fact that the only
remedy applied was the same old nostrum—more credit. The
Federal Reserve Banks, in the hope of breathing a new life into
the exhausted spirit of credit, had by May, 1931, reduced the
discount rate to 1.5 per cent (in New York) and were flooding
the market with reserve credit by open market purchases. During the early years of the depression, the problem was still one of
banking—technical insolvency due to a drop in the value of
investments and actual insolvency due to an inability to liquidate
loans and investments. The government currency was still unquestioned. To aid the banks, the banking and currency laws
were relaxed by a series of measures.† Early in 1932 (January
22) a huge lending corporation, the Reconstruction Finance
Corporation, was created with a credit power of $2,000,000,000
supplied by the United States Treasury, to bolster the credit
structure of the country by loans to embarrassed banks, insurance and other financial companies, to railroads, to states and

---

* Albania, Lithuania, Danzig, and the Dutch East Indies were also
on the gold standard.

† (a) Banks were permitted to value investments at prices above the
market value; (b) the privilege of issuing national bank notes against
government securities was expanded (Act of July 27, 1932); (c) loans
by banks to veterans against adjusted service certificates were made
eligible for rediscount with Federal Reserve Banks (Act of July 21,
1932). This was a violation of Federal Reserve theory, which held that
Federal Reserve credit should be created only to finance short term commercial transactions.

political bodies, and finally to certain types of private corporations.

All these efforts were to no avail. Business revived slightly in 1932, then a new wave of bank failures swept the country, a foreign run on American gold reserves began, and the virus finally reached the government monetary system itself. Everywhere deposits were being withdrawn in gold and government paper money was being presented to the Federal Reserve Banks and the United States Treasury for redemption in gold. In February, 1933, banks began to close their doors in whole sections of the country, and when Franklin D. Roosevelt took over the reins of government from Herbert Hoover, on March 4, he faced a great nation in which every bank was closed tight. By nightfall the redemption of money in gold had been definitely suspended by the wealthiest government in the world.

ৰ্জ ইৎ

As we survey the monetary situation in this period we discover that the distortions and convulsions which developed were the result of a people relying increasingly upon money to facilitate its commercial exchanges, while at the same time progressively weakening and deteriorating its money system. A vast and splendid structure of technical economy, of organized commerce and integrated industry had been built upon the foundation of money, and while we were building this structure we were undermining the foundation by the device of deposit credit. We saddled upon money the burden of our entire economic functioning, the complicated and extensive machinery for the creation and distribution of goods, and then progressively weakened our money until it was no longer able to support the weight. In the years preceding the great stock market collapse of 1929 we had been going through a progressive inflation of the money, comparable in character, if not in degree, to that which had been going on in the countries of Europe.

Under the conditions that grew up around a situation of constantly expanding banking operations based on steadily diminishing reserves it was inevitable that a crash should occur. There was too little gold to support these vast commitments of the banking system to pay out on demand gold (or lawful money which in turn was redeemable in gold) against demands for withdrawal. The stupendous house of banking had been built upon sand—public confidence in the infallibility and capacity of the institution—and when the sand began to shift, the whole structure toppled like an Egyptian monolith.

As so often has happened in history, the lessons of the epoch were never learned. The outbreak of a second world war—the genesis of which many scholars[2] trace to the economic policies, and particularly to the monetary policies, pursued before and following the first—brought opportunity for reform; but the events were used rather as excuse for perpetuation of the old evils, and with them the acceptance of a more ancient evil that free men had long since thought to have exorcised. We refer to the resurgence of state monopolization of the principal agencies for the creation and distribution of goods, beginning with the money mechanism.

The progress of these developments in the forty years since the first edition of this work will conclude this account of the destiny of money. Before entering upon this account, however, it is necessary to pause and review some of the concepts that direct the management of the institution, in particular, the theory of debt. The period that began with the end of World War I and closed with the Great Depression is appropriate for such a review: it is sufficiently distant in history to afford perspective; the debacle with which it closed is without parallel in its range and intensity; and the skeleton of the carcass is so exposed as to offer ample data for analysis.

Book Eleven. A PAUSE FOR PERSPECTIVE

M ONEY, it becomes apparent as we survey its modern development, is nothing more than debt—a vast structure
of lead thinly veneered with gold. What men accept for their
daily toil and for the product of the field or work bench is not a
tangible substance endowed with intrinsic value but an evidence
of debt. In this country, in England, and to a smaller degree in
other countries, this evidence of debt consists of deposit credit,
the obligation of a bank to pay out a certain sum of money on
demand. Elsewhere, in less developed countries, the paper note
of the government serves the same purpose. Yet so accustomed
have men become to this form of money that its perils and consequences must be argued before a hostile court of economic
opinion. Such a task we now undertake.

I. The Cost of Bank Money

LET us note first the dilemma of those who oppose fiat paper
issued by the state, but agree to the use of checkbook money and
private bankers' notes. This dilemma is that of the interest burden such a system imposes, and the necessity of encouraging
the incubus of debt.

"Under democracy," says Professor Frederick Soddy, who
analyzed the system in Great Britain, "the prerogative of the
issue of money has been usurped by private financial companies,
and the state money is reduced to a trivial proportion of the
whole. Clearly the profits of the issue of money should belong
to the community. A counterfeiter issuing money is punished, if
convicted, for treason rather than theft. But the banks, by the
check system, have invented a means of issuing money without
coining it or even issuing a bank note. . . . In this way, well over
£2,000,000,000 worth of wealth has been taken from the public

237

and is owed to the banks by those who have borrowed it, and by
the banks to their clients. . . . *

☙ ❧

Bank checks, to explain Professor Soddy's thesis in its American application, which serve as the medium for some 90 per cent
of payments, are drafts upon bank deposits; these bank deposits,
as we have noted, arise from loans made by banks to customers,
for the use of which the banks receive interest payments. Though
individual borrowers may be perfectly willing to pay interest for
the use of their loans, the total amount so paid becomes a tax
upon commerce for the use of a medium of payment.

This becomes more apparent when we consider that the price
structure of the country is built up in relation to the vast amount
of purchasing power represented by bank deposits, rather than
in relation to the smaller amount of actual money outstanding,
and that the stability of the price structure is conditioned upon a
corresponding stability in the amount of bank credit outstanding. Most proposals for "reflation," for instance, imply a re-
ëxpansion of bank credit: this means that borrowers must be
found to absorb the bank credit it is proposed to issue, and that
interest must be paid to the banking system for the use of the new
check-money with which the country is to be supplied. In other
words, a system of bank deposit money must be constantly supported by a flow of interest payments to the banking system for
its services in providing the medium of payment.

As interest payments themselves are made in this same deposit currency, the process involves a constant increase of credit
money in order to supply the necessary funds for these interest
payments. This is obvious if we realize that to support the nearly
forty-three billion dollars of commercial deposits outstanding in
1930, at an interest rate of 3 per cent, required over a billion
and a quarter dollars annually. To discharge such a sum in
actual money (gold) would have required some three times as

---

* From *Money versus Man* (London, 1931). Professor Soddy was
not a professional economist, but a distinguished English chemist, and
his observations, penetrating as they are, put him on the other horn of
the dilemma—the acceptance of fiat paper money.

much gold as was produced by the world in that year. A system of deposit money supported by debt and its handmaiden, interest, necessarily feeds upon itself, and must forever be increasing. Let it cease to grow, and it must collapse.

≈§ §≈

A frequently heard argument for managed money is the necessity of maintaining a stable price level. Unfortunately, the operation of this theory has never been dispassionately examined. Instead, the catastrophic effects of sudden rises or falls in the price level are displayed to the electorate. Men are reminded of the fearful effects of falling prices—factories closed, millions thrust into idleness, homes and farms foreclosed, businesses thrust into bankruptcy—all because of a drop in the market. Since rising prices generally proceed more gradually than falling prices, and carry with them a train of speculative profits, the dangers of inflation are less frequently preached and more dubiously received. Yet a vast amount of fruitless effort, just as catastrophic in effect, may be expended under the influence of rising prices. Equally destructive are differences *within* the price structure—the scissorlike movements that price indexes tend to conceal. Such differences were particularly wide in the decade 1920–30, but were either overlooked or ignored by analysts. These differences became acute in the cases of prices for agricultural products and manufactured products; of capital goods (securities and real estate) and consumption goods; of wage rates and costs of food, clothing, and shelter. They were characteristic also of the 1974–75 recession, in which prices of real estate soared while security prices collapsed. The unnoticed paradox is that these divergencies have been accentuated and aggravated by the system of bank money, that is, check-book money.

When banks extend credit they create purchasing power, and when this movement is on a broad front, a decisive effect upon the price level follows. To explain this process let us revert again to the early goldsmiths.

Here are two London merchants, dealers in rugs, who keep their cash on deposit with a goldsmith. A shipmaster arrives from the Orient with a cargo of rugs which he wishes to sell, and with the proceeds to buy a cargo of cloth. As the two merchants know how much gold they have on deposit in the goldsmith's strong box, they know how much they can bid for the rugs, and the resulting price will be within range of their particular ideas of value.

Now a shrewd and adventurous young merchant conceives that he can successfully buy and sell the rugs if he can obtain the cash for the original purchase. He approaches the goldsmith and urges from him a loan, not of gold, but of a written receipt for the gold. He convinces the goldsmith that when the shipmaster has sold the rugs, he will use the receipt in turn to purchase his cargo of cloth, and that consequently the gold will not be called for. The young merchant, on his part, will repay the loan with interest when he has sold the rugs.

Now, instead of two competitors for the rugs there are three. The total purchasing power of the community has been increased. With three merchants bidding for the rugs, the price rises. A new factor in price making has been created which clearly tends to advance prices.[1]

If the buyer of the rugs is to dispose of them in the market and so repay the loan to the goldsmith, new buyers able to pay the enhanced price must in turn be found. To aid these secondary purchases, the use of the goldsmith's credit may again be called into play. He finances these purchasers, and so the circle of debt widens, and with each new increment of debt, a new hoist is given to the general level of prices. Everyone is happy, but whether everyone is better off is questionable.

ᴖᔥ ᔥᴖ

The effect of the system is to place the price structure upon a basis that is purely psychic, rather than upon the actual relationships existing among commodities in the market, and between goods and needs. Primarily, the level is sustained by confidence in the goldsmith's receipt, and beyond that, upon the future productive power of the community. For the increments of purchasing power are derived from debt, and the willingness to go into debt, or to extend credit, is based upon confidence in the future.

The future is a world into which we can never enter but which we can populate with all the creatures of the imagination. Ages of it stretch ahead, a magnificent vista lambent with wealth and power. By the mystic formula of credit, this wealth is tapped and made to flow in a copious stream into the arid valley of the present. By mortgaging the future, pledging the productive power of unopened mines, uncut forests, unbuilt factories and unborn generations, a tremendous demand may be created for wares already produced in the markets.

At the end of 1929, the total net debt of the country—public, corporate, and private—stood at $190 billion or double the total national wealth of thirty years earlier.[2] By any definition, this debt represented the exchange of tangible, created wealth for uncreated wealth existing only in the future. That future embraced in one generation, both the severest economic depression and the most disastrous war in history. Yet such was the extent to which that uncertain future was mortgaged that over $1.2 billion of debt existed in 1929 with a maturity three generations distant—that is, after A.D. 2000—burdening each generation with an interest cost equivalent to the corpus of the debt. The editors of *Fortune* reported that Florida land sold at a price that would have required for its amortization the income of a building 200 stories high with all offices rented in perpetuity. (And despite this experience, to this day development land continues to command prices that can only be validated by a continuation of inflation.)

During the years prior to 1929, the price structure seemed firmly founded, so stable indeed that leading economists doubted the existence of a credit inflation. The delusive character of the structure was revealed when the psychic foundations began to weaken. The credit resources of the country were being strained to the limit—not that there was insufficient gold at the time to support the banking operations under the legal reserve requirements, but that the imagination was becoming exhausted. It was, for instance, being stretched to the limits of human capacity to envision a future productive power in South American countries capable of sustaining interest and amortization service on the millions of dollars of bonds that were being offered in this market. It was being hard put to sustain its faith in a banking system in which over five thousand institutions had failed. It was finding hard the task of populating innumerable skyscrapers with swarms of busy workers. And when, finally, it was asked to believe that poverty had been abolished and want annihilated, it succumbed in exhaustion.

ᴈᶘ ᶘᴈ

Not only does the system of bank money tend to enhance prices and to sustain them at an artificial level, but it aggravates and intensifies what otherwise might be a natural adjustment downward. Bank credit is not only dependent upon future productive power but upon the future prices at which this production will be sold. If the prices of commodities upon which credit is extended tend to weaken, the basis of the credit is destroyed, and immediately the whole house is pulled down.

Let us assume that another shipmaster, learning of the high prices received for rugs in England, leaves his normal route and hastens thither with a fresh cargo of rugs. The market is now glutted. The goldsmith, seeing his security vanishing, demands a repayment of the loan from the young merchant. To pay the loan the young merchant must hurriedly sell everything he has. These forced sales break the market, other debtors are involved, other loans are called, and as the circle widens the ruin increases.

The contraction of bank credit produces a strange paradox. In four years after the stock market debacle of 1929, for instance, commercial bank deposits dropped by about $14,000,000,000, or a decline of 30 per cent from the peak. The decline in bank deposits meant, essentially, that borrowers at banks were, willingly or unwillingly, paying off loans. It meant that the country was, to that degree, getting out of debt. That a process which should be wholesome and salutary should have the opposite effect, should provoke such disaster as to lead the country to the verge of revolution, can be accounted for only by the deceptiveness of the money system.

The obverse of this paradox is the situation produced by the frantic efforts to expand the money system by "pumping credit" into the banking structure by way of the Federal Reserve System —central bank credit policy, it is called—in the hope that it will be absorbed by the commercial community. To alleviate the burdens of a people already so bowed with a burden of personal, corporate and governmental debt that they are almost prostrate, by a process of inducing them to assume more debt, is like relieving anaemia by the medieval process of bloodletting.

It is of course, a recourse that has a certain method in its madness. Our perfectly enormous debt structure was never intended to be paid off. It is liquidated only by means of fresh debt. If in prosperous times people began paying off their debts— which never happens, of course—the results upon the money and economic system would be just as disastrous. Once we have allowed the pillars of debt to rest upon our shoulders we are in the position of Atlas—let us budge an inch and the skies tremble.

◆§ §◆

Still another harmful effect of the system of bank money upon the price structure is the inequalities which it creates within the structure itself. Bankers, no more than society women, are not immune to fashion trends. Because of the compactness of the money market and the influence of Wall Street, certain types of investment risks acquire favor and status. Thus, after World War I, the shortage of commodities attracted banking interest. Bankers thought it good business to lend against inventories of cotton, copper, sugar, silk and the like. When a buyer's strike— which meant no more and no less than that consumers could not pay the prices demanded (for consumer's credit was still in swaddling clothes)—finally broke the market, havoc was widespread.

The banking system, its fingers burned by this experience, but with credit power untouched, expanding under the credit policies of the Federal Reserve System and ready to flow into whatever new channels might be opened, now turned to securities. Securities were marketable, theoretically, and apparently satisfied the requirement of "liquidity." And so the banking system, as we have seen, went heavily into security purchases and the financing of security flotations. And while the banking house reviews were complacently taking note of the stability of the commodity price index and the low state of inventories—"hand to mouth buying" had become the new rule of industry—a tremendous inflation was piling up in the field of capital goods, securities and real estate.

During the 1920–30 decade, for instance, the country experienced a building boom, but only in specialized types of construction—types which were conveniently financed, such as office buildings and expensive multi-family dwellings. After the storm had passed, and the skies cleared, observers looked about to discover a forest of office buildings rising gaunt and empty in the evening sky, while at the same time the American people were living under perfectly wretched conditions of housing. In New York City, for instance, where at least four skyscrapers were built in these years with the only object, apparently, of surpassing the record for the world's tallest building, from a quarter to a third of the population, say 1,800,000 persons, still occupied houses that had been outlawed thirty-three years earlier by the Tenement House Act of 1901.[3]

The availability of quick and easy credit against collateral has provided leverage for violent fluctuations in the stock market, particularly in stocks that enjoy favor among bankers and investment managers. We cannot attribute such fluctuations to the bankers, but there can be no doubt that the leverage of credit increases the range. "Styles" in stocks—glamour stocks—are a well known phenomenon of the market. Thus, in 1916 steels were the darling of investors; in 1927, mail order companies; in 1940, cement companies; in 1960, life insurance held the stage. The recent craze has been for companies growing by acquisitions known as the conglomerates, from the disparate variety of enterprises brought under single control.

Thus, those who demand credit expansion fail to realize that purchasing power created by the banking system is unevenly distributed—going mainly to those enjoying banking connections and in position to take advantage of distressed markets while the rest of the community must wait. Efforts by the monetary authorities, or by legislation, are at best only mildly effective. Credit is rightly "liquid" and finds ways of flowing through legislative fences. The result is to widen the gap between rich and poor.

و§ ۟ه

The increasing control over the banking system by the Federal Reserve and the increasing intervention of government in the economy, both through control of private banking and by the proliferation of government lending agencies, have not changed the character of the phenomenon. Rather, they have sharpened the problem. But for our purposes, instead of speaking of the banking system we must speak of the money managers.

Thus, we say that their power to direct the flow of credit and purchasing capacity has become even more vicious both in times of prosperity and in times of depression. This leads directly into a field of inquiry which comprehends not only our economic system but the fundamental social and political relationships of men upon which the solidarity of the existing order depends.

II. Credit Imperator

GOING into debt through "buy now, pay later" has become such an accepted pattern of modern life that anyone who rises to question the institution of credit is apt to be regarded as a little queer. Credit buying not only is stimulated by merchants and manufacturers and by all those who have goods to sell, but is practically dictated by our income tax administration which finds a check better evidence of a deductible expense item than the taxpayer's ledger. Despite the jokes about the uses of credit, it has become a matter of prestige and status to pay for everything on time. Celebrities, like movie stars, with income in the millions, boast that they never carry more than $50 in cash. Wallets that formerly held coins, and later paper money, are now stuffed with credit cards. With proper credit identification, one may travel around the world with hardly a penny in cash.

This phenomenon creates new problems for the monetary economist in defining money, or the quantity of money in being. Nevertheless, though we be charged with fighting windmills, we propose to examine some of the less obvious consequences of the use of credit.

An immediate consequence of the credit inflation of the nineteen twenties was the concentration of wealth into the hands of a few. Doubtless there were many other factors that fostered differences in the ownership of wealth—the natural disposition of men, for one: some being thriftless, others thrifty; some lazy, others industrious; some generous, others acquisitive; some ascetic or poetical, others practical and materialistic; some healthy or vigorous, others sickly. Laws like those of copyright and patent have tended to enhance the rewards of endeavor in certain fields, though not in others—ideas themselves not being subject to patent or copyright, but once released, belong to the world like the raven which Noah sent forth. Differences in the resources of the earth, and private title to these resources, also make for differences of wealth. Yet among all these various influences none has been more significant in modern times than access to credit as a means to affluence.

The concentration of wealth by use of banking power became a phenomenon of the nineteen twenties that attracted attention of scholars and statesmen.[1] That its importance declined in subsequent decades is accounted for by the shift in the direction of credit from private users to public: the banking mechanism, operated mainly through the Federal Reserve System and the government bond market, became a chief agency after 1930 in transferring economic power and monopoly from private hands to the state. This development we shall survey further on.

Employing its power to create purchasing power—a power limited only by a superficial relationship to the amount of gold laid in bars and coin in the vaults of the Federal Reserve Banks —the banking system lent its resources to finance industrial consolidations and corporate structures that were stupendous for the times and for even a later generation inured to speaking of billions instead of millions. Many of these financial empires, particularly the utility holding companies, had no justification other than financial—an increase in monetary profits. Frequently, these owed their existence to credit granted in the first instance by a commercial bank to a promoter, for the purchase of securities, and subsequently, by the commercial banks to the investment banks for the flotation of securities issued by the promoter for the expansion of his enterprise.

The researches of Berle and Means on the concentration of wealth became politically explosive. They disclosed that in 1930, of the wealth represented by the 303,000 corporations filing income tax returns, over half was in the hands of 200 large corporations; among them were 45 railroads, 58 public utilities, and 97 industrial corporations.[2]

These huge corporations did not, with few exceptions like the Ford Motor Company, grow out of earnings. Thus, a huge amusement enterprise embracing motion picture producing companies and a nation-wide chain of motion picture theaters, accumulated by William Fox, became possible largely through commercial bank credit which Fox was able to command—and when he no longer held the confidence of the bankers his enterprise toppled and he disappeared into obscurity. In 1929 the United Corporation was formed under the influence and assistance of the House of Morgan; within a year it held effective control of 22.6 per cent of the electrical production of the country.[3] By his ability to hoodwink a group of Wall Street bankers, a Swedish promoter by the name of Ivar Kreuger—of whom little was known beyond his name—became lender to impecunious governments throughout the world, obtaining in return valuable monopolies together with the sobriquet of "the Match King." Two real estate operators in Cleveland, the Van Swearingen brothers, with the assistance of Cleveland and Wall Street bankers, became masters of railroad properties of over $2 billion in assets.

ఆర్ సెవ

The method by which these concentrations of wealth were brought about is of interest.[4] Essentially, it depended upon two instruments of leverage—(a) a commercial bank willing to lend upon the unsecured note of a customer, and (b), a hierarchy of securities ranging from mortgage bonds secured by physical properties through unsecured bonds, simple debentures, preferred stock, non-voting common stock, common stock, and sometimes merely rights to subscribe to common stock. The operation would begin with a short-term loan to the promoter by means of which he would acquire a certain amount of stock of a nucleus company—a company with a history of earnings and well-seasoned marketable securities. This stock would be used as collateral for further bank borrowing, and when the word got around that so-and-so was buying, the price would move up enough to provide a margin of collateral to satisfy the banker. When sufficient securities had been acquired, a holding company would be organized to which they would be transferred—frequently at a profit to the promoter—and a friendly investment house would then undertake to sell to the public the bonds or senior securities of the holding company, and thereby put it in funds for further expansion. There would be layers of holding companies, some holding each other's securities, all creating more baffling relationships than those displayed in the *Almanach de Gotha,* and some of them requiring years to untangle after the Public Utility Holding Company Act in 1934 decreed their demise.

The Van Swearingens acquired control of the Chesapeake & Ohio Railroad with an ownership of less than 1 per cent of the stock, and with this property in their grasp eventually dominated railway systems spanning the continent. All this power was brought under their hand by means of a holding company in which they had an initial investment of only $1,700,000, and it was brought out in the Senate hearings that the brothers had obtained this $1,700,000 by a bank loan.[5]

H. L. Doherty and Company, with the ownership of stock of a par value of one million dollars, controlled one billion dollars of assets in the Cities Service Corporation. In 1929 a group (the Byllesby interests) with an investment of one million dollars in Standard Gas and Electric Company was able to vote 41 per cent of the shares outstanding and control a billion dollars of assets. As it happened, a year or so later another Wall Street group discovered a technical flaw in the complex system of control and was able to effect a coup and wrest control of this gigantic corporation by a similar insignificant investment.

The virus of speculation, like that of cancer in remission, remained quiescent for a generation. Then, warmed by easy credit policies, it erupted in the sixties, its fever feeding a devouring hunger for conglomerates—those corporate mastodons that grew by "trading on equities" until, in the seventies, they withered like Jonah's gourd in the burning heat of the new inflation.

Book Twelve. MONEY IN DISINTEGRATION

B Y the eighteenth century the spirit of individualism and freedom that had been fermenting since the Renaissance broke
forth in political revolt. The War of the American Revolution,
precursor to the French Revolution, was as much a rebellion
against the idea of autocracy as against particular grievances.
In the sixteenth and seventeenth centuries, as we have briefly
noted,[1] sovereignties asserted not only absolute political prerogative, but economic monopoly as well. The use of the word
"royalty," as fee to a proprietor for the exploitation of a work or
property, derives from the period when the sovereign assumed
title to all wealth of the realm. It was the struggle for freedom
from these encroachments of the state that chiefly marked the
nineteenth century, and established everywhere constitutional
regimes of limited authority.

I. The New Authoritarianism

In the twentieth century, however, we have witnessed a gradual and almost unresisted movement back to state authoritar-
ianism, primarily in the economic sphere, accompanied by the
spread of state monopoly and intervention. This new authori-
tarianism is as pervasive in its way as in 1600 when the English
merchant who was not a member of one of the state-chartered
trading companies was excluded from trade everywhere except
France, Spain, and Portugal.

What is significant for our discussion is the manner in which
statism and state monopoly have expanded, with the silence of
a cat and the enveloping quality of fog, by means of the money
mechanism.

The Federal Reserve System had been set up, as has been
noted,[2] with the idea of an elastic currency to meet the seasonal

needs of business. Money supply was to be expanded or contracted in accordance with commercial, rather than public, needs, and by the process of purchasing ("discounting") short-term notes executed to finance the production or marketing of goods. The banks could issue their credit either in the form of deposit credits or circulating notes, so long as gold was held to the extent of 40 per cent or 35 per cent of the credit outstanding. Theoretically, as the note matured and was paid off the money supply would be contracted. The organization was given a great deal of autonomy and it was to be largely independent of government interference. Two-thirds of the directors of the Reserve Banks were to be chosen by member banks, but the System's board of governors, who appointed the other directors and also supervised the operations of the System, were named by the President.

It is at once paradoxical and in accord with the times that the Constitutional authority for the creation of the Federal Reserve System has never been seriously challenged. Yet a cursory glance at the document will reveal on what fragile grounds this system of bank notes is. The Constitution specifically forbad the States to make anything legal tender but gold and silver coins or to emit bills of credit (paper money). At the same time the Constitutional convention, debating the question and having in mind the flagrant issues of Continental currency, while confiding to Congress the power "to coin money and regulate the value thereof" pointedly omitted the authority to issue paper money. Nevertheless, the Federal Reserve banks, not an organ of Congress and with practically no Congressional oversight, have enjoyed this power to issue paper money.[3]

While the Federal Reserve System was thus given quasi-independent status, it was implicit that its power would be exercised in behalf of a planned economy in which the interests of the state were paramount. Its policies were, at the first, to be directed toward maintenance of an even flow of credit to moderate the seasonal or episodic characteristics of the economy.

It was not long before its powers were directed toward the more primary needs of the state. This was the necessity of financing a war—an excuse that is chronic in the history of central banking. At the end of 1917 the Federal Reserve Banks held $660 million of commercial paper sold to them by member banks and $121 million of government bonds. Bills discounted reached a maximum in 1920, when the average amount held by the Federal Reserve Banks was $2.5 billion, and thereafter declined to only $5 million at the outbreak of World War II. Meantime, Federal Reserve credit was flowing into government account, through purchases of Treasury securities. The flow was modest at first, never exceeding $300 million during World War I, but rapidly accelerating after the Crash and the coming of the New Deal with its philosophy of expanded government intervention in the economy. As trade diminished, and the amount of bills offered for rediscount dwindled, credit was pumped into the economy by the purchase of Treasury bills; the amount rose to nearly $1.9 billion at the end of 1932 and hovered around $2.5 billion until the outbreak of World War II. Thereafter the Federal Reserve System became the chief creditor of the government, and primarily a mechanism for monetizing the public debt. The result was that the money system ceased to respond to the fluctuating demands of business, but responded instead to the political fluctuations of Washington; a condition obtained in which a traditional policy of fiscal prudence, of a balanced budget, and a reduction of public debt—processes formerly regarded as highly favorable to business—was not only contemned, but actually declared to be harmful to the economy, by reason of its effect on the money supply.

A few figures will illustrate: by the end of World War II, holdings of Treasury obligations by the Reserve Banks had risen to $24 billion, while discounts and advances were less than $250 million. The end of the war did not mean, however, an end to the monetization of the public debt; twenty-one years later, Reserve Bank holdings of Treasury securities had risen to $42 billion, and advances were less than $1 billion (figures are for the Reserve Banks only). Each dollar deposit with a Reserve Bank had a credit leverage of from 4 to 6 dollars in the commercial bank system. The enormous funds released by these operations found outlet in government bond purchases by the commercial banks instead of loans for commercial and industrial enterprises. Again, let the figures speak. In 1917 all commercial banks had loans outstanding of $18 billion and investments in United States government securities of $1.5 billion. At the end of 1939 loans were $17 billion and government bonds held were $16 billion, but of loans only $6.4 billion were classified as business loans, the remainder being loans for the purchase of securities and for other purposes. By the end of World War II, holdings of government bonds had increased to $90.6 billion while business loans had increased to only $9.6 billion. Subsequently, the banks did manage to shift some of their activity back to their original function of commercial lending, and by the end of 1965 had increased their business loans to $71 billion, while reducing their government portfolio to $59½ billion; but business loans at that date represented less than a fourth of their investments, the balance being in securities, both public and corporate, and various other forms of loans, including real estate mortgages and consumer credit. Commercial banking had in fact ceased to be commercial banking and had become a mongrel form of investment banking.

Meantime, government was infiltrating the economy by means of lending institutions, government owned or fostered and financed through the fountains of Federal Reserve credit. The American Bankers Association reported in 1934 that the Federal Government had created or participated in the capitalization and operation of approximately 5,700 lending agencies and corporations, exclusive of its direct participation in banking through the purchase of notes or capital stock of existing banks. In addition, the Reconstruction Finance Corporation, the mammoth government corporation established by the Hoover administration to combat the depression by more loans, had been putting funds in the banking system by way of purchases of bank stocks and debentures, and by March 6, 1934, had by this means acquired an interest in 6,191 banks, or about 44 per cent of the unrestricted (freely operating) institutions of the country.[4]

A survey of the way in which bureaucracy has interposed itself into business since World War I is beyond our limits here: the territory is immense. We can only refer to the expansion in the field of finance. Thus, a 1960 report of the Joint Economic Committee of Congress on Subsidy and Subsidy-like Programs of the United States Government offered the following list of Federal lending and loan guarantee activities: "purchase of government-insured mortgages on houses, loans to local public agencies for slum clearance and urban renewal, loans to colleges and universities, loans to local authorities for construction of low-rent public housing, loans to war veterans for housing, loans to co-operatives to provide electric power and telephone service to rural areas, loans to farmers to 'strengthen the family-type farm and encourage better farming methods,' loans to farmers on the security of farm products, loans for construction of ships and fishing vessels, loans for student financial aid and construction and acquisition of teaching equipment, loans to American firms and foreign governments of foreign currency proceeds from sale of surplus agricultural products, loans to governments of underdeveloped nations or organizations and persons therein, loans to finance exports and imports and to promote economic development in lesser developed countries, business loans to small business, disaster loans to small business, loans to small business investment companies, loans to State and local development companies, loans for the development of technological processes or production of essential materials for war use"; in addition, "guarantees of real estate loans, loans to veterans for various purposes, farm ownership and soil and water conservation loans, loans on commodities, loans on passenger and cargo-carrying vessels, loans for purchase of aircraft by small concerns, loans to railroads for certain purposes, loans to defense contractors, loans to governments of underdeveloped nations and their citizens."

II. Money and the New Internationalism

MEDIATING in the twentieth century between those who would settle the world's problems by the sword and those who would rely upon the Cross, has arisen a dominant element who would determine matters with the check book. As in the days of the Medici and the Fuggers, the direction of international diplomacy has come again under the influence of bankers and accountants and financial experts who would use the power of money rather than arms or morals to control and direct affairs. To their credit let us add that they have been importantly on the side of peace and conciliation through the years and principally the architects of the institutions of international co-operation.

To rebuild devastated Belgium following World War I, bankers were called in and they floated a loan. This became a favorite process of restoration and a main instrument of the League of Nations. Austria was given an injection of a League of Nations loan. Defeated Germany was not allowed to collapse completely, but a Dawes Committee came to the rescue with a loan, and the subsequent Young Committee sired both a loan and a bank.

None of these efforts succeeded in preserving the peace, and there is ground for arguing that by dealing in palliatives rather than cures they only aggravated the condition that brought on World War II.

When the struggle began, American sympathies were soon manifested in the specious lend-lease program whereby billions of dollars of war materials and strategic commodities were provided to the Allies under the pretext of a loan rather than the gift they proved to be in large degree.*

As the defeat of Germany merely served to elevate into the annals of history two vaster antagonists, Soviet Russia and the United States, around which the lesser sovereignties of the earth were to cluster as satellites, the institutions of finance were again invoked to maintain the peace and to support alliances. The task of distributing money naturally fell to the United States, where $25 billion in gold had accumulated, or some 70 per cent of the

* Total lend-lease aid amounted to $46,728 million less offsetting aid in kind received from Allies totaling $7,819 million. Fifteen years after the end of the war, $3,258 million had been paid on account and the balance had been written down to $1,734 million. See *U.S. Foreign Aid*, prepared by Legislative Reference Service, Library of Congress (Washington, 1959).

world stock. Later, the Soviet Union, more accustomed to political than economic warfare, would embark upon a subtle diplomacy of purchase which, like its money, consisted more of promises than of substance.

❦❧

The first of the post-war dollar aid programs was that of the United Nations Relief and Rehabilitation Administration, toward which the United States contributed $2,670 millions of aid. In 1947, when Soviet political pressure on Greece and Turkey threatened the independence of these powers, the United States undertook to support their governments with military and financial aid. Military aid was limited to military supplies and technical assistance. Chief reliance was upon a program of economic aid for which an initial appropriation of $400 million was made. Meantime, a post-war lassitude in Europe, accompanied by commercial stagnation and a deepening political discontent, prompted the United States Government in 1948 to offer what became known as the Marshall Plan—a five-year program of financial assistance to co-operating European countries in the prospective sum of $20 billion.

The psychological effect of this proposal was as striking as the financial. The offer of American economic aid, the objective researchers of the Library of Congress found, "had the effect of lifting European morale and providing a leadership that gave promise of helping Europe to save itself."[1] In Germany, where the money had again depreciated to zero, monetary reforms in 1948 had an electrifying effect. As Jacques Rueff and André Piettre reported:

"The black market suddenly disappeared, shop windows were full of goods, factory chimneys were smoking; and the streets swarmed with lorries. Everywhere the noise of new buildings going up replaced the deathly silence of the ruins. If the state of recovery was a surprise, then its swiftness was even more so. In all sections of economic life it began as the clocks struck on the day of currency reform. Only an eyewitness can give an account of the sudden effect which currency reform had on the size of stocks and the wealth of goods on display. Shops filled up with goods from one day to the next; the factories began to work.

On the eve of currency reform the Germans were aimlessly wandering about their towns in search of a few additional items of food. One day apathy was mirrored on their faces while on the next a whole nation looked happily into the future."[2]

The moral and psychological factors in European recovery were overlooked or ignored among policy framers, however, for the official line adopted was that the world suffered from a "dollar shortage" and insufficient capital investment. In 1949 President Truman announced his famous Point Four, making United States financial and technical assistance available to the "underdeveloped" countries as a continuing policy. This program was enthusiastically accepted by the electorate for motives that are somewhat mystifying—a mixture of shrewd mercantilism, of naïve philanthropy, of moral obligation, of fear of the "evil eye" of envy, and a conviction, fostered by many economists of the Marxian, economic-determinism school, that people could be reformed, discontent allayed, and communism resisted by economic-financial programs designed to raise the standards of living.[3]

Despite the doubtful constitutional authority to tax the citizens for largesse to foreign sovereignties, and increasing evidence of the ineffectuality of the program, of waste and corruption in its administration, the Congress continued to vote, year after year, with little opposition, enormous sums for foreign aid. By the end of 1970 some $210 billion had been expended in various forms.

This immense employment of finance as an instrument of diplomacy did not increase the general sense of security or allay the universal unrest; the burden of armament continued to mount, and the United States found itself engaged in a monstrous arms race with Soviet Russia of the very sort that public opinion had so fervently deplored in the case of Europe two generations earlier. By 1960, before the beginning of United States involvement in southeast Asia, the arms budget was of the order of $40 billion, or more than 10 per cent of the gross national product* of the country—more than twice the relative

* A statistical measurement in monetary terms of the value of goods and services produced.

burden carried by other members of the North Atlantic Treaty
Organization.

⋅◦§ §◦⋅

Not unexpectedly, the evolution of this new diplomacy of
purchase was a burgeoning of official financial institutions. By
mid-century the financial center, not only of the United States,
but of the world, was centered in Washington. In 1934, as part
of the New Deal, the Export-Import Bank of Washington had
been created to finance exports by loans to foreign governments
and enterprises. Following World War II, the political planning
for the peace resulted in the creation of two international financial agencies—the International Monetary Fund and the International Bank for Reconstruction and Development—as adjuncts to the United Nations. The International Monetary Fund
was a reserve of gold and United States dollars, originally subscribed in varying amounts by member governments, upon
which they were in turn permitted to draw to meet deficits in
their balance of international payments and to stabilize their
currencies. In practice the principal reserve was United States
dollars, which had become the accepted international currency;
at the end of 1959, of $3,451 million currencies drawn down by
Fund members, $3,084 million consisted of United States
dollars.[4]

The International Bank for Reconstruction and Development, with a subscribed capital (1966) of $22.6 billion, lends
to member governments for economic development purposes,
and by the end of 1966 had lent some $7½ billion, of which
nearly $5 billion was in dollars.*

Other official institutions began to sprout—among them the
International Finance Corporation (1956) for development
loans to private enterprises; the Development Loan Fund
(1957) for "soft" loans to poorer countries, that is, loans in
dollars that could be repaid in the inconvertible currencies of
the borrowing countries; the Inter-American Development Bank
(1960), a regional organization for loans to Latin America; the

* By 1974, however, due to the decay of the dollar, the bulk of the
loans were repayable in other currencies.

vaguely conceived and vaguely dedicated International Development Association (1960); and in 1966 the Asian Development Bank, a counterpart of the Inter-American Development Bank, but designed to accumulate Asian support for the U.S. war involvement in Viet Nam.

The unnoticed phenomenon about these developments was the transfer of enormous aggregations of power to little groups of financial managers over whom only the barest shreds of control existed. As agents responsible to forty or more different governments, with the chain of authority filtering through a maze of bureaus and ministries, these officials were practically immune to interference; they were given a lofty prestige and were endowed with more power than many a Caesar. In former times the degree of risk and the value of a security was assessed by the democratic processes of the market place, functioning through several thousand security dealers reflecting the judgments of millions of individual investors. These judgments were now exercised in an absolute fashion by a few score officials almost completely isolated from the currents of the market. That the defects of this financial monopoly were not immediately exposed is due to the fact that the early managers were generally men drawn from the market place—practical bankers and businessmen—not yet inebriated with power.

III. The Ghost of Hamlet's Father

At the end of the seventh decade of the twentieth century, nearly 1.2 billion ounces of gold was held by the central banks of the world's sovereignties. Although more and more of new mine production was being used in industry or privately hoarded as a result of rising inflation and distrust of currencies, the official stock represented some 45 per cent of the estimated total output of gold since the discovery of America. At the same time, thanks to the cyanamid process of gold extraction and the deposits in South Africa, newly mined gold continued to come into the market at the rate of 40 million ounces annually.

Yet no anxiety was more dissimulated among the monetary managers than that occasioned by a prospective shortage of gold. In Soviet Russia few secrets are more carefully guarded than the gold reserve of the state bank and the current output of the mines. Disclosure of such information is a high crime with penalties as severe as for treason.

Here is a paradox. Everywhere the leading monetary economists were contemptuous or skeptical of the importance of gold as money. Lenin is variously quoted as saying that in the classless society they would use the gold to pave the public privies, and economists of the capitalist "camp" have not been much kinder in their references to the metal. Some have proposed, with some acuity, that instead of keeping such a vast quantity of gold in vaults built deep in the earth at such expense, we simply dump it all into the sea. This school of economists, of whom John Maynard Keynes became the principal exponent,[1] held that, more important than the intrinsic value of the standard were the wisdom and skill of the central bank authorities in controlling the quantity of money and the uses to which it was put. These objects the bank managers achieved by means of the official interest rate and by intervention in the market by buying or selling securities and thereby affecting the general flow of bank credit. So influential was this school that by mid-century few central banks were under any restriction so far as gold reserves were concerned, or as to the amount of circulating notes or bank credit they might create; they were governed only by their reaction to the movement of the price indexes, the indexes of employment and production and other criteria.

In the United States, which held the greatest reserve stock of the metal, the official Treasury policy began to disparage gold and advocate its demonetization—a view, however, that found little support among the electorate or among the foreign central banks.

≈§ §≈

The premises and postulates of the managed money school rested upon a seemingly firm ground of historical experience. For years there had been in progress a process of "economizing gold," as the economists called it, by which lesser and lesser amounts of gold were made to carry the burdens of money, or rather, heavier and heavier burdens of money were saddled on to the available supplies of gold. First, there had been the fractional reserve system by which circulating notes were issued to several times the amount of gold they were presumed to represent as resting in the vaults of the issuing authority. This device contrived to make the same gold unit serve in several places at the same time for the transfer of value. There followed the development of "check-book" money, by which banks created credits for customers and thereby invested them with purchasing power through demand drafts the total of which represented liabilities of the banks several times the amount of actual funds held by the banks.

In the nineteen twenties, as we have noted, the practice developed abroad by which central banks substituted for gold in their vaults, and treated as reserves equivalent to gold, credits of foreign central banks—particularly the Bank of England and the Federal Reserve Banks—that were payable in gold. Despite the general suspension of convertibility from 1930 on, the system survived and expanded. It survived because the United States Treasury continued until 1971 to deliver gold to foreign central banks against notes or deposits here, although it had suspended redemption of notes and deposits held by its own citizens. The gradual effect of this, combined with the movement of gold to this country until 1950, was that by mid-century half the reserves of the central banks of the rest of the world consisted of dollar exchange and deposits in United States banks. Thus, a bank deposit credit of one dollar in the United States, against which there might be in reserve only a few cents in gold, was equated with gold of the value of a dollar in the reserve of a foreign central bank, against which it was able in turn to create the equivalent of several dollars' purchasing power in the form of circulating notes and deposits.[2]

❧ ❧

Just before the Great Depression, as we have observed,[3] the United States gold stock had fallen to less than 10 per cent of the note and deposit liabilities of the money system, and in 1933 the system collapsed.

The means employed to meet the crisis were the time-hallowed methods we have observed in Athens, in Rome, in medieval Europe, in France in the time of Louis XIV. By the Agricultural Adjustment Act of May 12, 1933 (the Thomas Amendment) and the Gold Reserve Act of January 30, 1934, the President was authorized to fix the gold content of the dollar from time to time, within limits of 50 to 60 per cent of its former value. This was tacit recognition of the inflated state of the money mechanism and acknowledgment that the country was bankrupt and that the only way to restore solvency was to write down all liabilities accordingly in correspondence with the value of the assets. The proclamation of the President on January 31, 1934, officially devaluing the dollar to 59.06[4] per cent of its former value, was in effect a reduction of the gold value of the mass of outstanding debt. Under authority of the legislation all gold was withdrawn from circulation and United States citizens were forbidden, under severe penalties, to hold monetary gold; all domestic trade in gold was also effectively prohibited. Gold became a monopoly of the government.

Thus, the gold dollar established in 1834 lasted just one hundred years—a better record than most moneys, not so good as some.

IV. Dethronement of the Dollar

AFTER World War II, as after World War I, the United States was called upon to contribute its resources to the restoration of a devastated Europe. By 1949 the United States Treasury controlled some 24½ billion of gold (at the $35 an ounce parity) or around 70 per cent of the visible world stock. United States policy was to redistribute this treasure. With the help of the Marshall Plan, the foreign aid program, and the various international lending agencies referred to in a preceding section, Europe recovered its productive capacity—but monetary stability proved more elusive.

An attempt to restore convertibility to sterling in 1947 lasted only six weeks, and in 1949 the pound was devalued to a fine gold equivalent of 2.48828 grams (compared with a 1914 equivalent of 7.332382 grams) and to the equivalent of $2.80 in terms of the post-1934 devalued dollar. In 1954 the London gold market that had been closed since 1939 was reopened to foreign trading in the hopes of restoring confidence in sterling, but it remained closed to British subjects.

Germany, where the mark had become so worthless that by 1947 cigarettes supplied to United States occupation troops became the common media of exchange, had greater success in regaining stability. In 1948 a new *Deutschmark* was introduced, along with a new bank of issue modeled after the Federal Reserve banks, and in 1953 the mark was given a gold value and convertibility.

In France, postwar inflation and depreciation of the franc continued until the revolutionary crisis that brought Charles de Gaulle to power in 1958. As with Bismarck, as with Napoleon, as with Constantine the Great, almost the first step by de Gaulle in the reform of the state was the restoration of a sound currency. On December 29, 1958, the French franc, now worth about a quarter of a United States cent, was abolished in favor of a new *franc* equivalent to .18 grams fine gold (United States $.2025). The value of the new standard was maintained *de facto* rather than *de jure* by an open gold market and official exchange operations.

Following these reforms, European currencies gained the appearance of stability through increased reserves of gold and foreign exchange. Unfortunately, these reserves had been acquired largely at the expense of the United States economy. The United States, as we have noted, lost gold steadily after 1949. The effect of creating dollar credits both abroad and at home forced up the domestic price level, that is, lowered the purchasing power of the dollar, which by 1966 had dropped to nearly half its 1945 level.*

* As measured by the Bureau of Labor Statistics index of consumer prices. By 1975 the dollar had dropped another one-third in value. The

The same inflationary trend in prices—depreciation of currencies—was happening abroad in varying degrees, the effect of creating currency and credit on the mixed base of gold and United States dollar deposits. (Foreign-held dollar deposits, under the commitments assumed by the United States in organizing the International Monetary Fund, were convertible into gold at $35 an ounce, and hence under the gold-exchange standard were treated as equivalent to gold.)

The inevitable consequence was a growing but generally unperceived distrust of currencies in favor of gold. Despite the immense amount of new gold production, more and more was being taken by private buyers ("hoarding"), with central banks getting only the crumbs.* At one time in 1960 private buying bid the London bullion price up to $40 an ounce. Since the literal meaning of this was to degrade all so-called gold currencies, the event sent a shock wave through the board rooms of central banks all over the world.

In 1962 public demand for gold again pushed the open market price above statutory parity, and an international run on gold became imminent. The first overseas transmission of television pictures was one of President Kennedy dramatically assuring the world of United States determination to maintain the value of the dollar at $35 an ounce. At the same time, the principal central banks formed the International Gold Pool to provide gold to the market through the agency of the Bank of England, with quotas assigned to various central banks and the United States Treasury furnishing the moiety.

Public uneasiness continued, accompanied by gold buying and a massive outflow of gold from the United States stock. In 1965, to assure a gold supply in the market, Congress abolished the gold reserve requirement for Federal Reserve deposit liabilities. In 1967, Great Britain again devalued the pound, and, in 1968, under United States pressure, the "two tier" system was

---

steady depreciation of the dollar is concealed by periodically adjusting the index to a new base.

* Almost everywhere except in the two richest countries of the world —Great Britain and the United States—where private holding of gold money was forbidden.

evolved by which all central banks ceased selling gold in the market—in effect suspended convertibility—but maintained the parity of their currencies with each other by exchanging gold at the official rate. To sustain the fiction of official gold values of currencies, the United States undertook to sell gold at the official rate to other central banks that adhered to this agreement.

Further manifestation of both the corrosive inflation in prices and public dismay with what was happening to money was a spurting demand for Federal Reserve notes. From an increment of some $300 million annually, circulation now began to increase by $2 billion annually. The American public, so docile in monetary matters, was becoming mutely agitated over the increasing insecurity of their money and fearing perhaps another bank holiday, but unable, like the French and the Germans, to put away some gold coins as defense, were fortifying themselves with a feeble barricade of paper notes.

Since the circulation, by law, required a gold backing of 25 per cent, the obvious was done. In 1968, by act of Congress, the gold reserve against the note issue was summarily removed, thereby breaking the last fragile tie of the United States monetary system to gold.

To bolster the appearance of reality to money, however, a further fiction was introduced. Members of the International Monetary Fund were permitted to treat as prime reserves—that is, equivalent to gold—rights to a quota of certain currencies upon which they could draw to settle their international obligations to other central banks. These were known as Special Drawing Rights, and were defined as the equivalent of .888676 grams of fine gold (the gold content of the United States dollar at $35 an ounce). On August 15, 1971, the United States suspended all gold convertibility, and although Congress acted to revalue the dollar at $38 an ounce, and again to $42.22 in 1973, to all effect the United States dollar, which had become the standard of the world, was no more than a piece of paper. To justify this development the Treasury declared official policy henceforth to be that of demonetizing gold. On this question, however, Congress, which had the last word, hesitated to speak, and on the contrary, each legislative act devaluing the dollar continued to declare its new value in terms of so many grains of fine gold.

On December 31, 1974, by Congressional act, United States citizens were again permitted to own and trade in gold. Gold trading soon began at a level some four times the official price, as further confirmation of the collapse of the fractional reserve system of money and the incapacity of man to manage a fiat money system.

Such is the record which the school of monetary management has to offer in support of its theories.

V. The Phoenix—Silver

BEFORE concluding this account of money it is necessary to treat again the metal that for some three thousand years of historical record prior to 1871 had served mankind as the principal medium of commerce, substance of adornment, and repository of accumulated wealth. No understanding of money can be complete without a grasp of the historical service of silver in the commerce of mankind.

Although bronze, silver, and gold were being struck in uniform pieces, or coins, as early as the eighth century B.C., silver, until late modern times, was the most accepted and widely used in ordinary commerce. Gold was reserved as the tribute to emperors, the ransom of kings, the indemnity of war, the ornament of princes, the plating of idols. While gold is mentioned very early in the Genesis account of Creation, as found in one of the rivers of Paradise—"Pison, where there is gold: and the gold of that land is good"[1]—all early references to money payments were in terms of silver, measured by *shekels* of the Sanctuary standard of weight and fineness.

Until 1871, in modern times, Great Britain was the only major power that used gold as the standard of value. In that year Germany, flush with its victory over France and in possession of a 5-billion-franc indemnity, inaugurated the German Empire with the adoption of a gold coinage and standard. Following this lead the countries of Europe and North America rapidly demonetized silver as a standard of value, though retaining silver as a medium of payments in the form of subsidiary coinage. In 1900, with the shift of the Indian currency system to a gold-sterling base, most of Asia followed suit.

The consequence of these official actions was not to replace silver with gold in circulation but silver with paper and to throw vast quantities of demonetized silver upon the market. The depressing effect upon the substantial United States silver mining industry led to the enactment of various silver purchase laws, some of which we have already noted.[2]

In 1932 the price of silver reached the lowest in history, of twenty-five cents an ounce compared with the statutory value of $1.29 an ounce by which the dollar had been coined since 1837, and under the Silver Purchase Act of 1934 the Treasury was directed to purchase silver at its discretion until the monetary stock of silver was equal to one-fourth the total monetary stock of gold and silver.

Under this program and succeeding legislation the Treasury stock of silver reached a total of 2.43 billion ounces in 1942, of which about half was held in coined dollars or in bullion as reserve against silver certificates issued; the balance, representing the seignorage,* was held in the Treasury general fund.

The program was only partially successful so far as the mining interest was concerned, for silver production went into a secular decline. By 1960 there was only a handful of silver mines in operation, silver production was less than two-thirds of the production at the beginning of the century and nearly two-thirds of that production came as a by-product of the smelting of copper, lead, and zinc ores. Prices had recovered to ninety-one cents an ounce by 1960, but by comparison with prices for other non-ferrous metals in 1900 and 1960, or in consideration of the historical relationship with gold, silver was a cheap metal.

Unlooked for consequences of the demonetization of silver and the United States silver purchase program were the disappearance of a visible silver supply throughout the world and a

* That is, the profit between the price paid for the silver and its monetized value of $1.29 an ounce.

United States monopoly of the available stocks. The importance of this monopoly became apparent in two world wars, but its actual and potential significance was ignored among Treasury and central bank officials, monetary economists, and the silver manufacturing interest.

                                                      ✎§ §✍

When World War I broke out, the British Government discovered that the people of its Indian empire were increasingly suspicious of the paper money secured by sterling credits in London and demanded good silver in exchange for their goods and services. As Britain had demonetized silver, it had insufficient supply and appealed to the United States. Under the Pittman Act, 200 million ounces were made available by melting down silver dollars held by the Treasury.

Hardly had the war ended when this salutary lesson in monetary economics was forgotten. In fact, during the following decade, under the influence of prevailing monetary concepts, various American "money doctors" went about the world prescribing central banks on the model of the Federal Reserve System, and recommending the demonetization of silver. By the time World War II broke out, the only power in the world employing silver as an official element of its monetary system was the United States and the only paper money anywhere in the world fully covered by the metal it purported to represent was the United States silver certificate.*

With the renewal of war in 1939, a demand again arose in Asia for silver. Despite decades of acquaintance with paper money, and despite official efforts to wean the populations from silver coin, the masses of working people rebelled against paper

---

* It is arguable of course that the silver certificate was equally fiat money since the silver behind the certificate was valued at $1.29 an ounce, whereas the market price since 1920 had never exceeded 91 cents an ounce. However, since Federal Reserve notes were backed only by 25 per cent gold, silver certificates backed by silver worth anything above 35 cents an ounce in the market were somewhat more reliable, particularly as redemption of the certificates in the metal was never suspended, whereas the holder of a Federal Reserve note could only whistle for his gold.

money. Again the United States Treasury vaults were opened, and through the mechanics of the Lend-Lease Act, 410 million ounces of silver were shipped to Asia and the South Seas to maintain confidence and allay unrest.

~§ §~

What the money managers had overlooked is that while silver might be dethroned as a medium of payment or standard of reckoning, it retained a vast importance in Asia as a store of value. Among these poverty stricken millions, a piece of honest silver saved from the day's or week's earnings was the beginning of financial security, independence, and contentment. When the colonial and other sovereignties began to substitute paper money and debased silver for good silver coinage they opened the flood gates to political discontent and revolution.

The experience of Iran is of interest. In 1294 A.D., Kai Khatu, the Mongol ruler of Persia, on the advice of his vizier and in imitation of his brother monarch, Kublai Khan in China, introduced paper money into his realm. This action aroused such resentment among the merchants that a riot ensued. The vizier was seized by the mob, torn to pieces, and thrown to the dogs. The edict establishing paper money was withdrawn and no Persian monarch until the twentieth century dared impose paper money upon his subjects.[3]

The standard of value and the common medium of exchange continued to be silver of high purity. Paper money was an alien device until 1931, when the modern-minded Reza Shah introduced a national bank of issue and gradually withdrew and melted down the silver coinage in circulation.

It is of interest to record that Reza Shah lost his throne just ten years later, and while the one event was not the cause of the other, it nevertheless facilitated the execution of the other.

When the Soviet and British governments concerted in 1941 on the occupation of Iran, the Shah's forces were able to offer only feeble resistance, and the Shah was compelled to abdicate. The two powers, however, affirmed the juridical independence of the country and forswore any interference with the internal administration. By these declarations they excluded the prerogative of a conqueror, of levying taxes, and they were consequently compelled to find means of financing their occupation.

Twenty years earlier, during World War I, when Great Britain sent an expeditionary force into Persia, the unfamiliarity of the people with notes and exchange compelled the commander to carry quantities of British gold sovereigns; with these, however, he had been able to buy supplies, recruit workers to clear the passes of snow, and even to organize a guerrilla force.[4]

Now, a simpler and less expensive procedure was available. It was to set the printing presses to rolling. The occupying powers coerced the supine Iranian government into financial agreements by which the Iranian national bank was compelled to provide unlimited quantities of *rials* in exchange for sterling and dollar exchange at a fixed rate. Subsequently the British government agreed to convert 40 per cent of the sterling credits into gold at the official parity, stipulating, however, that the gold be kept either in Canada or South Africa.

To the consternation of the occupying authorities, the *rial,* which was theoretically the most heavily insured currency in the world, began a precipitate depreciation that carried with it— since they were tied by the exchange agreement—the pound sterling and the United States dollar.* Chaos spread in the market, goods disappeared into hoarding, including precious wheat and copper, and famine gnawed at the country.

⊷ ৡৈ

Within the year conditions had grown so beyond the feeble powers of the government that it was counseled to seek fiscal advisers from abroad, and among these the author was appointed Treasurer General by action of the Iranian Parliament. At the time of his arrival, in January, 1943, such was the disruption of the markets and the depreciation of the currency that an automobile tire that normally sold for $40 cost $700 in the bazaar.

The author had some familiarity with the country from resi-

---

* Also the ruble, but the ruble had no international value in any case, and the Soviet government had guaranteed in sterling and dollars its drawings of *rials.*

dence twenty years earlier, when he served as a teacher in northern Iran and relief worker in the Soviet Caucasus. He had observed the relative economic stability of the Iranian villages despite the breakdown of political authority and an almost non-existent administration, and for contrast the chaos and prostration of the cities of the Caucasus, ruthlessly governed by an all-powerful Communist dictatorship. In the one region, trade and livelihood persisted with the aid of a plentiful supply of good silver coinage; in the other such anemic trade as one could see was done by means of a depreciated paper currency so worthless that it often went by weight—a bundle of notes in one scale, a loaf of bread in the other.

Persuaded that only with the precious metals freely available as a medium of payment and store of value would the hoards of grain and copper be released and prices stabilized, he proposed that the minting of silver *rials* be resumed. As the dies had been broken and the mint had fallen into disrepair, this idea had to be abandoned.

He thereupon recommended that instead of keeping the gold locked up it be put to work to discharge its historic functions. He proposed that the occupying powers finance their costs with gold instead of sterling and dollar exchange, and that gold be sold directly in the market, to relieve the strain on the printing press. Not only would the process stop the expansion of the note issue, but it would reduce the costs of occupation, since the bazaar price of gold was equivalent to $70 to $80 an ounce, as against the $35 an ounce at which dollars and pounds were being sold to the Iranian national bank for *rials*. Importantly, hoarders would have a more effective means of storing their wealth than wheat and copper, and these commodities would return to the market.

The recommendation was adopted and the United States Treasury offered to provide the gold. As it was prohibited by law from exporting coin, it shipped instead quantities of gold bars, and these were put on sale along with gold of various coinages held by the Iranian national bank. The success of the operation was limited by the fact that the market for gold bars, since they were expensive, was restricted; nevertheless, it proved sufficiently effective and it was extended throughout the Middle East War Theatre.

و§ §و

Similar testimony to the importance of good silver money in the maintenance of economic and political stability among the vast populations of Asia and Africa is afforded by John Leighton Stuart, for over forty years a missionary in China and ambassador to China during the Nationalist-Communist war of 1946–1949. The United States Government was supporting the Nationalists with arms, munitions, and gold, but the authorities were keeping the gold impounded in Taiwan, and issuing against it notes termed *Gold Yuan*. In his recollection of these events Stuart commented:

"More crucial than strategy were silver coins with which to pay the troops. They did not want Gold Yuan, but four silver dollars per month apiece—two U.S. dollars—or even two of these would sustain their morale. Otherwise, Communist agents could buy them off with hard money or even promises. The government had nearly 300 million U.S. dollars in gold and silver bullion, but most of this was safely in Taiwan."[5]

Two developments following World War II served to restore the question to public importance. The first was an immense expansion in the consumption of silver in industry. Since the invention of photography and the motion picture, large quantities of silver were being consumed in photographic silver. Technology now found new uses for which silver was particularly adapted—in brazing alloys in a vast range of appliances, for electrical contacts, in ceramics for the electronics industry, for electrical storage batteries, as a catalyst in the chemical industry, and for water sterilization. By 1960 industrial consumption in the United States required 100 million ounces annually, about three times United States mine production, while consumption elsewhere took an equal amount.

In addition, the development of coin vending machines and the parking meter created a new demand for subsidiary coinage. Silver for this purpose began to take from 40 to 50 million ounces annually in the United States. Abroad, governments were discovering that only the precious metals were adequate to the dignity of sovereignty and began to replace their small denomination paper notes and base metal coinage with silver. Including coinage, total free world consumption of silver began to exceed 300 million ounces annually, against world production of around 225 million ounces.

This difference between consumption and mine production was met largely from the seigniorage (general fund) silver held by the United States Treasury. Under the Act of 1946, the Treasury was permitted to sell this silver at not less than 90½ cents an ounce, and increasing amounts began to flow into the market. By 1961 the stock, which had amounted to nearly 1¼ billion ounces in 1942, had been reduced to around 22 million ounces, and on recommendation of the Treasury the President, on November 28, 1961, ordered suspension of further sales at 90½ cents. Thereafter Treasury silver was available to the market only by redemption of silver certificates. Market prices moved upward and in July, 1963, reached $1.31 an ounce at which price it was profitable to melt down silver dollars.

Congress now took the historic step of demonetizing silver. The Silver Purchase acts were repealed, and the free silver market was restored by repeal of the prohibitive Transactions tax.[6] The only silver money, apart from subsidiary silver coinage, was that represented by silver certificates, and as the market was now at the mint price the amount of these certificates continually diminished as notes were presented for redemption in exchange for silver bullion.[7]

Meantime a voracious demand developed for small silver, which was coined at $1.38+ per ounce, and this demand was added to by the minting of commemorative half dollars with the image of the assassinated President Kennedy. These disappeared as rapidly as they came from the mint. In 1964 coinage took over 200 million ounces of silver, and in 1965 over 320 million ounces. These figures compare with 56 million ounces in 1961. Congress now, under pressure from the Treasury, abolished silver coinage, except for a debased half dollar containing only 40 per cent silver, but fraudulently deceptive by means of a cladding of 80 per cent silver hiding a core consisting mainly of copper.[8] As a substitute that would have the electrical properties needed to activate coin vending machines (that were made to work with silver) hermaphroditic "sandwich" dimes and quarters were devised, made of a layer of copper between layers of nickel-copper alloy.

The new coinage resulted in reduced consumption of silver in coinage but did not allay the public demand for the metal, which now fed upon the silver reserve. By presenting certificates for redemption the public drew down the Treasury stock from 1.9 billion ounces at the beginning of 1964 to 703 million ounces at the end of 1966, and by 1970 the Treasury supply was substantially exhausted, save for 165 million ounces set aside as a strategic reserve.

There remained, however, a stock of some $484 million silver dollars in circulation, profitable to melt at above $1.29 an ounce, and some $2 billion subsidiary silver, profitable to melt at above $1.38 an ounce. These supplies began to go into the pot or the mattress, and in 1967 the open market breached the mint parities and rose to $1.87 in New York. In 1970 the Treasury, its reserves exhausted, ceased all silver mintage, and thus ended the last vestige of precious metal coinage in the United States.

VI. Retrospect

THE evidence of modern history confirms the inability of mankind to maintain a standard of value and means of payment based upon a combination of gold and silver. Bimetallism proved unworkable. Whether a monetary system based upon one of the metals could survive in the complexities of modern commerce is still to be discovered, for the gold standard, that became general after 1871, was soon degraded to a gold-debt standard, the stability of which was dependent upon the wisdom of the money managers. The incapacity of the money managers is also evident.

Is it possible to return to a metallic money? The principal

argument offered to the contrary is the scarcity of gold, but a substance of which some 45 per cent or more of the total known production is still in existence can hardly be called scarce. It is scarce only in regard to the amount of currency related to gold at a given ratio of value. An appropriate revaluation of the price of gold would provide abundance of the metal for monetary use. A mechanism by which such revaluation of the dollar could be undertaken without a convulsion of the debt structure was proposed in the 1934 edition of this work. Other methods are currently under discussion; the task is not insurmountable; the details need not detain us here.

What is more to the point is the capacity of mankind, and more specifically the people of the United States, to exercise the restraint necessary for the maintenance of a monetary system linked to a precious metal, the total quantity of which is relatively stable. It is the moral dimension of the money problem with which we must deal.

Money, first of all, is a measure—a common and accepted standard of value for current transactions and future payments.* The requirements of a measure were given by Moses to the children of Israel three thousand and more years ago, and the requirements are imbedded in the moral structure of Western culture: "Just weights, just balances, a just ephah, and a just hin, shall ye have: I am the Lord your God."[1]

It was in acknowledgment of this principle that President Roosevelt declared to the World Monetary and Economic Conference in London in 1933, that "the U.S. objective would be that of giving currencies a continuing purchasing power that does not vary greatly in terms of commodities and need of modern civilization" and added, "The U.S. seeks the kind of dollar which a generation hence will have the same purchasing and debt paying power as the dollar value we hope to attain in the near future."

We pass over what has happened to the purchasing power of the dollar in the years since. Despite this hopeful promise, the

---

* Most authorities also say that it must have intrinsic value, and serve as a store of value, and argue the relative indestructibility of gold for this purpose.

seeds of inflation had already taken root in the fertile soil of the Federal Reserve System. In 1921 the board had adopted a major policy decision, that a principal function of the System was to maintain a stable price level. Euphemistically reasonable, this meant that the maintenance of a sound currency through adequate reserves of gold was no longer the substance and object of monetary management. Since the whole purpose of industrial technology is to make goods more abundant, hence cheaper, the effect of the policy was to direct the money system in the interest of creditors rather than debtors, producers rather than consumers.

We have in previous sections surveyed the record of misuse of the monetary power to finance government deficits and various kinds of speculation. We may now note the other major divergence from correct monetary principle. The Employment Act of 1946 declared public policy to promote conditions of useful employment for all, and the monetary system has since been manipulated to this end, particularly by forcing Federal Reserve credit into the commercial banking system regardless of the state of commercial need and indifferent to the integrity of the standard.

Growing fascination by economists and government administrators with state planning, as practiced by soviet-style governments, led in 1975 to the introduction by two leading senators of a bill to provide for a state planning board headed by an official of cabinet status. A plan without a program is a mere intellectual exercise: materials and human resources must be moved about in conformity with the plan. In a country not yet a police state the means to the end is money. Since taxes are onerous, the easiest way to produce money is by the printing press. Abetting this procedure is a school of economists who advocate a steady, mathematical increase in the supply regardless of the reserves to maintain its integrity.

&§ §&

The principal theoretical argument of the monetarists—as they are called—is not a defense, but an attack. The use of gold

—since the Renaissance, the ultimate standard of value—is derided as a relic of barbarism, and the mining of gold, only to store it in Fort Knox, as arrant folly. Gold has but limited commercial or industrial use, we are told, and hence no meaning in a monetary system.

It should be elementary, of course, that if gold has no importance for the individual, it has little monetary importance to government, and can be dismissed in monetary discussion. Gold reserves in central banks would be as useful as a warehouse of pork in Saudi Arabia. It is evident, however, that despite the protestations of theorists, gold remains of immense importance to individuals, and so long as it does it will be useful as money.

The reason for this importance is not hard to discover: it lies in the corruptibility of governments and the uncertainty of personal security. Despite the spreading influence throughout the world of the Prince of Peace, despite all the paraphernalia of the United Nations and networks of treaties and alliances, despite the polarization of influence between two great powers, each avoiding a confrontation, the possibility of war, or at least of political turmoil, continues to enter into the considerations of the prudent. With them, as with the millions who remember, or who have witnessed or experienced, the devastation of war, the disruptions of trade and industry, the uprooting of populations, a stock of the precious metals, however small, is a shield, however feeble, against the shocks of fortune.*

◄§ §►

Whatever may be the arguments for or against a metallic money, the subject is not closed until we consider the alternatives. In the absence of metal, the substance of money is no more than debt, the fragile promises of men and the hopes upon which they are based. A consideration of man and his money cannot be complete without some reference to the phenomenon of debt in the modern world.

* Recent examples are the influx of refugees from Cuba and from Southeast Asia, and the flight of Portuguese from Angola.

VII. The Incubus of Debt

As debt is the essence of modern money, so the problem of money is the problem of coping with debt. Debt is not only a system of money and financial status, but an attitude of mind. It is also a canker which is gnawing deep into the vitals of society. With the monetary system as the source of infection, it has spread through the veins of economic enterprise, penetrating with its poison every organ of production and distribution. Indeed, so imbedded has the idea of debt become in the conception and attitudes of people, so coated over with the nacre of terminology—debt is no longer "debt" but "credit," "personal finance," "deferred payments," "securities," and the like—that the nation has insensibly saddled itself with a mountain of monetary obligations that may require a revolution to remove.

Before pursuing further the implications of the money-debt system, let us examine the extent of debt. The researches of the Twentieth Century Fund, completed in 1933, give us a summary of the debt structure of this country at that now distant period:

In 1913–1914, total long-term debt amounted to thirty-eight billion dollars, or equivalent to 19.7 per cent of the dollar estimate of national wealth ($192,000,000,000) and the debt service amounted to $2,143,000,000, or a 6 per cent charge upon the national income ($36,000,000,000). In 1921, the post-war depression year, total long-term debt amounted to seventy-five billion dollars, or 23.4 per cent of the national wealth ($321,000,000,000) and debt service consumed 7 per cent of the national income ($66,000,000,000). At the height of prosperity, in 1929, the long-term debt amounted to 126 billion dollars, or 32.7 per cent of the national wealth ($385,000,000,000) and debt service consumed 9 per cent of the national income ($85,000,000,000). The depression that set in at the close of 1929 reduced the monetary value of the national wealth to $300,000,000,000 in 1931–1932, but the long-term debt increased to 134 billion dollars, or 44.7 per cent of the national wealth, and debt service consumed 19.8 per cent of the reduced national income ($40,000,000,000).

In addition to the long-term debt, there was a steadily increasing amount of short-term debt, which rose from fifty-one billion dollars at the end of 1913 to 150 billion dollars at the end of 1929, and 103 billion dollars at the end of 1932. At the end of 1932, therefore, the combined total of short- and long-term debt was 237 billion dollars, against an estimated national wealth of 300 billion dollars.[1]

By 1970, total assets of the United States, as estimated by the Federal Reserve Board in the Flow of Funds Accounts, amounted to $4,076 billion, while total debt had risen to $3,208 billion, or to nearly 80 per cent of assets, while the debt service, at the interest rates occasioned by the rising tide of inflation must be calculated at around $225 billion a year, or 23 per cent of national income.*

More disturbing than these figures are the data for personal debt, or "consumer credit," fostered by charge accounts and installment buying. Department of Commerce compilations report this form of debt has risen from $5.7 billion at the end of World War II (1945) to $127 billion 25 years later, a multiplication of twenty-two times. A more recent phenomenon is the growth of credit and finance, the outstanding balances of which increased in the three years 1967 to 1970 from $828 million to over $3 billion.[2]

Attempts to portray the debt burden statistically are, however, apt to be misleading. Debt is also credit; bonds in the hands of investors constitute wealth to them and the interest therefrom, income. Bonds, evidences of long-term debt, may be used as security, or collateral, to obtain short-term loans; the debts thus overlap and multiply. Obviously, also, a monetary conception of national wealth is deceptive. Wealth is tangible goods and property; the dollar expression is merely the market value. The reduction of eighty-five billion dollars in estimated national wealth between 1929 and 1933 did not mean any destruction of

* Figures are for gross debt, which includes certain duplicating governmental and corporate debt (chain of debt). Net debt in 1970 is estimated by the Dept. of Commerce at $1,844 billion, an increase from $125 billion in 1932 and $490 billion in 1950.

actual wealth, except in those cases of disintegration and destruction caused by the malfunctioning of the money mechanism
—properties sold under foreclosure and passing into the hands
of less capable management, factories dismantled and farms
abandoned because they did not earn interest and taxes, conscious restriction of productive activity in order to create an
artificial scarcity and thereby raise prices, and such like.

The real effect of the money debt system can perhaps be more
fully appreciated from the theoretical approach. The fundamental opposition of interest growth and natural growth was
argued by Lawrence Dennis in a 1932[3] work, and analyzed
statistically by Bassett Jones.[4]

To restate their thesis, the burden of debt service constantly
tends to overreach the capacity of industry to support it, and
the pressure of interest upon income produces the recurrent
cataclysms of depression, default and bankruptcy. Debt tends
to mount at a compound interest rate. Investors in savings banks,
and investors who follow the policy of diversifying risks, operate
upon this principle: a dollar compounded at 3 per cent annually
is doubled in twenty-four years; at 6 per cent, in twelve years.
So long as the institution of debt is stable, the law is inexorable.
"Capitalism," as Stuart Chase phrased it, "operates to a definite
rhythm, the rhythm being a curve of development which substantially takes the form of a 3 to 5 per cent compound interest
graph—varying at different times and in different countries."[5]

On the other hand, the physical growth of wealth and economic activity necessary to support the interest on debt cannot
proceed at any compound interest rate beyond certain definite
limits. Neither the laws of physics nor of biology permit an indefinite growth of physical goods or population. Although physical growth has expanded at an inordinate rate in this country,
the process may now be slowing up. Obviously therefore, either
the interest rate must steadily decline until it approaches zero,
in order to bring the growth of debt to correspond with the
growth of physical wealth and activity, or, as Dennis argued,
there must occur periodical collapses of the debt structure in
order to bring it within a proper relationship to wealth. We
appear, in this eighth decade of the twentieth century, to be

going through one of these periodical collapses of the debt bubble.

ন্ট ঈৈ

It is not necessary to discuss, in such a study as this, the social and moral effects of debt upon society. Materialism, lack of restraint, mania for speculation, are characteristics of modern life all too prevalent to allow complacency over the wholesomeness of the age. These qualities are certainly stimulated by the ease of going into debt. On the other hand, the necessity for repayment of debt, especially when times are hard, induces a loss of independence, unrest, discontent, and political and social unsettlement.

ন্ট ঈৈ

There is, however, one phase of the debt problem which has generally been overlooked and to which attention must be called. That is the fact that our system of money based on debt has destroyed one of the principal functions of money—that of serving as a store of value. At the same time that it has aggravated the business cycle, by encouraging speculation, it has made it almost impossible to build up reserves against the day of inevitable collapse. Under our system of money, it is well nigh hopeless for the average man to save against a rainy day. For savings, under our scheme, are not reserves; they are used by the banking system, they are spent in the capital markets, and when they are needed, they are discovered to be immobilized, to be invested in bonds and loans the value of which is dependent upon a continuation of prosperity.

The effects of this process are made clearer by analogy to a householder whose barn is destroyed in a storm. If he has a golden guinea saved away, he may rebuild his barn. But under the system of deposit money, in which money is representative not of gold, but of wealth, or debt, the barn is also his money, and when it is gone, the money is gone. Stated more definitely, when national calamity strikes—be it the result of economic maladjustments, physical disaster, or war—purchasing power, if money is sound and substantial, is always available for rebuilding, for taking up market surpluses, for discharging debt.

But deposit money floats with the tide. Being based upon debt, it becomes worthless when any considerable body of bank customers are no longer able to discharge their obligations. The bank fails, carrying with it the purchasing power of the community, especially that portion of the community which has husbanded its resources and has converted them into the promises to pay of the bank, as deposits. With the whole purchasing power of the community destroyed there is no one left able to come to the rescue. Properties and commodities are thrown frantically on the market in the hope of finding a buyer, until there is a glut for which there is no effective demand; prices are forced lower and lower to meet the shrunken buying power, and the whole structure of society topples in ruins.

To examine the problem more concretely: in 1935 the Social Security System was set up by which employers and employees were to pay into a reserve against old age requirements. For the next 40 years the reserve continued to grow, invested in United States securities, as payments to annuitants were less than contributions to the Fund. By 1974 the reserve amounted to $45 billion, but the actuarial realities overtook the System, which was now faced with the necessity of drawing upon its reserves. With a federal budget deficit of $44 billion, how could the System liquidate its Treasury securities on the market to acquire cash except by crowding all other borrowers from the capital market and depriving industry and trade of funds necessary to carry on their functions?

❧ ☙

The reverse of debt is credit—to believe. The inherent defect of a monetary system based upon debt is that it rests upon the sands of confidence. The sands run out, and the whole structure topples.

Runs occur on the soundest banks, as on the weakest, and as for the whole system, whether it is supported by nothing but confidence, or whether only the last dollar outstanding is so supported, the whole structure is shaken by every wind of popular apprehension.

❧ ☙

Inescapably we are brought to the conclusion that our money system will not achieve the stability and strength necessary to enable it to support the vast and complicated structure of modern economy until the moral dimension of the question is faced. Whether, as a practical matter, a money system is based on debt, as at present, upon the good faith and credit of the sovereignty creating it, or whether money should be intrinsic, a metallic coinage or a metallic reserve freely available to note holders, the ultimate answer is a moral response. In the words of a resolution adopted by the Institute for Monetary Research, Inc.,

"The essence of the money problem is moral more than technical—that as money is the standard of economic value and measure of commerce the manipulation of money is evil, whether in the interest of creditors or debtors, industry or labor, producers or consumers, government or taxpayers; that the integrity of money should be maintained by clearly defined content and composition, and by adherence to the definition."

BIBLIOGRAPHY

Book I

H. J. Davenport, *Economics of Enterprise*. New York, 1913.

Thorstein Veblen, *The Vested Interests*. New York, 1920.

————, *The Theory of Business Enterprise*. New York, 1910.

R. H. Tawney, *The Acquisitive Society*. New York, 1920.

Book II

Alexander Del Mar, *History of Money in Ancient Countries*. London, 1885.

A. R. Burns, *Money and Monetary Policy in Early Times*. New York, 1927.

Jules Toutain, *Economic Life of the Ancient World* (translated by M. R. Dobie). New York, 1930.

William Kemp, *Precious Metals as Money*. London, 1923.

Ivan M. Linforth, *Solon the Athenian*. University of California Press, 1919.

Gustave Glotz, *Ancient Greece at Work* (*Le Travail dans la Grèce Ancienne*). New York, 1926.

George Grote, *Greece*, chap. xi. London, 1846–1856.

Kathleen Freeman, *Work and Life of Solon*. London, 1926.

Augustus Boeckh, *Public Economy of the Athenians* (translated by Anthony Lamb). London, 1857.

William Ridgway, *The Origin of Metallic Currency and Weight Standards*. Cambridge, 1892.

Ernest Babelon, *Les Origines de la Monnaie*. Paris, 1897.

Charles Theodore Seltman, *Athens: Its History and Coinage befor the Persian Invasion*. Cambridge, 1924.

William Linn Westermann, "Warehousing and Trapezite Banking in Antiquity," *Journal of Economic and Business History*, III (1930), 30–54.

Aristotle, *Politics*, Book V.

Plutarch, *Solon, Theseus*.

Strabo, *Geography*, Books VI, VII.

Polybius, Book VIII.

Herodotus, Book I.

Pliny, *Natural History*, XXXIII.

Karl Helfferich, *Money* (translated by Louis Infield). New York, 1927, 2 vols.

Carl Knies, *Geld und Kredit*, Vol. I of *Das Geld*. Berlin, 1888.

Benjamin M. Anderson, Jr., *The Value of Money*. New York, 1926.

Irving Fisher, *Purchasing Power of Money*. New York, 1920.

Francis A. Walker, *Money*. New York, 1891.

————, *Money and Its Relation to Trade and Industry*. New York, 1891.

Horace White, *Money and Banking*. New York, 1895.

Hartley Withers, *The Meaning of Money*. London, 1909.

Henry Dunning MacLeod, *The Theory and Practice of Banking*. London, 1923 (new impression).

W. T. Foster and W. Catchings, *Money*. Boston, 1903.

W. S. Jevons, *Money and the Mechanism of Exchange*. London, 1893.

C. F. Dunbar, *The Theory and History of Banking*. New York, 1922.

Book III

Theodore Mommsen, *History of Rome* (English translation by Rev. Wm. P. Dickson). London, 1868.

————, *Histoire de la Monnaie Romaine* (translated by Louis C. P. Casimir, duc de Blacas). Paris, 1865.

Léon Homo, *L'Empire Romain*. Paris, 1925.

Ferdinand Lot, *End of the Ancient World*. New York, 1931.

Jules Toutain, *Economic Life of the Ancient World*. New York, 1930.

A. R. Burns, *Money and Monetary Policy in Early Times*. New York, 1927.

Alexander Del Mar, *History of Money in Ancient Countries*. London, 1885.

————, *Money and Civilization*. London, 1886.

W. W. Carlile, *Evolution of Modern Money*. New York, 1901.

George Finlay, "Roman and Byzantine Money," in his *History of Greece*, Appendix, Vol. I. Oxford, 1877.

François Lenormant, *La Monnaie dans l'Antiquité*. Paris, 1878. 3 vols.

Frank F. Abbot, *The Common People of Ancient Rome*. New York, 1911.

Book IV

A. A. Vasilev, *History of the Byzantine Empire* (translated by

Mrs. S. Ragozin). University of Wisconsin Studies. Madison, 1928.

Charles Diehl, *History of the Byzantine Empire* (translated by Geo. B. Ives). Princeton, 1925.

Theodore Mommsen, *Histoire de la Monnaie Romaine*. (translated by Le duc de Blacas). Paris, 1873.

Alexander Del Mar, *History of Monetary Systems*. New York, 1903.

————, *Money and Civilization.*

————, *History of Money in Ancient Countries.*

Sewell, "Roman Coins in India," *Journal of Asiatic Society*, Vol. XXXVI. London, 1904.

Ernest Nys, *Researches in the History of Economics* (translated by N. F. and A. R. Dryhurst). London, 1899.

George Finlay, *History of Greece from its Conquest by the Romans to the Present Time*. Oxford, 1877.

J. B. Bury, *A History of the Later Roman Empire, from Arcadius to Irene*. London, 1889.

————, *History of Eastern Roman Empire from Fall of Irene to Ascension of Basil I* (A.D. *802–867*). London, 1912.

————, *The Imperial Administrative System in the Ninth Century*. London, 1910.

Cambridge Medieval History, Vol. II, chap. iii, "Roman Law," by H. J. Roby. London, 1926.

Robert Byron, *The Byzantine Achievement*. London, 1924.

Book V

Alexander Del Mar, *Money and Civilization.*

————, *History of Precious Metals*. New York, 1902.

Ernest Nys, *Researches in the History of Economics.*

W. A. Shaw, *History of Currency, 1252–1894*. London, 1896.

Richard Ehrenberg, *Capital and Finance in the Age of the Renaissance* (translated by H. M. Lucas). London, 1928.

R. H. Tawney, *Religion and the Rise of Capitalism*. London, 1926.

P. Boissonade, *Life and Work in Medieval Europe* (translated by Eileen Power). New York, 1927.

W. Cunningham, *Western Civilization in its Economic Aspects*. London, 1924.

George Unwin, *Finance and Trade under Edward III*. London, 1918.

Le Vicomte G. D'Avenel, *Histoire économique de la Propriété, des Salaires, des Denrées, etc., 1200–1800*. Paris, 1894.

Book VI

Franklin W. Ryan, *Usury and Usury Laws*. New York, 1924.

R. H. Tawney, *Religion and the Rise of Capitalism*. London, 1926.

Ernest Nys, *Researches in the History of Economics*.

J. E. Thorold Rogers, *Economic Interpretation of History*. London, 1888.

A. E. Monroe, *Monetary Theory before Adam Smith*. Cambridge (Massachusetts), 1923.

Clive Day, *History of Commerce*. London, 1907, 1917.

J. W. Horrocks, *A Short History of Mercantilism*. New York, 1925.

W. Cunningham, *Western Civilization in its Economic Aspects*.

Richard Ehrenberg, *Capital and Finance in the Age of the Renaissance*.

Thomas Wilson, *A Discourse upon Usury* (edited by R. H. Tawney). London, 1925.

Jacob Strieder, *Jacob Fugger the Rich* (translated by Mildred L. Hartsough). New York, 1931.

Henri Sée, *Les Origines du Capitalisme moderne*. Paris, 1926. Translated into English as *Modern Capitalism* by Homer B. Vanderblue. New York, 1928.

John A. Hobson, *The Evolution of Modern Capitalism*. London, 1906.

Abbot Payson Usher, "Deposit Banking in Barcelona," *Journal of Economics and Business History*, Vol. IV (1934), No. 1.

———, "Origins of Banking," *Economic History Review*, Vol. IV (1934), No. 4.

C. F. Dunbar, "The Bank of Venice," *Quarterly Journal of Economics*, VI, (1892), 308–335.

Book VII

Thomas Francis Carter, *Invention of Printing in China and Its Spread Westward*. New York, 1925.

W. Vissering, *On Chinese Currency*. Leiden, 1877.

W. A. Shaw, *Theory and Principles of Central Banking*. London, 1930.

Horace White, *Money and Banking*. New York, 1895.

Albert Despaux, *L'Inflation dans l'Histoire*. Paris, 1922.

Le Duc de Saint Simon, *Memoires*. (Universal Classics Library.)

John Law, *Money and Trade Considered*. Edinburgh, 1705.

Georges Oudard, *The Amazing Life of John Law* (*La Très Curi-*

euse Vie de Law), translation by G. E. C. Massé. New York, 1928.
    Adolphe Thiers, *John Law and the Mississippi Bubble* (*Law et son système des finances*). Paris, 1826. (American translation, 1859.)
    E. Levasseur, *Recherches historiques sur le système de Law.* Paris, 1854.
    James Breck Perkins, *France under the Regency.* New York, 1892.
    Viscount Erleigh, *The South Sea Bubble.* New York, 1933.
    R. H. Mottram, *History of Financial Speculation.* London, 1929.
    Charles Mackay, *Extraordinary Popular Delusions and the Madness of Crowds.* 1841. (Reprinted, Boston, 1932.)
    Alexander Del Mar, *Money and Civilization.*
    ———, *History of Monetary Systems.*

Book VIII
    W. A. Shaw, *History of Currency, 1252–1894.*
    Alexander Del Mar, *History of Monetary Systems.*
    ———, *Money and Civilization.*
    ———, *History of the Precious Metals.*
    ———, *Barbara Villers.* New York, 1899.
    Karl Helfferich, *Money* (*Das Geld*).
    J. Laurence Laughlin, *History of Bimetallism in the United States.* New York, 1885, 1896.
    H. Parker Willis, *A History of the Latin Monetary Union.* University of Chicago Press, 1901.

Book IX
    William B. Weeden, *Indian Money as a Factor in New England Civilization.* Johns Hopkins University Studies in Historical and Political Science, Second Series, VIII–IX. Baltimore, 1884.
    W. Z. Ripley, *Financial History of Virginia.* Studies in History, Economics and Public Law, edited by the University Faculty of Political Science of Columbia College. New York, 1893.
    C. P. Gould, *Money and Transportation in Maryland* (*1720–1765*). Johns Hopkins University Studies in Historical and Political Science, Thirty-Third Series. Baltimore, 1915.
    John Thomas Holdsworth and Davis R. Dewey, *The First and Second Banks of the United States.* Publications of the National Monetary Commission. Washington, 1910.
    W. A. Shaw, *Theory and Principles of Central Banking.*
    Charles A. Conant, *A History of Modern Banks of Issue.* New York, 1896, 1902, 1927.

Noble Foster Hoggson, *Epochs in American Banking*. New York, 1929.

H. Parker Willis and B. H. Beckhart, *Foreign Banking Systems*. New York, 1929.

J. E. Thorold Rogers, *First Nine Years of the Bank of England*. Oxford, 1887.

A. Andréadès, *History of the Bank of England, 1640 to 1903*. London, 1924.

Harry E. Miller, *Banking Theories in the United States Before 1860*. Cambridge (Massachusetts), 1927.

Margaret B. Myers, *The New York Money Market*, Vol. I, *Origins and Development*. New York, 1931.

Walter Bagehot, *Lombard Street*. London, 14th ed. 1914; reprinted 1924.

Robbert E. Chaddock, *The Safety Fund Banking System in New York, 1829–1866*. Publications of the National Monetary Commission. Washington, 1910.

Davis R. Dewey, *State Banking Before the Civil War*. Publications of the National Monetary Commission. Washington, 1910.

A. Barton Hepburn, *History of Currency in the United States*. New York, 1924.

Leland Hamilton Jenks, *The Migration of British Capital to 1875*. New York, 1927.

Arthur Kemp, *The Legal Qualities of Money*. New York, 1956.

Nelson W. Aldrich, *Interviews on the Banking and Currency Systems of England, Scotland, France, Germany, Switzerland and Italy*. Publications of the National Monetary Commission. Washington, 1910.

Alexander Hamilton, *Papers on Public Credit, Commerce and Finance*, edited by Samuel McKee, Jr. New York, 1934.

Book X

O. M. W. Sprague, *History of Crises Under the National Banking System*. Publications of the National Monetary Commission. Washington, 1910.

Frank A. Vanderlip, *Tomorrow's Money*. New York, 1934.

David Kinley, *The Use of Credit Instruments in Payments in the United States*. Publications of the National Monetary Commission. Washington, 1910.

Dickson H. Leavens, *Silver Money*. Bloomington, Indiana, 1939.

Harold G. Moulton, *Principles of Money and Banking*. Chicago, 1916.

W. Jett Lauck, *The Causes of the Panic of 1893*. Boston and New York, 1907.

Federal Reserve Board, *Report of the Committee on Member Bank Reserves of the Federal Reserve System*. Washington, 1931.

Paul M. Warburg, *The Federal Reserve System: Its Origin and Growth*. New York, 1930.

H. Parker Willis, *The Federal Reserve System*. New York, 1923.

H. Parker Willis and B. H. Beckhart, *Foreign Banking Systems*.

Seymour E. Harris, *Monetary Problems of the British Empire*. New York, 1931.

Harold L. Reed, *Federal Reserve Policy 1921–1930*. New York, 1930.

Frank D. Graham, *Exchange, Prices and Production in Hyper-Inflation Germany*. Princeton, 1930.

James Harvey Rogers, *Inflation in France*. New York, 1929.

Book XI

Frederick Soddy, *Wealth, Virtual Wealth and Debt*. London, 1926.

———, *Money Versus Man*. London, 1931.

Harry W. Laidler, *Concentration in American Industry*. New York, 1931.

Maurice Wormser, *Frankenstein, Incorporated*. New York, 1931.

Berle and Means, *The Modern Corporation and Private Property*. New York, 1932.

Louis Brandeis, *Other People's Money*. New York, 1914.

Book XII

Evans Clark, editor, *The Internal Debts of the United States*. New York, 1933.

Lawrence Dennis, *Is Capitalism Doomed?* New York, 1932.

Stuart Chase, *Economy of Abundance*. New York, 1934.

Bassett Jones, *Horses and Apples*. New York, 1934.

———, *Debt and Production*. New York, 1933.

Robert R. Doane, *The Measurement of American Wealth*. New York, 1934.

John T. Flynn, *Security Speculation*. New York, 1934.

Hearings of the Senate Committee on Banking and Currency on Stock Market Practices. Washington, 1933.

Wiggins and Schoeck, ed., *Foreign Aid Re-examined*. Washington, 1958.

J. M. Keynes, *General Theory of Employment, Interest and Money*. New York, 1936.

Franz Pick, *Pick's Currency Year Book*. New York, annual editions.

Elgin Groseclose, *Introduction to Iran*. New York, 1947.

————, *The Decay of Money*. Monograph No. 1. Washington: Institute for Monetary Research, 1962.

————, *Silver as Money*. Monograph No. 2. Washington: Institute for Monetary Research, 1965.

————, *The Silken Metal—Silver: Past, Present, Prospective*. Monograph No. 3. Washington: Institute for Monetary Research, 1975.

Maj. Gen. L. C. Dunsterville, *The Adventures of Dunsterforce*. London, 1921.

John Leighton Stuart, *Fifty Years in China*. New York, 1954.

Ludwig von Mises, *Theory of Money and Credit*. New York, 1934.

Henry Hazlitt, *Critics of Keynesian Economics*. New York, 1960.

R. S. Sayers, *Central Banking after Bagehot*. London, 1957.

Sir Henry Clay, *Lord Norman*. London, 1957.

Charles Rist, *The Triumph of Gold* (translated by Philip Cortney). New York, 1961.

NOTES

INTRODUCTION
1. Exodus iii, 14.

BOOK ONE—CHAPTER II
1. Matthew, xxii, 17–21.
2. Leviticus, xix, 19; Deuteronomy, xxii, 10.
3. Leviticus, xix, 36.
4. *Cruden's Complete Concordance* (Philadelphia, 1930), *Art. Brass.*
5. Exodus, xxx, 15.
6. See Leo Kadman, *The Coins of the Jewish War of 66–73*, Vol. III in the *Corpus Nummorum Palaestinensium* (Tel-Aviv-Jerusalem, 1960).
7. Amos, viii, 5.

BOOK ONE—CHAPTER III
1. Thomas Babington Macaulay, *The History of England* (London, 1848), chap. xxi.

BOOK TWO—CHAPTER II
1. Herodotus, Book I, sec. 94; Strabo, *Geography*, Book VII, chap. iii, sec. 33; Plutarch, *Theseus* (London, 1876), p. 150.
2. Aristotle, *Politics*, Book V, chap. ix.
3. Theodore Mommsen, *History of Rome*, translation of Rev. Wm. P. Dickson (London, 1862–1875), I, 251; Homer *Iliad*, VI, 236, VII, 274; Pliny, *Natural History*, XXXIII, 3. The "oxen" theory of money is disputed by various authorities. See Alexander Del Mar, *History of Money in Ancient Countries* (London, 1885), p. 195; A. R. Burns, *Money and Monetary Policy in Early Times* (New York, 1927), p. 6.

BOOK TWO—CHAPTER IV
1. George Grote, *History of Greece*, chap. xi.
2. Augustus Boeckh, *Public Economy of the Athenians*, translated by Anthony Lamb (London, 1857), pp. 67 ff.

BOOK TWO—CHAPTER V
1. Karl Helfferich, *Money*, translated by Louis Infield (New York, 1927), I, 281.
2. Carl Knies, *Geld und Kredit* (2d ed.: Berlin, 1888), Vol. 1, *Das Geld,* p. 147.

3. Irving Fisher, *Purchasing Power of Money* (New York, 1920), pp. 31–32.

4. Helfferich, *op. cit.*, II, 494.

5. Benjamin M. Anderson, Jr., *The Value of Money* (New York, 1926), p. 153.

6. Book V, chaps. viii to xii.

BOOK THREE—CHAPTER II

1. Léon Homo, *L'Empire Romain* (Paris, 1925), p. 341.

2. Ferdinand Lot, *The End of the Ancient World* (New York, 1931), p. 55.

BOOK THREE—CHAPTER IV

1. George Finlay, *History of Greece* (Oxford, 1877), Appendix I, 432.

2. Theodore Mommsen, *History of Roman Money*, Part III, chap. v, sec. 10 (I, 147, 148, in translation of Le duc de Blacas, Paris, 1873).

3. Mommsen, *op. cit.*, Part III, Chap. v, sec. 11 (III, 149, 150).

BOOK FOUR—CHAPTER II

1. George Finlay, *History of Greece* (Oxford, 1877), II, 213.

2. Karl Helfferich, *Money*, Infield translation (New York, 1927), I, 88. See also Alexander Del Mar, *History of the Precious Metals* (New York, 1902), p. 199. Del Mar states the treasure in gold and silver taken from Peru to have been equivalent to 217,000 ounces of gold.

3. Helfferich, *op. cit.*, I, 169. Charles A. Conant, *History of Modern Banks of Issue* (New York, 1902), p. 193 (p. 197 in revised edition of 1927).

4. Helfferich, *op. cit.*, I, 210.

5. See Sewell, "Roman Coins in India," *Journal of Asiatic Society*, XXXVI (1904), 620–21.

6. See Thomas Madox, *History of the Exchequer* (London, 1769, 2 vols.).

7. *Christian Topography*, Lib. XI.

8. *Ibid.*

9. *Le livre du préfet ou l'édit de l'empereur Léon le Sage sur les corporations de Constantinople*, French translation from the Geneva text by Jules Nicole, p. 38. Cited by Ernest Nys, *Researches in the History of Economics*, translation of N. F. and A. R. Dryhurst (London, 1899), p. 203.

10. *Byzantinische Kulturgeschichte* (Tübingen, 1909), p. 78.

BOOK FIVE—CHAPTER I

1. Herman Schmidt, *Tate's "Cambist"* (London, 1880), p. 43.

2. Le Vicomte G. D'Avenel, *Histoire économique de la propriété*,

des salaires, des denrées, etc. 1200–1800 (Paris, 1894), I, 62. Also I, 37–39, 482–494.

3. Alexander Del Mar, *Money and Civilization* (London, 1885), pp. 11, 12.

4. *Ibid.*, p. 10.

5. H. Pigeonneau, *Histoire du commerce de la France*, I, 82, cited by Ernest Nys, *Researches in the History of Economics* (London, 1899), p. 237.

6. Nys, *op. cit.*, p. 239.

7. *Op. cit.*, p. 37.

8. W. A. Shaw, *History of Currency, 1252–1894* (London, 1896), pp. 4 ff.

9. See his chapter, "Sacred Character of Gold," in *History of Monetary Systems* (New York, 1903).

BOOK FIVE—CHAPTER II

1. Article "Livre" in the *Encyclopédie*, quoted, Molinari, *Cours d'économie politique*, and in J. Schoenhof, *Money and Prices* (New York, 1896), p. 99.

2. W. A. Shaw, *op. cit.*, Appendix V.

3. *Ibid.*, p. 44.

4. *History of Monetary Systems*, p. 232.

BOOK FIVE—CHAPTER IV

1. Cited by Nys, *op. cit.*, p. 249.

2. *Ibid.*, p. 252.

BOOK SIX—CHAPTER I

1. Franklin W. Ryan, *Usury and Usury Laws* (New York, 1924), pp. 42 ff.

2. R. H. Tawney, *Religion and the Rise of Capitalism* (London, 1926), p. 43.

3. *Ibid.*, p. 35.

4. *Ibid.*, p. 42.

5. Ryan, *op. cit.*

BOOK SIX—CHAPTER II

1. *Cambridge Medieval History* (London, 1926), Vol. II, chap. iii, "Roman Law," by H. J. Roby.

2. Richard Ehrenberg, *Capital and Finance in the Age of the Renaissance*, translation of H. M. Lucas (London, 1928), pp. 34, 35.

BOOK SIX—CHAPTER III

1. Jacob Strieder, *Jacob Fugger the Rich*, translation of Mildred L. Hartsough (New York, 1931), p. 1.

2. *Ibid.*, p. 3.
3. Nys, *op. cit.*, pp. 284, 285.

BOOK SIX—CHAPTER IV

1. William Linn Westermann, "Warehousing and Trapezite Banking in Antiquity," *Journal of Economic and Business History* (1930), III, 30–54; Abbott Payson Usher, "Deposit Banking in Barcelona," *ibid.* (1931), IV, 121–155; *idem*, "Origins of Banking," *Economic History Review* (1934), IV, 399–428.

2. Pompeo Molmenti, *Venice*, translated by Horatio F. Brown (London, 1906), I, 15; Nys, *op. cit.*, p. 205; C. F. Dunbar, "The Bank of Venice," *Quarterly Journal of Economics* (1892), VI, 308–335.

3. Charles A. Conant, *History of Modern Banks of Issue* (New York, 1902), p. 195 (p. 199 in edition of 1927).

BOOK SIX—CHAPTER V

1. Clive Day, *History of Commerce* (London, 1907, 1917), p. 155.
2. Ehrenberg, *op. cit.*, pp. 243 ff.
3. *Ibid.*, p. 242.
4. *Ibid.*, p. 243.
5. *Ibid.*

BOOK SIX—CHAPTER VI

1. J. W. Jeudwine, *Studies in Empire and Trade* (London, 1923), p. 278.
2. *Ibid.*

BOOK SEVEN—CHAPTER I

1. See W. Vissering, *On Chinese Currency* (Leiden, 1877); also Jules Heinrich Klaproth, "Sur l'origine du papier monnaie," *Journal Asiatique*, Vol. I (1822). Also in pamphlet form.

2. Del Mar, *History of Monetary Systems*, p. 182.

3. Del Mar, *Money and Civilization*, p. 29.

4. Thomas Francis Carter, *Invention of Printing in China and Its Spread Westward*, p. 100.

5. Carl Richard Greer, *Advertising and its Mechanical Preparation* (New York, 1931), p. 357.

6. W. A. Shaw, *Theory and Principles of Central Banking* (London, 1930), pp. 26, 27.

7. William B. Weeden, *Indian Money as a Factor in New England Civilization*, Johns Hopkins University Studies in Historical and Political Science, Second Series, VIII–IX (Baltimore, August and September, 1884).

8. Horace White, *Money and Banking* (New York, 1895), pp. 3–9.

9. Noble Foster Hoggson, *Epochs in American Banking* (New York, 1929), p. 32.

10. W. Z. Ripley, *Financial History of Virginia*, Studies in History, Economics, and Public Law, edited by the University Faculty of Political Science of Columbia College (New York, 1893), pp. 145 ff.; Horace White, *op. cit.*, pp. 3–9; See also C. P. Gould, *Money and Transportation in Maryland (1720–1765)*, Johns Hopkins University Studies in Historical and Political Science, Thirty-third Series (1915).

11. Noble Foster Hoggson, *op. cit.*, pp. 49 ff.

BOOK SEVEN—CHAPTER II

1. Albert Despaux, *L'Inflation dans l'Histoire* (Paris, 1922), p. 159.
2. *France Under the Regency* (New York, 1892), p. 283.
3. Jean la Bruyère, *De l'homme*, chap. ii.

BOOK SEVEN—CHAPTER III

1. *La très Curieuse Vie de Law*, translated by G. E. C. Massé (New York, 1928).
2. *Theory and Practice of Banking* (new impression, London, 1923), II, 243 ff.

BOOK SEVEN—CHAPTER IV

1. Saint-Simon, Louis de Rouv Roy, duc de, *Memoires* (Paris, 1788), chap. vii.

BOOK SEVEN—CHAPTER VI

1. *Lettres sur le nouveau systéme des finances* (May 18, 1720).

BOOK SEVEN—CHAPTER VII

1. Letter in *Mercure de France* (May, 1720).

BOOK EIGHT—CHAPTER I

1. W. A. Shaw, *op. cit.*, pp. 18–23.

BOOK EIGHT—CHAPTER II

1. *Ibid.*, pp. 160, 161.

BOOK EIGHT—CHAPTER III

1. Karl Helfferich, *Money*, Infield translation (New York, 1927), I, 115 ff.
2. J. Laurence Laughlin, *History of Bimetallism in the United States* (New York, 1885, 1886), p. 23.
3. "Report on the Establishment of a Mint" (in *Report of the International Monetary Conference of 1878*), pp. 454–484. Also, *Reports of the Secretary of the Treasury (Report on the Finances 1790–1814)* Vol. I (Washington, 1837).
4. J. Laurence Laughlin, *op. cit.*, p. 53.

5. Actually 15.98 to 1. The Act of 1837 readjusted the alloy in the silver and gold coins to bring them both to a standard fineness of .900. The result was a slight adjustment in the ratio of 16 to 1 set by the Act of 1834.

6. J. Laurence Laughlin, *op. cit.*, pp. 66, 67.

BOOK EIGHT—CHAPTER IV

1. H. Parker Willis, *A History of the Latin Monetary Union* (University of Chicago Press, 1901), pp. 32, 36.

2. See H. Parker Willis, *op. cit.*, pp. 59 ff. Dr. Willis, after careful investigation, comes to the same conclusion as Dr. Soetbeer (*Währungsfrage*, p. 29), whose views are also adopted by Laughlin (*op. cit.*, p. 148).

3. Helfferich, *op. cit.*, I, 148.

4. According to the tables of the United States Director of the Mint.

5. Helfferich, *op. cit.*, I, 181.

BOOK NINE—CHAPTER II

1. W. A. Shaw, *Theory and Principles of Central Banking* (London, 1930), pp. 31, 32.

BOOK NINE—CHAPTER III

1. Charles A. Conant, *A History of Modern Banks of Issue* (New York, 1902), pp. 90, 91.

2. *Op. cit.*, p. 122.

BOOK NINE—CHAPTER IV

1. Noble Foster Hoggson, *Epochs in American Banking* (New York, 1929), p. 100.

2. This classification is based upon Charles A. Conant, *A History of Modern Banks of Issue* (New York, 1902, 1927), chap. xiv, whose account of the state banking systems is classic.

3. Conant, *op. cit.*, p. 360 (1927 edition).

4. *Ibid.*, pp. 361 ff.

5. *Ibid.*, p. 378.

6. *Money and Its Laws* (New York, 1877), p. 540.

7. See the admirable work on the subject, *The Legal Qualities of Money*, by Arthur Kemp, (New York, 1956).

BOOK NINE—CHAPTER V

1. John Stuart Mill, *Principles of Political Economy*, III, chap. xxiv.

2. *Op. cit.*, p. 125 (1927 edition).

3. For further details see the author's *The Decay of Money* (monograph) (Washington: Institute for Monetary Research, 1962).

BOOK NINE—CHAPTER VI

1. J. E. Thorold Rogers, *First Nine Years of the Bank of England*

(Oxford, 1887), p. 8.

2. *Ibid.*, p. 9.

3. A. Andréadès, *History of the Bank of England, 1640 to 1903* (London, 1924), p. 276.

4. Harry E. Miller, *Banking Theories in the United States Before 1860* (Cambridge: Harvard University Press, 1927).

5. Vethake, *The Principles of Political Economy* (1838), cited in *The New York Money Market*, by Margaret G. Myers (New York, 1931), I, 87.

6. Margaret G. Myers, *op. cit.*, I, 87.

7. Harry E. Miller, *op. cit.*, p. 12.

8. *Op. cit.* I, 88.

9. Hamilton, "Report on a National Bank" (1790), *American State Papers*, Finance, I, 68. Also in *Papers on Public Credit, Commerce and Finance* (New York: Columbia University Press, 1934), pp. 53–95.

10. Albert Gallatin, *Considerations on the Currency and Banking System of the United States* (1831), p. 31.

11. Henry E. Miller, *op. cit.*, p. 110.

BOOK TEN—CHAPTER I

1. Reports of the Director of the Mint.

2. See the author's *The Silken Metal—Silver: Past, Present, Prospective* (Monograph) (Washington: Institute for Monetary Research, 1975); also, Dickson H. Leavens, *Silver Money* (Bloomington, Indiana 1939).

3. David Kinley, *The Use of Credit Instruments in Payments in the United States*, Publications of the National Monetary Commission (Washington, 1910).

BOOK TEN—CHAPTER II

1. Conant, *op. cit.*, pp. 538, 539.

BOOK TEN—CHAPTER III

1. Harold G. Moulton, *Principles of Money and Banking* (Chicago, 1916), p. 295.

2. Adapted from the *Federal Reserve Act* (Boston News Bureau Co., 1914), pp. 10–11, 38; Harold G. Moulton, *op. cit.*, p. 264.

3. Subsequently, in 1968, the gold reserve requirement for notes was abolished.

4. *Report of the Committee on Member Bank Reserves of the Federal Reserve System* (Washington, 1931).

5. In 1965, the gold reserve requirement against deposit liabilities was abolished.

6. United States Government securities, and certain types of agricultural credit obligations, municipal warrants, trade acceptances and bankers' bills.

7. Section 14, Federal Reserve Act.

BOOK TEN—CHAPTER IV

1. *Recent Social Changes* (New York, 1933), I, 256.

2. *New York American* (November 9–15, 1931).

3. Letter from Moody's Investors' Service. The figures are given annually in *Moody's Manual of Investments, Government and Municipal* (New York), blue page section.

4. Franklin W. Ryan, "Family Finance in the United States," *Journal of Business of the University of Chicago*, Vol. III, No. 4 (October, 1930).

BOOK TEN—CHAPTER V

1. Helfferich, *op. cit.*, I, 212; Willis and Beckhart, *Foreign Banking Systems* (New York, 1929), p. 1205.

2. Helfferich, *op. cit.*, I, 220.

3. W. A. Shaw, *The Theory and Principles of Central Banking* (London, 1930), Preface, vi.

4. Adapted from Madden and Nadler, *Foreign Securities* (New York, 1920), pp. 13–14.

BOOK TEN—CHAPTER VI

1. *League of Nations' Monthly Bulletin of Statistics*, Special Number (May, 1933).

2. See, for instance, J. M. Keynes, *The Economic Consequences of the Peace* (New York, 1920).

BOOK ELEVEN—CHAPTER I

1. Adapted from Frank A. Vanderlip, *Tomorrow's Money* (New York, 1934), pp. 16–18.

2. U.S. Dept. of Com., *Historical Statistics of the U.S.* (Washington, 1960), and *Statistical Abstract of the U.S.* (annual issues).

3. *Housing America*, by the editors of *Fortune* (New York, 1933); also *Fortune* (March, 1932).

BOOK ELEVEN—CHAPTER II

1. See Harry W. Laidler, *Concentration of American Industry* (New York, 1931); Maurice Wormser, *Frankenstein, Incorporated* (New York, 1931); Berle and Means, *The Modern Corporation and Private Property* (New York, 1932).

2. Berle and Means, *op. cit.*, chap. iii.

3. Laidler, *op. cit.*, p. 53.

4. For a detailed description of the process, see Berle and Means, *op. cit.*; also John T. Flynn, *Security Speculation* (New York, 1934).

5. *Hearings of the Senate Committee on Banking and Currency on Stock Exchange Practices*, Part II (May 26 to June 9, 1933).

BOOK TWELVE—CHAPTER I

1. *Supra*, Book Six, Chapter V.
2. *Supra*, Book Ten, Chapter III.
3. Congressman Wright Patman, for years one of the most powerful figures in Congress as Chairman of the House Banking and Currency Committee, was never able to obtain an audit of the Federal Reserve System. Former Justice Arthur Goldberg, questioned as to the indifference of the courts to the Constitutional question stated that the courts were always reluctant to question the power of Congress, either to exercise or to delegate, on economic questions.
4. *New York Times*, March 7, 1934; April 22, 1934.

BOOK TWELVE—CHAPTER II

1. *U.S. Foreign Aid* (Legislative Reference Service, Library of Congress, Washington, 1959).
2. Quoted in *Prosperity Through Competition—The Economics of the German Miracle*, by its creator, Ludwig Erhard, Vice Chancellor and Minister for Economic Affairs of the German Federal Republic (New York, 1958), pp. 12, 13.
3. For a critical discussion of the foreign aid program, see *Foreign Aid Re-examined*, a symposium held at Emory University, 1957, ed. by Wiggins and Schoeck (Washington, 1958).
4. International Monetary Fund, *Annual Report for 1960* (Washington, 1960), p. 177.

BOOK TWELVE—CHAPTER III

1. See his *General Theory of Employment, Interest and Money* (New York, 1936).
2. *Supra*, Book Ten, Chapter V. By 1970, of total reserves of the world's central banks, of $92½ billion, only $37 billion was in gold.
3. *Supra*, Book Ten, Chapter III.
4. From 23.22 fine grains gold to 13 10/14 fine grains, or a value of $35 per ounce.

BOOK TWELVE—CHAPTER V

1. Genesis ii, 11, 12.
2. *Supra*, Book Eight, Chapter IV; Book Ten, Chapters I, II, III.
3. See the author's *Introduction to Iran* (New York, 1947), pp. 51, 157 ff., 164 ff., 176 ff.
4. See Maj. Gen. L. C. Dunsterville, *The Adventure of Dunsterforce* (London, 1921), for an account of this expedition.
5. *Fifty Years in China* (New York, 1954), p. 228.
6. Public Law 88–36, approved June 4, 1963.

7. Since silver had not been coined since 1934, the mint was authorized to deliver silver bullion at the mint price of $1.29 an ounce.

8. "Coinage Act of 1965" (Public Law 89–81), approved July 23, 1965.

BOOK TWELVE—CHAPTER VI
1. Leviticus, xix, 36.

BOOK TWELVE—CHAPTER VII
1. *The Internal Debts of the United States*, edited by Evans Clark (New York, 1933).

2. U.S. Board of Governors of Federal Reserve System, in *Statistical Abstracts of the U.S.*

3. *Is Capitalism Doomed?* (New York, 1932), chap. iii.

4. *Debt and Production* (New York, 1933).

5. *The Economy of Abundance* (New York, 1934), p. 133.

INDEX

302

ABOUT THE AUTHOR

Elgin Groseclose is well known as a financial analyst and consultant. At one time a specialist in far eastern finance with the United States Department of Commerce, he became the first financial editor of *Fortune* magazine and subsequently taught at the University of Oklahoma. He returned to Washington as chief financial economist of the Special Telephone Investigation and as economist for the Treasury Department.

Since 1944 he has headed his own firm of financial and investment consultants. In 1961 he founded the Institute for Monetary Research, Inc., which he continues to serve as executive secretary. He has also been lecturer on money and banking at the City College of New York and on investment analysis in the Graduate School of the American University in Washington, D.C.

Familiar with the effects of currency debasement through service as a relief worker in Iran and the Soviet Caucasus after World War I, Mr. Groseclose is author of five novels dealing with Christian missions. His *Ararat*, 1939 winner of the American Booksellers' Award and of the Foundation for Literature Award, was republished in 1974 in a major paperback edition. His works have been translated into Swedish, Norwegian, Italian, Spanish, and Persian. He is also founder of Welfare of the Blind, Inc., a Christian agency for the sightless of the Middle East, which maintains a center for the blind in Teheran.